SECOND EDITION

B1 PRELIMINARY
SUCCESS WITH
BUSINESS

SUCCESS WITH BUSINESS resources (including audio and answer sheets for the practice exam)

http://www.eltexampreparation.com/success/success-business

Password: succ!BUS#2

TEACHER'S BOOK

National Geographic Learning,
a Cengage Company

Success with Business Preliminary Teacher's Book
2nd Edition
John Hughes, Rolf Cook, Mara Pedretti

Publisher: Sharon Jervis

Project Manager: Hattie Fell

Editorial Manager: Claire Merchant

Head of Strategic Marketing ELT: Charlotte Ellis

Product Marketing Manager ELT: Victoria Taylor

Head of Production and Design: Celia Jones

Senior Content Project Manager: Sue Povey

Manufacturing Manager: Eyvett Davis

Composition: emc design ltd

Cover Design: emc design ltd

Audio Producer: James Richardson

For permission to use material from this text or product,
submit all requests online at **www.cengage.com/permissions**

Further permissions questions can be emailed to
permissionrequest@cengage.com

ISBN: 978-1-4737-7250-2

National Geographic Learning
Cheriton House, North Way
Andover, Hampshire, SP10 5BE
United Kingdom

Locate your local office at **international.cengage.com/region**

Visit National Geographic Learning online at **ELTNGL.com**
Visit our corporate website at **www.cengage.com**

Printed in the United Kingdom by Ashford Colour Press
Print Number: 01   Print Year: 2019

B1 PRELIMINARY
SUCCESS WITH
BUSINESS

NATIONAL
GEOGRAPHIC
L E A R N I N G

Australia · Brazil · Mexico · Singapore · United Kingdom · United States

Contents

Overview of the course

Student's Book

The Student's Books for all levels contain 12 modules divided into the core lessons of *Business topic*, *Business skills* and *Exam spotlight*. This modular division of material makes it easy to adapt the book for the specific needs of your class:

Students preparing for the Cambridge Business English exams – teach everything; the course provides complete exam preparation

Students who don't want to take the exam – teach everything except the *Exam spotlight* lessons

Students who want to focus on vocabulary and grammar – teach the *Business topic* lessons

Students who need a specific focus on business skills – teach the *Business skills* lessons

Business topic lessons

Twelve vocabulary / grammar lessons of four pages (six in Higher), covering all Cambridge Business English syllabus topics. See pages 10 and 11 for a breakdown
of topic coverage.

Business skills lessons

Twelve function / grammar lessons of four pages (two in Higher), covering high-frequency business skills. See pages 10 and 11 for a breakdown of topic coverage.

Exam spotlight lessons

- background information to all the papers
- exam skills
- exam practice

Back of book material

Each Student's Book contains additional material at the back of the book, including:

- pairwork / group work materials
- useful expressions
- listening scripts
- key information about the Cambridge Business English exam (B1 Preliminary and C1 Higher – this information is integrated into the lessons in B2 Vantage)
- grammar reference (B2 Vantage only)
- business idioms (C1 Higher only)

Workbook

Each Workbook contains the answer key.
They feature stimulating input texts and motivating activities which consolidate and extend the topics and skills presented in the Student's Books. They also provide further exam practice.

Audio

There are audio files for each level online. You can access all the listening material for the core lessons, all the speaking and listening tests for the *Exam Spotlight* lessons, and all the audio for the *Practice Exam Listening Test*. To access the audio please go to:
http://www.eltexampreparation.com/success/success-business
Password: succ!BUS#2

Teacher's Book

The Teacher's Books are very comprehensive and contain:
- reduced Student's Book spreads for easy reference as you teach
- step-by-step teaching notes and answers
- listening scripts
- extra activities
- suggestions for alternative activities / how to modify the book activity for pre-work students
- twenty-four photocopiable activities and teaching notes
- suggestions in the lesson notes for when to do the photocopiable activities
- answer sheets for the *Practice Exam* online. To access the answer sheets please go to:
  http://www.eltexampreparation.com/success/success-business
  Password: succ!BUS#2

Success with Business and the Cambridge Business English exam

Where do the Cambridge Business English exams fit into the bigger picture?

The table below shows the correspondence in linguistic ability between the Cambridge Business English exams, Cambridge English's suite of general English exams and the Common European Framework of Reference.

Cambridge Business English	Equivalent General English Exam	Common European Framework of Reference (CEFR)
	C2 Proficiency	C2
C1 Business Higher	C1 Advanced	C1
B2 Business Vantage	B2 First	B2
B1 Business Preliminary	B1 Preliminary	B1
	A2 Key	A2

How does *Success with Business* prepare students for the Cambridge Business English exams?

Success with Business specifically prepares students for the Cambridge Business English exams in the following ways:

- *Exam spotlight* lessons in the Student's Books covering all the test papers
- *Exam success* boxes throughout the Student's Books, giving tips
- exam-type exercises used extensively in the core lessons in the Student's Book
- complete coverage of Cambridge Business English topics. See pages 10 and 11 for a breakdown.
- exam lessons in the Workbooks

You may photocopy the *Exam checklist* on the facing page for your students. It's a good idea to give them a copy of this exam checklist in the last lesson before the Cambridge Business English exam, so that the advice is fresh in their minds.

Exam checklist

Read the advice before you do your Cambridge Business English exam.

READING AND LISTENING

1 **Each question carries the same marks.**
   Do those parts of the paper you find easiest first and don't get stuck for a long time on a particular question.

2 **Don't leave any answer blank.**
   The computer / examiner can't tell if you've guessed or not!

3 **Leave enough time to mark the answers on the answer sheet.**
   This is your responsibility and there are no excuses.

4 **There is only one correct answer to each question.**
   Don't give more than one answer.

5 **Write your answers in block capitals.**
   This will avoid any confusion.

WRITING AND SPEAKING

1 **Read the instructions carefully.**

2 **Answer the question you are asked.**
   Cover all the points mentioned in the question or prompt.

3 **Don't write more than you need to.**
   The examiner will look to see that you have covered all the points, but will only assess your written English up to the word limit.

4 **You can ask the examiner to repeat a question, but not to explain it.**
   The examiner is not allowed to rephrase a question or explain words you don't know.

5 **Organise your writing and speaking.**
   Use clear paragraphs, bullet points in writing, and a clear introduction and conclusion in speaking. This will make life easier for the examiner.

How do I know *Success with Business* covers all the topic areas that will come up in the Cambridge Business English exams?

In general, the topics listed below will recur across the three levels of the Cambridge Business English examinations. As the level of the exam increases, the linguistic and skills requirements become more advanced. Some topics, eg 'Personal identification' are more suited to the lower levels. You can see in the table below how the topic coverage in *Success with Business* reflects this shift in emphasis.

If you are using the course selectively, focusing either on skills or vocabulary, you may wish to take this mapping into account, to ensure adequate coverage of all the topics. The business topic lessons are labelled 1.1, 2.1, 3.1, etc. The business skills lessons are labelled 1.2, 2.2, 3.2, etc. The flexibility of this organisation allows each topic to be approached from the most suitable angle.

Topic area	*Success with Business* B1 Business Preliminary
Personal identification	1.1 World of work 1.2 Personal and professional details 3.1 Company biography 12.2 Job applications
The office, general business environment and routine	2.2 Making arrangements 5.1 Career choices 9.2 Meetings
Entertainment of clients, free time, relationships with colleagues and clients	10.2 Organising a conference
Travel and meetings	6.1 Business travel 6.2 Travel arrangements
Using the telephone	4.2 Business communications
Health and safety	11.1 Health and safety 11.2 Reporting accidents
Buying and selling	4.1 International business 7.2 Orders and contracts
Company structures, systems, processes	2.1 Work in progress 8.1 Manufacturing processes 8.2 Problems and solutions 12.1 The job market
Products and services	7.1 Products and services
Results and achievements	3.2 Company performance 5.2 Achievements and plans
Business issues	9.1 The future 10.1 Career development

Success with Business B2 Business Vantage	Success with Business C1 Business Higher
1.1 Ways of working	1.1 The gig economy
5.2 Participating in a meeting 6.2 Electronic communication 7.1 Job qualities	3.1 Communication at work 3.2 Email exchange 5.2 Discussing options 7.2 Report writing 8.2 Formal meetings 10.2 The language of proposals 11.2 Effective writing
5.1 The workplace	12.1 Crossing cultures 12.2 Social English
1.2 Making contacts	10.1 Travel and entertainment
3.2 Leaving and taking messages 9.2 Getting through	6.2 Telephoning
Secondary focus in other lessons	1.2 Asking and answering questions
7.2 Selling 11.1 Ethical economics	4.1 The art of selling 6.1 Purchasing power
2.1 Company benefits 2.2 Presenting your company 6.1 Recruitment 10.2 Solving problems	9.1 Innovation
12.2 Handling questions	9.2 Negotiating
11.2 Discussing trends	2.1 Growing the company 2.2 Presenting facts 4.2 Presenting figures
3.1 Starting a business 4.1 Advertising 4.2 Delegating 8.1 Training 8.2 Showing you're listening 9.1 Branding 10.1 Management 12.1 Business law	5.1 Money and finance 7.1 Managing people 8.1 Being responsible 11.1 The economy

Assessment criteria for the productive skills

The Cambridge *Business Handbook* and the Cambridge English website www. cambridgeenglish.org provide useful information about the marking schemes and assessment criteria. The following tables outline the criteria for assessing the speaking and writing tests.

Speaking

The two examiners in the Speaking Test give independent marks. The Interlocutor (the examiner who speaks to the candidates) gives one global mark and the Assessor (the examiner who observes) gives four separate marks for the areas listed in the table below.

Area and criteria	Minimum adequate performance		
	Preliminary	*Vantage*	*Higher*
Grammar and Vocabulary This refers to the range and accuracy of grammatical and lexical forms.	At this level candidates should be accurate enough, and use sufficiently appropriate vocabulary, to convey their intended meaning.	At this level candidates should be accurate enough, and use sufficiently appropriate vocabulary, to convey their intended meaning.	At this level a range of grammar and vocabulary is needed to deal with the tasks. At this level grammar is mainly accurate and vocabulary is used effectively.
Discourse Management This refers to the coherence, extent and relevance of each candidate's individual performance.	Contributions should be adequate to deal with the B1 Business Preliminary level tasks. At times, candidates' utterances may be inappropriate in length and some utterances may lack coherence.	Contributions should be adequate to deal with the B2 Business Vantage level tasks. At times, candidates' utterances may be inappropriate in length.	Contributions should be adequate to deal with the C1 Business Higher level tasks. Candidates should produce utterances which are appropriate in length.
Pronunciation This refers to the candidate's ability to produce comprehensible utterances.	At this level, most meanings are conveyed through the appropriate use of stress, rhythm, intonation and clear individual sounds, although there may be some strain on the listener.	At this level, meanings are conveyed through the appropriate use of stress, rhythm, intonation and clear individual sounds, although there may be occasional difficulty for the listener.	At this level, meanings are conveyed through the appropriate use of stress, rhythm, intonation and clear individual sounds, although there may be occasional difficulty for the listener.
Interactive Communication This refers to the candidate's ability to take an active part in the development of the discourse.	At this level, candidates should be able to take turns and keep the interaction going by initiating and responding appropriately. Hesitation may demand patience of the listener.	At this level, candidates should be sensitive to turn-taking and sustain the interaction by initiating and responding appropriately. Hesitation may, at times, demand patience of the listener.	At this level, candidates should be sensitive to turn-taking throughout most of the test and hesitation should not demand patience of the listener.

Writing

An impression mark is awarded to each piece of writing. The *General Mark Scheme* is used in conjunction with a *Task-specific Mark Scheme*, which focuses on criteria specific to each particular task.

The table below shows the *Summary of General Mark Scheme (Part 2)* for Preliminary. Examiners, who are co-ordinated prior to each examination session, work with a more detailed version, which is subject to updating. The other levels follow broadly the same criteria. Full details are available in the Cambridge *Business Handbook* or on the Cambridge English website www.cambridgeenglish.org.

BAND 5 All four content points achieved.
- Good range of structure and vocabulary.
- Confident control of language; a few non-impeding errors may be present.
- Effectively organised, with appropriate cohesion.
- Register and format consistently appropriate.

Full realisation of the task set.

Very positive effect on the reader.

BAND 4 Three or four content points achieved.
- More than adequate range of structure and vocabulary.
- Some errors, mostly non-impeding.
- Generally well-organised, with attention paid to cohesion.
- Register and format on the whole appropriate.

Good realisation of the task set.

Positive effect on the reader.

BAND 3 Likely maximum for scripts of 25–50 words.

Three or four content points achieved.
- Adequate range of structure and vocabulary.
- A number of errors may be present, several of which may be impeding.
- Organisation and cohesion is satisfactory, on the whole.
- Register and format reasonable, although not entirely successful.

Reasonable achievement of the task set.

Satisfactory effect on the reader.

BAND 2 Maximum for scripts of fewer than 25 words.

Two or three content points achieved.
- Limited range of structure and vocabulary.
- Numerous errors, several of which impede communication.
- Content is not clearly organised or linked, causing some confusion.
- Inappropriate register and format.

Inadequate attempt at task/task possibly misunderstood/response considerably irrelevant.

Negative effect on the reader.

BAND 1 Task misunderstood/response largely irrelevant.

Up to two content points achieved.
- Little evidence of structure and vocabulary required by task.
- Serious lack of control; frequent basic errors.
- Lack of organisation, causing a breakdown in communication.
- Little attempt at appropriate register and format.
- Poor attempt at the task.

Very negative effect on the reader.

BAND 0 Achieves nothing. Totally irrelevant or illegible.

CONTENTS

Overview

1.1 Business topic: World of work

READING — Training and workshops

LISTENING — What does your job involve?

GRAMMAR — The present simple; adverbs and expressions of frequency

SPEAKING — Work–life balance

1.2 Business skills: Personal and professional details

VOCABULARY — Meeting people

WRITING — Personal and professional profiles

VOCABULARY — *job* and *work*

READING — Employee of the Year Award

1.3 Exam spotlight: B1 Business Preliminary Exam Format and Reading Test Introduction

Understanding the B1 Business Preliminary Exam format

Understanding the Reading Test format

Useful language from Module 1

Wordlist

advert
advise sb on sth
allocate
ambitious
annual meeting
apply for a job
attend a workshop
auditing
author
award a prize
badge
balance
be in charge of
be responsible for
bonus
breed (v)
business administration
candidate
catering service
CFO = chief financial officer
Chronic Fatigue Syndrome
classmate
confectionery
consultancy
consultant
co-ordinate

criterion, criteria (pl)
deal with sth / sb
design
efficiency
electrical appliances
employ
employee
employer
engineering
eraser
feature
finance assistant
follow-up
gadget
gift
give sb advice on sth
goods
greet
have a master's degree in
head office
HR = human resources
in-company
interview
interviewee
interviewer
IT = information technology

IT consultant
job
job applicant
job title
leaflet
look for
magazine
maintain
make a contribution
marathon running
MD = managing director
memo
mentor
minute
one-to-one session
overall grade
overcome difficulties
owner
PA = personal assistant
pass grade
produce
production flow
production manager
provide
questionnaire

R&D = research and development
report
responsibility
run a business / courses / a factory
sales rep
sample
schedule
scuba diving
set a positive example
ship
show sb around
speaker
staff
supervise
supper
timetable
trainer
training
welcome
work
work for
workshop

Expressions

Do you like your job?
Do you often travel abroad?
Excuse me. Is your name ...?
How are you? – Not too bad, thanks.
How do you do?
How do you spell your name / surname?
I work for a company that ...
I'd like to welcome you all.
I'm a / an ...
I'm based in ...

May I introduce myself?
My name's ... / I'm ...
Nice / Pleased to meet you.
Nice to see you again.
Please, call me ...
What do you do?
What does your job involve?
When does your train leave?
Who's the managing director?

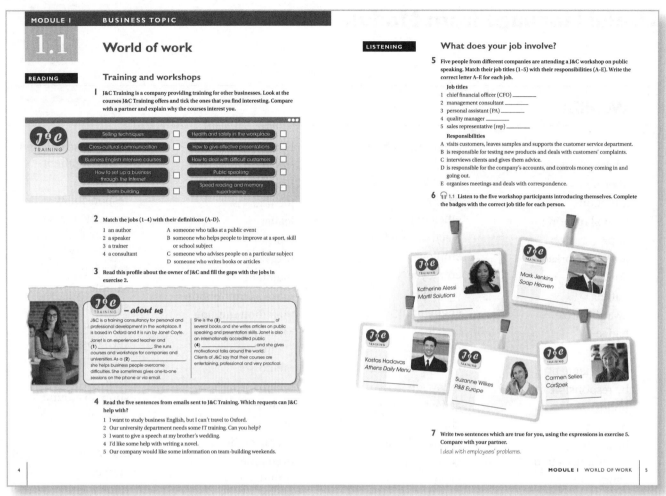

Student's Book pages 4 and 5

Training and workshops

READING

1 Start the exercise by telling students to keep their books closed. Ask them if they ever attend any training courses. Elicit students' experiences and write any relevant vocabulary on the board. Then write *J&C Training* on the board and say that this is a company that provides training services for businesses. Ask students what they think *J&C* stands for and to think of what type of training this company might provide. Write a few ideas on the board. Then ask students to open their books and compare the courses provided by J&C Training with the ones they've suggested.

Read the instructions with the students and check they understand what to do. Allow a few minutes to do the task. Students work alone. Tell them that if they don't know some of the words, they can ask you. Then they compare their choices with a partner and explain why they are interested in the courses.

2 Ask students to look at the first column (1–4) and cover the second one (A–D) with one hand, or a piece of paper. Ask students to explain what each of the people in (1–4) do. Now ask students to do the matching activity. Don't spend time explaining relative pronouns; treat them as passive knowledge for now.

Answers
1 D   2 A   3 B   4 C

3 Ask students to skim the text and find why the company is called *J&C Training*. When they've found the answer (it is run by Janet Coyte), they needn't go on reading. Ask students to give you the spelling of *Janet Coyte*.

Students then do exercise 3.

Answers
1 trainer   2 consultant   3 author   4 speaker

4 Ask students which requests J&C can help with and to give reasons.

Answers
1 Yes. (The text states that J&C is based in Oxford. It doesn't say that the training is provided at the training centre, so the assumption is that you can have a trainer at your university or in your company.)

2 No. (From the list of courses in exercise 1, none of them are IT courses. NB: *How to set up a business through the Internet* isn't a course on IT.)

3 Yes. (Janet is the author of books on public speaking and she also gives motivational talks. Therefore, she can probably help somebody to give a speech at a wedding.)

4 No. (From the list in exercise 1, J&C doesn't offer any creative writing courses.)

5 Yes. (From the list in exercise 1, J&C offers team building courses. As J&C runs courses for companies and universities, they probably organise this type of team-building course at weekends, when they can do outdoor activities, such as rock climbing, sailing and cycling.)

What does your job involve?

LISTENING

5 Before students do the exercise, point out the use of abbreviations in the job titles: *Rep* – sales representative; *PA* – personal assistant; *CFO* – chief financial officer. Students then match the job titles with their responsibilities.

Answers
1 D   2 C   3 E   4 B   5 A

Extension
Ask students if they know any other job titles that have abbreviations, eg: *CEO* – chief executive officer; *CIO* – chief information officer; *CCO* – chief communications officer; *MD* – managing director.

6 🎧 1.1 Ask students to look at the pictures of the people. Elicit what kind of job they think each person does. Accept any ideas. Students listen to the five participants of the workshop introducing themselves and find out whether their predictions were correct.

Play the recording twice. During the first listening, pause after each speaker so that students have enough time to write. Tell them to note down the abbreviations for the job titles as they listen, but they should write the job titles out in full on the badges after the second listening. Play the recording without pausing.

Remind students that in the exam they'll listen to the recordings twice and there won't be any pauses during the listening.

1.1 Listening script
J = Janet   K = Katherine   M = Mark
K = Kostas   S = Suzanne   C = Carmen

J Good morning, everyone. I'd like to welcome you all to this session about public speaking. My name's Janet Coyte, and I'll be your trainer for today and tomorrow. I can see your names and the companies you work for on your badges, but I'd like you to say something about your jobs and responsibilities. Katherine, would you like to start?

K Certainly. Hi, I'm Katherine Alessi and I work for Marfil Solutions. I'm a management consultant. Marfil Solutions gives companies advice on their markets, organisation and processes. I interview clients, identify problems and suggest solutions.

M Morning. My name's Mark Jenkins. I'm a sales rep for Soap Heaven. I visit customers and leave product samples. I look for new customers, and I support my company's customer service department.

K Hello, I'm Kostas Hadavas. I'm the personal assistant to the managing director of a company called Athens Daily Menu, which provides catering services. I arrange the MD's travel and accommodation for business trips, I organise his meetings, and I deal with correspondence.

S Good morning. My name's Suzanne Wilkes. I'm the chief financial officer of a company, P&B Europe, which designs gadgets and gifts. I'm responsible for the company's accounts, I advise the managing director on financial matters, and I control the money that comes in and goes out.

C Hello, I'm Carmen Selles. I'm the quality manager in a company that produces car seats and interiors. I arrange and carry out tests of our products and I deal with customers' complaints. Oh, the name of the company is CarSpek.

Answers
Katherine Alessi: management consultant
Mark Jenkins: sales representative
Kostas Hadavas: personal assistant
Suzanne Wilkes: chief financial officer
Carmen Selles: quality manager

7 Ask students to write the sentences on a piece of paper. Collect the sentences and read out some of them to the class. Students should guess whose descriptions are being read by the teacher. If you are teaching a small group, you'll probably have the time to read all of the sentences. If it is a large class, say that you are going to read only five or ten (you decide). Keep the other slips of paper for the following lesson. You can use them as a warmer activity.

The present simple

GRAMMAR

The present simple is used to talk about:
- permanent situations
  Q: *What do you do?*
  A: *I'm a sales rep. I work for a company that supplies computer software.*
- habits and frequency of activities
  Q: *Do you often travel abroad?*
  A: *Yes, I go to Italy two or three times a month.*
- timetables (with a time expression)
  Q: *When does your train leave?*
  A: *It leaves at 14:45.*

1 Complete the sentences with the present simple form of the verbs in brackets.

1 'What _____ your company _____?' (produce)
'It _____ electrical appliances.' (make)
2 'How many people _____ you _____?' (employ)
'We _____ 1,200 employees.' (have)
3 '_____ you _____ your goods abroad?' (export)
'Yes, we do. We _____ all over Europe.' (ship)
4 'How often _____ you _____ staff meetings?' (have)
'Once or twice a month. We _____ them every week.' (not hold)
5 'What time _____ the meetings _____?' (start)
'They usually _____ at 11 o'clock.' (begin)
6 '_____ Peta _____ you with your work?' (help)
'Yes, she does, but she _____ a lot of time.' (not have)

GRAMMAR

Adverbs and expressions of frequency

We often use these adverbs of frequency with the present simple:

always usually often sometimes rarely never

Adverbs of frequency usually go:
- before most verbs *She **often** prepares PowerPoint™ presentations.*
- after the verb *be He is **never** late.*

We also use expressions such as *once a week, twice a month, every Monday, on Thursdays.* These usually go at the end of the sentence.
We have a staff meeting every Monday / on Mondays / once a week.

2 Put the words in the correct order to make sentences.

1 meetings / month / we / every / have / two
_____

2 December / bonus / always / in / gets / a / he
_____

3 rarely / complaints / we / receive / any
_____

4 produce / catalogue / year / every / new / we / a
_____

5 she / schedule / behind / is / never
_____

SPEAKING   Work–life balance

3 Do you work or study too much? Or do you know how to balance your work with your life? Take this test to find out. Answer the questions by writing a number (0–5).

PERSONALITY QUIZ

HOW OFTEN ...

0 = never
1 = seldom / rarely
2 = occasionally
3 = frequently / often
4 = usually / normally
5 = always

1 do you plan your day's activities? ☐
2 do you sleep eight hours a night? ☐
3 do you find time to relax during the day? ☐
4 are you on time for appointments? ☐
5 do you spend more than an hour on lunch? ☐
6 do you see your friends at weekends? ☐
7 do you do exercise or sports during the week? ☐
8 do you read a magazine in the evening? ☐
9 do you wake up full of energy in the morning? ☐
10 do you laugh in a normal work day? ☐

TOTAL SCORE ☐

How to interpret the score:

41–50: Well done! You find it very easy to relax. But be careful – you are so relaxed that you are in danger of disappearing! Maybe you need to wake up and make sure people still know that you are there.

31–40: You find it quite easy to relax. People like being with you, because you are a positive presence.

21–30: You don't find relaxing very easy and life is a bit difficult for you.

11–20: You don't find relaxing easy at all – that's why you struggle so much at home and at work.

10 or below: You're making life hard for yourself – and maybe for the people around you too. Your health may even be suffering. Relax!

Exam Success

In Part Two of the Speaking Test, you will give a short presentation. There are two topics and you have to choose one of them. The heading on the topic sheet is *What is important when ...?*

4 Work in pairs.
Student A: Interview your partner using the questionnaire above.
Student B: Give as much information as you can.
A: Do you plan your day's activities?
B: Yes, I usually plan my day's activities the night before. I write appointments in my diary.
A: How often do you see your friends?
B: I see them once a week. We have supper together every Friday night.

5 Work in pairs. What things are important in maintaining a work-life balance?

Student's Book pages 6 and 7

The present simple

GRAMMAR

1 Before looking at the information about the present simple, ask students to think of some actions they normally do. Elicit two or three sentences in the present simple for the following uses: *permanent situations, habits and frequency, timetables*. Then look at the information with students and point out the different uses.

Tell students to work alone to do the following exercise. Ask them to put their pens down when they've finished. This will help you to monitor quick students and students who need more time.

Answers
1 does, produce, makes
2 do, employ, have
3 Do, export, ship
4 do, have, don't hold
5 do, start, begin
6 Does, help, doesn't have

Extension
Ask students to read the completed sentences in turns.

Adverbs and expressions of frequency

GRAMMAR

2 Draw a horizontal line on the board and write some expressions of frequency on it:

always   usually   often   sometimes   rarely   never

Discuss with students the idea of frequency given by each adverb. One way to do this is to use percentages, ie: *never 0%, always 100%*.

Ask students to suggest percentages to complete the diagram.

always	*usually*	*often*	*sometimes*	*rarely*	*never*
100%	*90%*	*70%*	*30%*	*10%*	*0%*

The percentages are approximate indications. However, the order is correct: *always > usually > often > sometimes > rarely > never.* Point out the position of these adverbs in the sentence.

Ask students to do the exercise orally first. Then they can write the correct sentences.

Answers

1 We have two meetings every month.
2 He always gets a bonus in December.
3 We rarely receive any complaints.
4 We produce a new catalogue every year.
5 She is never behind schedule.

Photocopiable activity

See page 160.

Work–life balance

SPEAKING

3   Write the headings *Work* and *Free time* on the board and ask students to give you at least five activities they regularly do at work / for work and five activities they regularly do in their free time. For example:

Work	Free time
get up early	*sleep*
discuss with boss	*read*
hurry	*relax*
eat at the canteen	*cook*
go to meetings	*go out with friends*

Ask students to read the questions in the quiz (*How often …?*) and see if their work / free time activities are in the list. Ask students if the time dedicated to work is balanced with their free time.

Before starting, remind students about the idea of frequency by pointing out the numbers that correspond to each frequency adverb. Students then do the quiz on their own. While students are doing the quiz, you can do it too!

Extension

Once students have calculated their scores, ask five students to read the five different descriptions. Tell them they should read the descriptions as if they are TV presenters.

4   Students work in pairs and interview each other.

5   Refer students to the Exam Success box. Tell students that this box contains useful information on taking the exam. This one in particular, gives information on the Speaking Test and it introduces the exercise.

BUSINESS SKILLS

1.2 Personal and professional details

VOCABULARY

Meeting people

1 Here are some phrases you can use when you greet somebody. Choose the best response (A–G) for each phrase (1–6).

0 Good morning. My name's Ros Cox.   A Not too bad, thanks. And you?
1 Hello. I'm Lothar Muller.   B No, I'm not.
2 Excuse me. Are you Linda Gordon?   C Pleased to meet you, Ms Cox.
3 Hello, Ms Leonardi. How are you?   D How do you do, Mr Muller?
4 Excuse me. Is your name Brown?   E Please, call me Peter.
5 Hi, George. Nice to see you again.   F Yes, it is.
6 Pleased to meet you, Mr Lehman.   G Nice to see you too.

2 Work in pairs to check your answers. Then practise saying the greetings and responses.

3 In which of the situations in exercise 1 are the people meeting for the first time?

4 Complete the conversation with the sentences in the box.

It's a real pleasure to work with her.	Nice to meet you, Ian.
Do you know her?	May I introduce myself?
My boss is in Sydney.	She's in Singapore, too.

Ian   Hello. (1) _____ My name's Ian and I work in the Asia-Pacific division.
Henry (2) _____ My name's Henry and this is my colleague, Sarah.
Sarah Hello, Ian. Do you work in the Sydney office?
Ian   No, not at the moment. (3) _____ But I'm based in Singapore.
Henry Look! There's Michelle over there. She's based somewhere in Asia. I can't remember where exactly. (4) _____
Ian   Yes, we're on the same project this year. (5) _____
Henry Ah, lucky you. She's really hardworking – and clever, too.
Ian   Yes, I know. (6) _____
Henry Sarah, do you know Michelle?
Sarah Yes, I do. Michelle, how lovely it is to see you again.

5 🎧 1.2 Listen to the conversation and check your answers.

8

WRITING

Personal and professional profiles

6 Find out about your classmates, using the questionnaire. First, work in pairs and prepare questions. Then interview your classmates and record the numbers.

0 Do you have a hobby?

Q Questionnaire

How many people:	Numbers
0 have a hobby?	_____
1 go abroad on holiday?	_____
2 haven't got any brothers or sisters?	_____
3 are single?	_____
4 have got a job?	_____
5 know three business words beginning with C?	_____
6 can play a musical instrument?	_____
7 don't like chocolate?	_____
8 can't name the levels of all three Cambridge Business English exams?	_____

7 Work with a new partner. Interview each other. Fill in the fact file with information about your partner.

Fact file

Name _____   Hobbies _____
Surname _____   Family _____
Town _____   Job title _____
Favourite destination for holidays _____
Reasons for learning English _____

8 With your partner, work with another pair of students. Introduce your partner to the other people in the group, using the information in exercise 7. Listen to the other presentations. Ask a follow-up question to each person.
Do you like living in ...?

9 Write a personal profile of your partner. Use the information from the fact file in exercise 7, but include one false sentence. Write 30–40 words.

10 Swap profiles with your partner. Read the profile about you and find the false sentence.

MODULE 1 PERSONAL AND PROFESSIONAL DETAILS   9

Student's Book pages 8 and 9

Meeting people

VOCABULARY

1 Elicit from students all the greetings they know in English. You may want to point out the different greetings for different parts of the day and also formal / informal greetings.

Answers
1 D   2 B   3 A   4 F   5 G   6 E

2 Students check answers by reading the lines in pairs out loud.

3 Ask students to look at exercise 1 again and decide in which of the situations the people are meeting for the first time.

Answers
People are meeting for the first time in:
0, 1, 2 (possible), 4 (possible), 6

4 Ask students to look at the picture. Elicit some information about the three people in the picture:

Where are they from?
Are they colleagues or friends?
Are they meeting for the first time?
How old are they?
Where are they? etc.

Then ask students to complete the dialogue, using the sentences provided. Don't check answers at this stage as this will be done in exercise 5.

5 🎧 1.2 Students listen and check their answers in exercise 4.

1.2 Listening script
I = Ian   H = Henry   S = Sarah

I Hello. May I introduce myself? My name's Ian and I work in the Asia–Pacific division.
H Nice to meet you, Ian. My name's Henry and this is my colleague, Sarah.
S Hello, Ian. Do you work in the Sydney office?
I No, not at the moment. My boss is in Sydney. But I'm based in Singapore.
H Look! There's Michelle over there. She's based somewhere in Asia. I can't remember where exactly. Do you know her?
I Yes, we're on the same project this year. She's in Singapore, too.
H Ah, lucky you. She's really hardworking – and clever, too.
I Yes, I know. It's a real pleasure to work with her.
H Sarah, do you know Michelle?
S Yes, I do ... Michelle, how lovely it is to see you again.

Answers

1 May I introduce myself?
2 Nice to meet you, Ian.
3 My boss is in Sydney.
4 Do you know her?
5 She's in Singapore, too.
6 It's a real pleasure to work with her.

Extension
After listening to the recording, ask three students to act the dialogue out.

Personal and professional profiles

WRITING

6 Ideally, students should be able to move around the classroom and find the classmates that have the characteristics described in 0–8. Allow 10–15 minutes to do this exercise. When the time is up, check the total number of students in each group.

Extension
Ask follow-up questions, such as:

Five students can play a musical instrument.

Who can play an instrument?

What instrument can he or she play?

7 Point out that students should work with a new partner. You may want to give a demonstration first. Ask one student:

What's your name?

And your surname?

Where do you live?

Do you have any hobbies?

8 Move around and listen to the students' presentations. Let them speak freely. Offer assistance or help only if they ask you. Leave feedback and correction time after the exercise.

Point out the importance of follow-up questions. Tell students that we become good communicators when we keep the conversation going, so asking for more details and additional information is a good technique. Tell them that the examiner will ask them some follow-up questions during the Speaking Test.

9 Allow 10–15 minutes to write the profile. Get the students to count the number of words, so that they start to become familiar with the length of the texts they will have to write in the Writing Test. Tell students that they will have to write 30–40 words in Writing Test Part One.

10 Ask students to read the profiles out loud, in pairs. Not only should they find the false sentence, but if they spot any mistakes, they should also underline them and discuss them with their partners.

Photocopiable activity
See page 161.

VOCABULARY *job* and *work*

1 Kostas Hadavas is a PA in a company that provides catering services. The in-company magazine interviews him. Write the correct form of the questions.

SPOTLIGHT ON STAFF

0 Q: What / name? *What's your name?*
A: Kostas Hadavas.
1 Q: How / spell / surname? _____
A: H-A-D-A-V-A-S.
2 Q: What / do? _____
A: I'm the personal assistant to the managing director of Athens Daily Menu.
3 Q: Who / managing director? _____
A: His name's Georgos Solomos.
4 Q: What / your job / involve? _____
A: I deal with clients, and I organise meetings and events.
5 Q: / write / reports too? _____
A: Yes, I often write reports and memos for our staff.
6 Q: / work / only in the Athens area? _____
A: No, we don't. We work in other parts of Greece, too.
7 Q: / like / your job? _____
A: Yes, I like it a lot.
8 Q: Why / like / it? _____
A: Because I'm always busy, and because of the variety of things I do.

Learning Tip
Make a note of the questions you got wrong. Try to analyse why you made the mistakes. Repeat the exercise next week and see if you improve.

2 🎧 1.3 Listen to the conversation and check your answers.

3 Use some of the information from the interview to write a profile of Kostas Hadavas for the magazine. Write 30–40 words.

4 Work in pairs to fill the gaps with *job* or *work*. Which word is both a verb and a noun? Which word is only a noun?

1 Do you like your _____ ?
2 'What's your _____?' 'I'm an electronics engineer.'
3 We _____ with several Asian companies.
4 Many students have a part-time _____ to earn extra money.
5 My brother starts his first _____ on Monday. He's very nervous about it.
6 Where do you _____ these days?
7 She always does a great _____ when she organises events.
8 It's my _____ to welcome visitors and show them around.
9 I like my new _____. The _____ is varied and interesting.
10 'Hi, Steve. Are you still at _____?' 'Yes, I'm still in the office.'

5 Work in pairs.
Student A: Write a list of jobs that are office based.
Student B: Write a list of jobs that involve travel.
Compare your lists and tell your partner which job(s) you would like to do and why.

READING

6 Rowan Barker Tate Inc. is a multinational confectionery company. Every year, at the annual meeting, the company awards a prize to its 'Employee of the Year'. Work in groups of four. Allocate one candidate (A–D) to each student in the group. Then read the criteria and the information about your candidate and decide why he/she should win.

ROWAN BARKER TATE INC.

Employee of the Year Award

The employee should:
• make a significant contribution to company efficiency, profit, product development or staff development.
• deal with professional or personal problems successfully.
• be a mentor or set a positive example to others.
• represent the company values of healthy living.

THIS YEAR'S CANDIDATES ARE:

A Ian Rogers is 40 years old. He's a production manager and he's based in Singapore. His responsibilities are to supervise projects and to co-ordinate resources. His professional background is in engineering. Ian usually goes scuba diving at weekends and he also enjoys marathon running and cooking. He runs a sports club for local children and he raises money for their training.

B Michelle Yong is 36. She's a finance assistant and she's based in Singapore. Michelle usually deals with Asia division accounts and sometimes does auditing for other divisions. She has a master's degree in business administration. In her free time Michelle likes painting, and she also does judo. Michelle suffers from Chronic Fatigue Syndrome and often works from home, but this does not stop her ambitious career plans.

C Sarah Mullen is 31 years old and based in the head office in Dallas. As the company's communications director, she deals with the company's internal and external communications. Sarah is also in charge of the company's successful new email system. She regularly works late to help colleagues or to attend external events. Sarah has a degree in journalism. Sarah's personal interests are writing detective stories, breeding Yorkshire terriers and showing her dogs in exhibitions.

D Henry King is 57 and is the research and development manager. Henry is based in Dallas. He manages R&D of new product ideas, including the best-selling new chocolate chewing gum range. Henry is famous for always thinking of new ideas and projects. Henry's professional background is in food technology, and in his free time he enjoys visits to museums, art galleries and the theatre.

7 Discuss the four candidates in your groups and choose a winner.

Useful language
I like Ian best. He ...
Michelle should win because she ...
I think Sarah is the best candidate. She ...
I think Henry should win because ...

Student's Book pages 10 and 11

---

job and *work*

VOCABULARY

1 Check that students understand the term *catering services*. Elicit the activities that a catering services company does, eg, it provides food and drinks at parties, receptions, business dinners.

Students work in pairs and write the correct form of the questions. Remind them that they need an auxiliary (*be* or *do*) in order to make the questions. Don't check answers at this stage as this will be done in exercise 2.

2 🎧 1.3 Students listen to the recording to check their answers. Ask them to underline any differences. Read through the Learning Tip with the students. In some cases students will understand the mistakes on their own, in others you may have to provide explanations.

1.3 Listening script
I = Interviewer   **K** = Kostas

I What's your name?
K Kostas Hadavas.
I How do you spell your surname?
K H-A-D-A-V-A-S.
I What do you do?

K I'm the personal assistant to the managing director of Athens Daily Menu.
I Who's the managing director?
K His name's Georgos Solomos.
I What does your job involve?
K I deal with clients, and I organise meetings and events.
I Do you write reports too?
K Yes, I often write reports and memos for our staff.
I Do you work only in the Athens area?
K No, we don't. We work in other parts of Greece, too.
I Do you like your job?
K Yes, I like it a lot.
I Why do you like it?
K Because I'm always busy, and because of the variety of things I do.

Answers
1 How do you spell your surname?
2 What do you do?
3 Who's the managing director?
4 What does your job involve?
5 Do you write reports too?
6 Do you work only in the Athens area?
7 Do you like your job?
8 Why do you like it?

Extension
Ask students to read the audio script out loud, in pairs.

3 You may want to elicit some of the points to be covered, eg:
- name
- surname
- job
- responsibility
- reasons for liking this job

Then elicit the actions that Kostas performs everyday (*he deals with clients, he organises meetings and events, he writes reports, likes his job*, etc). Point out the use of *-s* for the third person singular and remind students they must add an *-s* when writing Kostas' profile.

4 You may want to point out the two different meanings and uses of *job* and *work*:

job (countable noun): the regular work that you do in order to earn money, profession.

work (uncountable noun): the activities that you have to do at school or for your job.

work (verb): to do a job, especially the job you do to earn money.

Answers
1 job (noun)
2 job (noun)
3 work (verb)
4 job (noun)
5 job (noun)
6 work (verb)
7 job (noun)
8 job (noun)
9 job, work (nouns)
10 work (noun)

5 Draw a vertical line on the board and write the headings *Office based* and *Travel*. Elicit at least three jobs that are usually based in an office, and three that usually involve travel. For example, they may suggest office-based jobs such as: *secretary, accountant, computer programmer,* and jobs that involve travel: *flight attendant, reporter, photographer.*

Ask students to work in pairs and continue the exercise. A dictionary might be helpful if they are using their own language. Encourage students to give reasons why they would like to do certain jobs.

Employee of the Year Award

READING

6 You may want to pre-teach or draw attention to the following words and phrases:

employee (someone who is paid to work for someone else)

employer (a person or organisation that employs people)

award a prize (to give money or a prize following an official decision)

criterion, criteria (a standard by which you judge, decide about or deal with something)

Tell students that they're going to read about a competition called *Employee of the Year*. Ask them if they've ever seen, heard of, or taken part in a similar competition, such as *Student of the Year, Manager of the Year, Best Person of the Year,* etc. Brainstorm ideas on the characteristics candidates should have. Tell students to read the criteria set by Rowan Barker Tate Inc.

Divide the class into groups of four. If possible, try to balance male and female students in each group. Each student in the group should read a candidate's profile out loud to the other members of the group.

Extension
Tell students that if they aren't familiar with some of the words, they can write them on the board. Once all of the profiles have been read, explain any words written on the board.

7 Students have five minutes to discuss and choose a winner. You can provide extra phrases such as:

I think Michelle is the ideal candidate, because she ...

Sarah should get the prize, because she ...

Henry is the person who best deserves the title of 'Employee of the Year,' because ...

Ian has all the good qualities of the best candidate, in fact ...

EXAM SPOTLIGHT

1.3

B1 Business Preliminary Exam Format and Reading Test

EXAM FORMAT

Exam Success

What are your strong and weak areas in English? Concentrate on the areas you have most difficulty with at first.

Introduction

The B1 Business Preliminary Exam has three papers and tests your reading, writing, listening and speaking skills.

Each skill is worth 30 marks (total = 120). The pass grade is around 65% (or around 80 marks). You pass or fail on your total marks. For example, if you fail one skill but your total is 90, you pass the exam.

The table below shows the length of each test and its structure. You will learn more about the structure of each test in this book.

Paper	Skill(s)	Marks	Length (minutes)	Structure
1	Reading & Writing	30 + 30	90 minutes (Reading: 60 minutes Writing: 30 minutes)	Reading: 7 parts Writing: 2 parts
2	Listening	30	40 minutes	4 parts
3	Speaking	30	12 minutes	3 parts

You will get your results approximately seven weeks after the exam. Your results show your overall grade (*Pass with Merit, Pass, Narrow Fail or Fail*) and your performance in each paper. If you pass, you will get your certificate about four weeks after your results.

1 Read about the format of the B1 Business Preliminary Exam above. Find the answers to these questions.

1 How many papers are there in the B1 Business Preliminary Exam?
2 What skills are tested?
3 What's the maximum number of marks you can get?
4 How many marks do you need to pass?
5 Do you have to pass all four skills to pass the exam?
6 Which is the longest paper: Reading & Writing, Listening or Speaking?
7 How many parts are there in the Reading Test?
8 How many parts are there in the Speaking Test?
9 When do you get your results?
10 What do the results tell you?
11 When do you get your certificate?
12 Does everyone get a certificate?

EXAM FORMAT

The Reading Test has seven parts, which are always in the same order:
- Parts One to Five test your general reading comprehension.
- Part Six tests your grammar.
- Part Seven tests your ability to complete a form with relevant information.
- Each part contains a reading text and a comprehension task.
- Many different types of text are used, such as notices, messages, adverts, timetables, leaflets, graphs, charts, business letters, product descriptions, reports, minutes, newspaper and magazine articles, memos. Column 4 in the table below shows which text types are used in each part of the exam.
- You have 60 minutes to answer 45 questions and to transfer your answers to the Answer Sheet in pencil. If you need to change an answer, use an eraser.
- You can make notes on the text but not on the Answer Sheet.
- The table below summarises all the features of the Reading Test.

Part	Questions	Task type	Text type	Example
1	5	Multiple choice	Notices, messages, timetables, adverts, leaflets, etc.	Unit 5, page 54
2	5	Matching	Notice, list, plan, contents page, etc.	Unit 5, page 54
3	5	Matching	Graphs, charts, tables, etc.	Unit 5, page 55
4	7	Right / Wrong / Doesn't say	Advert, business letter, product description, report, minutes, etc. (150–200 words)	Unit 9, page 94
5	6	Multiple choice	Newspaper or magazine article, advert, report, leaflet, etc. (300–400 words)	Unit 9, page 95
6	12	Multiple choice cloze	Newspaper or magazine article, advert, leaflet, etc. (125–150 words)	Unit 12, page 124
7	5	Form-filling, note completion	Short memos, letters, notices, adverts, etc.	Unit 12, page 125

2 Read about the format of the Reading Test above and decide whether the following statements are true or false. Tick ✓ as appropriate.

	True	False
1 There are five parts in the Reading Test.	☐	☐
2 Grammar is not tested in the Reading Test.	☐	☐
3 A wide variety of text types are used.	☐	☐
4 Graphs and charts containing figures are used as texts.	☐	☐
5 There are 45 questions in each part of the test.	☐	☐
6 You have 60 minutes to do the Reading Test.	☐	☐
7 You must write your answers in pencil.	☐	☐
8 You can't make notes on the Reading text.	☐	☐
9 The longest text has 300–400 words.	☐	☐
10 All the tasks are multiple choice.	☐	☐

Student's Book pages 12 and 13

EXAM FORMAT

Read the introduction with students. Stop at every sentence and check that students understand the main facts about the exam (number of papers, skills that are tested, marks, pass grade, etc).

Ask students to read the contents of the grid individually. When they've finished, they should work in pairs and ask each other at least three questions about the contents of the grid. Invite them to use questions starting with: *How many? How long? What?*

Then read the text about results and certificates. Pause at every sentence and check that students understand the main facts.

1 Tell students that they have two minutes to answer the following 12 questions. After two minutes, if some students haven't finished yet, tell them to continue the exercise in pairs.

Answers
1 Three.
2 Reading, Writing, Listening and Speaking.
3 120.
4 Around 80.
5 No.
6 Reading & Writing.
7 Seven.
8 Three.
9 Approximately seven weeks after the exam.
10 The overall grade, and your performance in each paper.
11 About four weeks after the results.
12 No. (Only if you pass.)

Look at the Exam Success tip with your students. Elicit their strong and weak areas in English.

Ask students to take a sheet of paper, divide it into two columns and make a list of their strong and weak points in English. Here is an example:

Strong	**Weak**
I'm very good at reading texts.	My vocabulary is limited.
I'm quite good at writing.	I need more grammar practice.
I always do my homework.	I'm not very good at listening.

Collect the pieces of paper as a reminder of your students' needs.

Reading Test

Read the information about the Reading Test with students. After reading each item in the list, pause to make sure that students understand, and to give them time to process the information.

Ask students to look at the table. Point out the number of parts in the Reading Test and the number of questions in each part. Also point out the different types of task. Ask students to browse through the book and find some examples of text types, eg: notices, timetables, charts, product description, etc. Tell students that they'll find examples of exam questions for reading on the pages listed.

Extension

Bring examples of the following to class: notices, messages, adverts, timetables, leaflets, graphs, charts, business letters, product descriptions, reports, minutes, newspaper and magazine articles, memos, so that when students read about these different types of texts, they'll see their format.

You might like to do something with the numbers in this text, so you can ask the students:

How many questions are there in Part Six?

How many words are there in Part Four?

Or you can ask the students to work in pairs and ask each other similar questions, choosing the numbers at random.

2   Students work alone to do exercise 2. When they've finished, they can check their answers with a partner. Then check answers as a whole class and ask students to explain why each answer is true or false.

Answers
 1 False (There are 7 parts.)
 2 False (Part Six tests grammar.)
 3 True
 4 True
 5 False (There are 45 questions altogether in the test.)
 6 True
 7 True
 8 False (You can make notes on the text, but not on the Answer sheet.)
 9 True
10 False (Only parts 1, 5 and 6 are multiple choice.)

Overview

2.1   Business topic: Work in progress

LISTENING   New projects

GRAMMAR   The present continuous

READING   Flexible working

SPEAKING   Pros and cons of flexible working

VOCABULARY   Hiring and firing

2.2   Business skills: Making arrangements

LISTENING   Arranging a meeting

WRITING   Confirming a meeting

GRAMMAR   Prepositions of time: *at, in, on*

WRITING   Accepting an invitation

2.3   Exam spotlight: Writing Test Introduction

Understanding the Writing Test format

Writing an email asking for information

Proofreading and correcting mistakes

Useful language from Module 2

Wordlist

abroad	hire	production plant	suggestion
amazing	invite	project	supervisor
attendance	job applicant	project manager	take on
branch	kid	quality inspector	take shape
career field	management	reception (a party)	target
check	marketing manager	reception (a place)	temp (n + v)
confirm	maternity leave	reservation	temporary
construction	minor (adj)	return flight	temporary employment
convention centre	mobile (n)	routine	agency
correspondence	opportunity	sack (v)	tour guide
discover	option	sales team	trade fair
dismiss	partner	scenery	uncertain
employ	pay rise / cut	self-employed	update (n + v)
experience (n + v)	perform	shopping centre	variety
finance director	period of transition	short-term	venue
fire	permanent	skill	workforce
for or against	potential client	strategy meeting	
frightening	present (n)	sub-contractors	

Expressions

ahead of / behind schedule

avoid mistakes

from day to day

give a presentation

How about ...?

How does ... sound?

I look forward to ... (verb + -ing)

I regret that ...

I'm very sorry, but ...

in progress

It will be a pleasure to ...

make photocopies

meet a deadline

proceed according to plan

Sounds great!

take time off

We will be delighted to ...

What about ...?

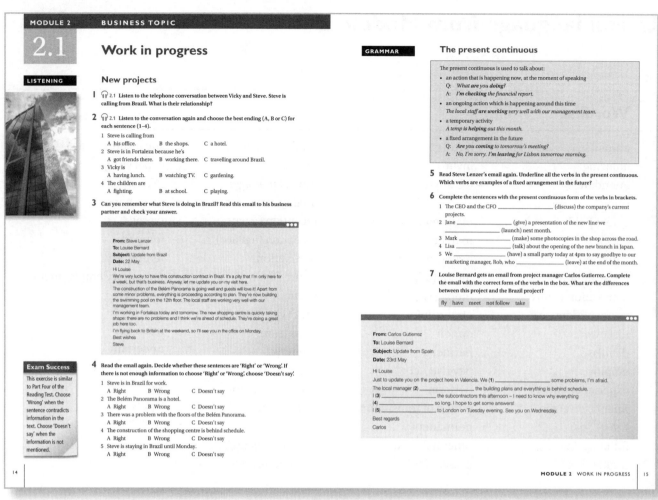

Student's Book pages 14 and 15

New Projects

LISTENING

1 🎧 **2.1** Before starting the listening task, tell students they're going to hear a telephone conversation between Vicky and Steve. Ask them these questions:

Who do you think Vicky and Steve are?

What is their conversation going to be about?

What do you think the relationship between Vicky and Steve is?

Ask students to listen to the recording and answer the question. Then check the answer with the class and ask students which phrase gives the answer.

2.1 Listening script
V = Vicky   **S** = Steve

V Hello.
S Hi, Vicky.
V Hi, darling. How are things in Brazil?
S Pretty good. And with you?
V Fine. Where are you calling from?
S My hotel in Fortaleza. It's on the north-east coast.
V Is it nice there?
S Yes, the scenery is amazing.
V And what are you doing in Fortaleza?

S I'm working on the plans for the shopping centre. What are you doing right now?
V Oh, it's sunny today, so I'm working in the garden.
S And what are the children doing?
V They're watching TV. No, that's not right. Tommy's playing on his computer, and Emma's with her friends, I think.
S Good. And are you doing anything nice this weekend ...

Answer
Vicky and Steve are a married couple.
(*Hi, darling. ... what are the children doing?*)

2 🎧 **2.1** Ask students to read the questions and to answer them if they can. Point out that *he's* in question 2 has two possible meanings, *he is* and *he has*: '*he has* got friends there', but '*he is* working there' and '*he is* travelling around Brazil'.

Play the recording again and tell students to check their answers.

Answers
1 C   2 B   3 C   4 C

3 Ask students if they can remember what Steve is doing in Brazil (*he's working on the plans for the shopping centre*). Tell students to read the email to check.

4 Tell students to read the questions first. They should then read the email again, and underline the information that either supports or contradicts the statement.

To help students choose the correct option, remind them that if the text contains
- information that supports the statement, mark 'A Right'
- information that contradicts the statement, mark 'B Wrong'
- no information that either supports or contradicts the statement, mark 'C Doesn't say'.

Answers
1 A (*construction contract*; *that's business*)
2 A (*the guests*; *swimming pool on the 12th floor* – NB: alternative answers might be possible)
3 C (*some minor problems*, but it doesn't say what)
4 B (*I think we're ahead of schedule*)
5 B (*I'm flying back to Britain at the weekend*)

The present continuous

GRAMMAR

5 Students work alone to do exercise 5. You could tell them to use different coloured pens if possible for the different uses.

Students then compare their answers with a partner.

Extension
Ask individual students to give an example of an action that's happening now from the text. Ask another student for the example of a temporary activity. Finally, ask a third student for the example of a fixed arrangement.

Actions happening now:
- The construction of the Belém Panorama is going well.
- ... everything is proceeding according to plan.
- They're now building the swimming pool ...
- The local staff are working very well with our management team.
- The new shopping centre is quickly taking shape ...
- They're doing a great job here too.

Temporary activity:
- I'm working in Fortaleza today and tomorrow.

Fixed arrangements:
- I'm flying back to Britain at the weekend ...

6 Students work alone to do exercise 6, then check their answers with a partner.

Check answers with the class. Then ask individual students to read out a sentence.

Answers
1 are discussing
2 is giving, 're launching
3 is making
4 is talking
5 're having, 's leaving

7 Students work in pairs. Ask them to write the verbs in the text, and then discuss the differences between the project in Spain and the Brazil project.

Answers
1 're having
2 isn't following
3 'm meeting
4 's talking
5 'm flying

Differences:
- They're having some problems in Valencia.
- The local manager is not following the building plans.
- Everything is behind schedule.

Photocopiable activity
See page 162.

Reproduced Student's Book pages 16 and 17

READING

Learning Tip

Don't try to understand every word in a reading text; concentrate on doing the tasks.

1 Read the title of the article. What do you think 'flexible working' means? How is it different from normal working? Tell the class your ideas.

2 Read the article and check your ideas.

Flexible working

Nowadays, many people are trying to balance their working life with a busy home life. Our hours extend beyond nine-to-five and with so much traffic on the road, the daily commute is also taking longer and longer – in the UK, the average worker spends two hours a day or more travelling to and from work. As a result, modern life is more stressful than ever.

However, technology is changing the way we work and we do more and more work from home or while we travel; for example, we can reply to emails on our phone on the train, or read a report at home on our tablet in the evening. Technology makes working more flexible and so we can work at different times of day, or maybe we don't have to go to the office at all because we can work from home.

More and more businesses are offering flexible working hours to staff. Some companies have a flexitime system so an employee can work, for example, any time between 8 in the morning and 8 in the evening. And on certain days, they can work from home.

Obviously, flexitime works well with some types of business such as financial services or technology-based industries which are screen-based. For companies who need staff talking face-to-face with customers, it doesn't work so well. Flexitime is also very popular with employees with young families. Flexible working can also include job-sharing when two people divide one job between them so they can be at home more often.

For flexible working, you need a quiet place at home. You also need a good Internet connection and a phone. Some employees discover that flexible working isn't right for them because they can't concentrate at home or separate their work responsibilities from their home life. But for others, flexible working is the perfect answer.

3 Read the text again and choose the best answer (A, B or C) for each question (1–4).

1 According to the text, which of the following statements is true?
   A Flexible working is very popular with people who travel for their job.
   B People find it difficult to balance the demands of a job and a home life.
   C More people are starting their own businesses at home.

2 According to the text, what has made flexible working possible?
   A Technology and the Internet
   B New types of business
   C Longer hours at work

3 According to the text, flexitime works well
   A in any type of company.
   B in customer service industries.
   C for jobs with less face-to-face contact.

4 According to the text, flexible working is the perfect answer if
   A you like working with technology.
   B you don't like working with other people.
   C you can manage your work from home.

4 Find words or phrases in the text that mean:
1 to make equal (paragraph 1)
2 the action of travelling to and from work every day (paragraph 1) _____
3 not relaxing (paragraph 1)
4 able to change (paragraph 2)
5 a system of work so you can work at different hours of the day or week (paragraph 3)
6 focus your attention on one activity (paragraph 5)
7 things you do as part of your job (Paragraph 5) _____

SPEAKING

Flexible working

5 Work in pairs. Read these comments about flexible working. Are they positive or negative comments? Tick ✔ as appropriate. Then add your own comments.

	Positive	Negative
A It's difficult to organise my time, so I often work at weekends as well when I'm at home.	☐	☐
B I like getting up later in the morning because I don't have to commute.	☐	☐
C We have three children at school, so we see them more in the evening.	☐	☐
D Sometimes I need to speak to my team, but they aren't always in the office.	☐	☐
E I get more work done in my living room because it's quiet all day.	☐	☐
F Last week my Internet didn't work. If I'm in the office, I can call IT and they fix it straight away.	☐	☐
G _____	☐	☐
H _____	☐	☐
I _____	☐	☐

VOCABULARY

Hiring and firing

6 Work in pairs. Look at the pictures and write the correct verb form in each gap.

1 How's work going, Joanna? / It's OK, but I really want to go abroad. I'm _____ (save) some money for a flight to Australia.

2 Hi, Joanna. _____ (you / come) for lunch? / No, thanks, Gerhard. I've got a meeting with Marta at 1.30. I want to ask her for a pay rise.

3 Joanna, I'm sorry. I can't give you a pay rise. I'm afraid we don't need you any more. / What! _____ (you / fire) me? / Yes, I'm afraid so. Your job was only temporary, after all.

4 Joanna, what's wrong? / Marta has decided to fire me! / No! I am sorry. / Oh, don't worry, Philippe. I _____ (go) to Australia next month. I've got a job as a tour guide.

7 Choose the appropriate words to complete the sentences.
1 The company is giving a pay rise / a pay cut to employees who meet their targets.
2 There's a lot more administration work with this project; we need to employ / dismiss more office staff.
3 Their sales are dropping, so they are taking on / sacking about 10 per cent of the workforce.
4 The department is hiring / firing employees who are performing badly.

Student's Book pages 16 and 17

Flexible working

READING

1 Class discussion. Before starting the reading task, write the word *Flexible Working* on the board. Ask students if they know what the word means.
Then ask:

Why do some people like flexible working?

Has any of you done a job which allowed some degree of flexible working?

Was it a good experience?

2 Ask students to read the article to find out more about flexible working. Refer students to the Learning Tip. Remind students that if they find a word they don't understand, they should think what it might mean from the context, and then they should continue reading. They might find that they can guess the meaning, or that they don't need to know precisely what the word means in order to do the exercise.

3 Tell students to read the questions and answers relating to the text first. Then ask them to read the text. As they read, they can underline any information that answers the questions. After the first reading, students should look for the answers in the text.

Answers
1 B People find it difficult to balance the demands of a job and a home life.
2 A Technology and the Internet
3 B for jobs with less face-to-face contact
4 C you can manage your work from home.

4 Tell students to look quickly through the text to find the words or phrases.

Answers
1 balance
2 commute
3 stressful
4 flexible
5 flexitime system
6 concentrate
7 work responsibilities

Flexible working

5 In pairs, students read about the positive and negative aspects of flexible working. They then discuss whether the comments are positive or negative with their partner and tick the appropriate box for each one. Ask them to build the discussion. For example:

One reason for more people to take up flexible working is the ability to manage their own schedule: You can arrange your day as you like.

That's true, but …

Ask students to add any additional comments about flexible working to the table.

Answers
A Negative
B Positive
C Positive
D Negative
E Positive
F Negative

Hiring and firing

VOCABULARY

6 Write the following on the board.
  – *an action happening now*
  – *a temporary activity*
  – *a fixed arrangement in the future*

Ask students to work in pairs and write one example of each of these uses of the present continuous.

After checking students' answers, write an example of each use on the board.

Students then write the correct form of the verb to complete the comic-strip story.

Extension
Ask students to work in pairs. They practise the dialogues together.

Then invite four students to the front of the class to read out the four dialogues. Philippe, Gerhard and Marta should stand in different parts of the classroom, and Joanna should move from one person to the next. Tell students to act as much as possible, eg: when Philippe asks Joanna what's wrong, it must be because he has seen that she's upset.

Answers
1 saving
2 Are you coming
3 Are you firing
4 'm going

7 Ask students to work on their own to complete the exercise. When they've finished, ask them to compare their answers with a partner.

After you've checked their answers, ask students to write new sentences, using the options that they haven't used.

Answers
1 a pay rise
2 employ
3 sacking
4 firing

BUSINESS SKILLS

2.2 Making arrangements

LISTENING

Arranging a meeting

1 🎧 2.2 It's Friday morning. Martina Möller is calling Dave Prakash to arrange a meeting. Listen to their conversation. When do they agree to meet?

Day _____   Time _____

2 🎧 2.2 Work in pairs. Listen to the conversation again.
Student A: Write in Martina's diary what she is doing next week.
Student B: Write in Dave's diary what he is doing next week.

Martina
Monday, 18
am   visit new plant
pm _____
Tuesday, 19
am _____
pm _____
Wednesday, 20
am _____
pm _____
Thursday, 21
am _____
pm _____
Friday, 22
am _____
pm _____

Dave
Monday, 18
am _____
pm   take time off
Tuesday, 19
am _____
pm _____
Wednesday, 20
am _____
pm _____
Thursday, 21
am _____
pm _____
Friday, 22
am _____
pm _____

3 Now tell your partner the information you have written in your diary.
Student A: Tell Student B what Martina is doing next week.
Martina's visiting the new plant on Monday morning.
Student B: Fill in Martina's diary.
Student B: Tell Student A what Dave is doing next week.
Dave's taking time off on Monday afternoon.
Student A: Fill in Dave's diary.

4 Read Martina's email to Dave Prakash. Choose the best 'Subject' line (A, B or C).
A Plans for the weekend
B Meeting next week
C Visit to the new plant

To: Dave Prakash
Subject: _____
Hi Dave
I'm just writing to confirm our meeting next Wednesday. I've booked a table at the Italian restaurant in Grey Street. It's quite quiet, so we can talk.
I'll see you in Reception at 12.30.
Have a good weekend!
Martina

5 Look at these questions from the conversation between Dave and Martina. Tick the suggestions.
When can we meet? ☐
How about Monday morning? ☐
Are you free on Thursday? ☐
Are you going to the trade fair? ☐
What about Tuesday, for lunch? ☐
How does 12.30 sound? ☐

WRITING

Confirming a meeting

6 Look at the list of activities below and choose three to do on Monday. Write them on the diary page and add another two activities of your own.

Memo
· present company to potential client
· meet sales team
· have lunch with Mark
· show quality inspectors around
· meet marketing manager
· visit production plant
· interview job applicant
· collect kids from school

MONDAY, 18
8AM _____   1PM _____
9AM _____   2PM _____
10AM _____   3PM _____
11AM _____   4PM _____
12AM _____   5PM _____

7 Work with a partner. Using your diary page in exercise 6, arrange to meet on Monday.

8 Write an email to your partner to confirm your meeting. Use the email in exercise 4 to help you.

To:
Subject:

Student's Book pages 18 and 19

Arranging a meeting

LISTENING

1 🎧 2.2 Tell students that they're going to hear a conversation between Martina and Dave arranging a meeting. Ask: *When do they agree to meet?* Then play the recording once.

2.2 Listening script
D = Dave   M = Martina

D Dave Prakash.
M Hi, Dave. It's Martina. Listen, I need to discuss the designs for the new R300 series with you. When can we meet?
D I can't make it today; I've got meetings all day. How about Monday morning?
M I'm visiting the new plant on Monday morning, but the afternoon is OK.
D I'm probably taking time off in the afternoon, actually.
M OK. Let me see … are you free on Thursday?
D No, I'm visiting clients on Thursday morning, and then I'm flying to Prague on Thursday afternoon.
M Are you going to the trade fair?
D Yes, that's on Friday morning. I'm coming back on Friday afternoon. Look, what about Tuesday, for lunch?
M No, I'm meeting the sales team on Tuesday and it's an all-day thing. That leaves Wednesday.

D Wednesday looks OK at the moment, but don't forget the strategy meeting at 10 o'clock.
M Oh, that's right, I'm going to that too. But I'm free after that. How does 12.30 sound? We could have lunch.
D Great, we can talk and eat on Wednesday. Now I must run. I've got a meeting with the finance director.

Answers
Day: Wednesday
Time: 12.30

2 🎧 2.2 Students work in pairs. Before playing the recording again, ask students what other activities Martina and Dave mentioned and the days that they're going to do them. Tell students to listen to the recording again; in each pair, one student fills in Martina's diary, and the other, Dave's diary.

Answers

> **Martina**
> **Monday, 18**
> am *Visit new plant.*
> pm –
> **Tuesday, 19**
> am *Meet sales team.*
> pm *Meet sales team.*
> **Wednesday, 20**
> am *Go to strategy meeting – 10 am.*
> pm *Meet Dave – 12.30.*
> **Thursday, 21**
> am –
> pm –
> **Friday, 22**
> am –
> pm –

> **Dave**
> **Monday, 18**
> am –
> pm *Take time off.*
> **Tuesday, 19**
> am –
> pm –
> **Wednesday, 20**
> am *Go to strategy meeting – 10 am.*
> pm *Meet Martina – 12.30.*
> **Thursday, 21**
> am *Visit clients.*
> pm *Fly to Prague.*
> **Friday, 22**
> am *Go to trade fair.*
> pm *Come back.*

3 Ask students to tell each other what they've written in their diaries.

4 Ask students to read the email and to discuss, in their pairs, which subject line is best and why.

Answers
Subject: Meeting next week

5 Ask students, in their pairs, to decide which of the questions are suggestions.

Answers
How about Monday morning? ✓
Are you free on Thursday? ✓
What about Tuesday, for lunch? ✓
How does 12.30 sound? ✓

Confirming a meeting

WRITING

6 Check that students understand what they have to do. They choose three items from the list and write them on the diary page, and add a further two activities of their own.

7 Students work in pairs. Ask them to arrange a meeting with their partner.

8 Ask students to read Martina's email to Dave Prakash again, and then write an email to their partner to confirm the day and time of their meeting.

Sample answer

> To: Carlos Martinez
> Subject: Meeting next week
> Hi Carlos
> I'm just writing to confirm our meeting next Thursday at 4.30.
> Have a good evening.
> Rebecca

Photocopiable activity
See page 163.

Student's Book page (reproduction)

Prepositions of time: *at*, *in*, *on*

We use *at*, *in* and *on* with the following time expressions:
- *at* + specific times, festivals in general; also *at lunchtime*, *at night*, *at the weekend*
- *in* + parts of the day, months, seasons, years, centuries
- *on* + days of the week and parts of named days, named festival days, dates

Note: *at the weekend* (UK English) and *on the weekend* (US English).

1 Fill the gaps with *at*, *in* or *on*.

0	in 2009	6	_____ the evening
1	_____ Christmas	7	_____ New Year's Day
2	_____ winter	8	_____ 20 July
3	_____ 7 o'clock	9	_____ the 21st century
4	_____ June	10	_____ Friday morning
5	_____ the afternoon	11	_____ half past six

2 Fill the gaps with the correct prepositions.

1 The design meeting is _____ Friday _____ 4.30.
2 We opened our Buenos Aires office _____ 2003. We're opening a second office _____ September.
3 I'm flying to Washington _____ Wednesday next week. My return flight is _____ 16 May.
4 I'm going to lunch now. Can I speak to you _____ the afternoon?
5 I don't have time to write the report today. I'll do it _____ Monday morning.
6 I'm self-employed. I find I often work best _____ night.

Accepting an invitation

3 Look at the letter. Who is it to? Who is it from?

New Directions
Osborne Park
Morpeth

2nd May 20___
Dear Mr Olaya

4 The sentences in the letter below are in the wrong order. Put them into the correct order (1-6).

_____ I look forward to seeing you again this year.
_____ Please confirm your attendance at both the fair and the reception.
_____ This year, the fair is taking place at the new convention centre in Morpeth, on 21st and 22nd June.
_____ You are also invited to a special reception at 8pm on 21st June, to celebrate the tenth anniversary of New Directions and our new venue.
_____ Best regards, Andrea Greer
_____ I am writing to invite you to the New Directions Book Fair in June.

5 Bob Olaya and Felix Lund of Menta Books are talking about the Book Fair. Complete the conversation with prepositions of time.

Bob Felix, are we planning to go to the New Directions Book Fair this year?
Felix Yes, I think so. It's always a good event. We usually make lots of new contacts. When is it?
Bob It's (1) _____ June this year. It's (2) _____ Thursday and Friday the 21st and 22nd.
Felix Oh, just a second. Aren't we going to Helsinki that week?
Bob No, the Helsinki conference is (3) _____ July.
Felix Oh yes, that's right. Fine, let's go to the Book Fair.
Bob There's a special reception (4) _____ the 21st.
Felix Is it (5) _____ lunchtime?
Bob No, it's (6) _____ the evening (7) _____ 8 o'clock.
Felix Sounds great! Can you get everything organised?
Bob No problem. I'll confirm our attendance.

6 🎧 2.3 Listen to the conversation and check your answers.

7 Write a reply to Andrea Greer to confirm your attendance at the fair and either accept or decline the invitation to the reception. Use some of the expressions from the Useful language box below in your letter. Write 60–80 words.

Andrea Greer
New Directions
Osborne Park
Morpeth

7th May 20___

Dear Ms Greer

MENTA BOOKS
London – Toronto – Sydney

Useful language

Thank you for …	We will be delighted to …
Many thanks for …	It will be a pleasure to …
We can confirm …	I'm very sorry, but …
I confirm our …	I regret that …

Student's Book pages 20 and 21

Teacher's notes

Prepositions of time: *at*, *in*, *on*

GRAMMAR

1 Ask some students which day they've arranged their meetings. Elicit: *on* + day.

Ask some students what time they've arranged their meetings. Elicit: *at* + time. Tell students that another preposition often used with time expressions is *in*. Refer to the information about prepositions.

Ask students to do exercise 1.

Answers
1 at   2 in   3 at   4 in   5 in   6 in
7 on   8 on   9 in   10 on   11 at

2 Ask students to work alone to do the exercise.

Answers
1 on, at
2 in, in
3 on, on
4 in
5 on
6 at

Accepting an invitation

WRITING

3 Ask students to look at the beginning of the letter. *Who is it to? Who is it from?*

Answers
The letter is to: Mr Olaya
The letter is from: New Directions

4 Ask students to decide on the correct order of the sentences to complete the letter. Students check their answers with a partner.

Answer
The correct order is: 5-4-2-3-6-1.

5 Ask students to complete the sentences alone. Then tell them to practise the conversation in pairs. If one student has made a mistake, the other can correct it. Students should then swap roles and read again. Don't check answers at this stage as this will be done in exercise 6.

6 🎧 2.3 Students listen and check their answers in exercise 5. Ask students what Bob and Felix said exactly. Ask students for any alternative sentences.

Point out to students that you say *the* and *of* when talking about dates, but you don't write these words, ie, *the 21st of June* (spoken), but *21st June* (written).

Nowadays, you can also leave out the ordinal letters when writing the date: *21 June.*

In American English, the day and month are usually inverted, and the cardinal number is often used: *June 21* (*twenty-one*).

Draw students' attention to the conversation in exercise 5. The article *the* appears before the dates, because the month is not written afterwards.

2.3 Listening script
B = Bob   **F** = Felix

B Felix, are we planning to go to the New Directions Book Fair this year?
F Yes, I think so. It's always a good event. We usually make lots of new contacts. When is it?
B It's in June this year. It's on Thursday and Friday the 21st and 22nd.
F Oh, just a second. Aren't we going to Helsinki that week?
B No, the Helsinki conference is in July.
F Oh yes, that's right. Fine, let's go to the Book Fair.
B There's a special reception on the 21st.
F Is it at lunchtime?
B No, it's in the evening at 8 o'clock.
F Sounds great! Can you get everything organised?
B No problem. I'll confirm our attendance.

Answers
1 in   2 on   3 in   4 on   5 at   6 in   7 at

7 Ask students to write a reply to Andrea Greer's letter to confirm their attendance at the fair. They should accept or decline the invitation to the special reception. They can use some of the expressions from the Useful language box.

Point out that this activity is like Part Two of the Writing Test, in which they have to write 60–80 words. A good way of increasing the word count is to add explanations, eg:

We will be delighted to attend the special reception on the 21st, as this will be a good opportunity to meet the other publishers.

Or:

I regret that I cannot attend the special reception because my company is giving a dinner for the sales team.

Sample answer

Dear Ms Greer

Thank you for your invitation to the New Directions Book Fair. I can confirm that we will be at the fair on both days.

Thank you also for the invitation to the special reception. I regret that neither I nor my colleague, Felix Lund, will be able to attend the reception, as my company have organised an event on Thursday evening. However, I look forward to seeing you again during the day.

Best wishes

Bob Olaya

EXAM SPOTLIGHT

2.3 Writing Test: Introduction

EXAM FORMAT

The Writing Test comes immediately after the Reading Test. You have 1 hour and 30 minutes to do the Reading and Writing Tests.

The Writing Test has two parts:
In Part One, you have to write a piece of internal communication, ie to someone in the company. You have to write 30–40 words.
In Part Two, you have to write a piece of business correspondence, ie to someone outside the company. You have to write 60–80 words.
You write both answers on the Answer Sheet.
There is a total of 30 marks for the Writing Test.

EXAM PRACTICE

Exam Success

During the exam, you must write your email on the Answer Sheet provided. The information for **To**, **Date** and **Subject** is given. You don't need to copy this onto the Answer Sheet.

1 Answer the exam question below.

- You are going to take your B1 Business Preliminary Exam.
- Write an **email** to your teacher:
  - telling her that you are preparing for the exam
  - asking her for more information about the Writing Test
  - asking her for any suggestions on how to avoid mistakes.
- **Write 30–40 words.**

To:	Ms Dilts
From:	
Date:	6 February
Subject:	Information on B1 Business Preliminary Exam

2 Read your teacher's reply. Which paragraph (1–5) is about the following?

A Part One of the Writing Test _____
B Part Two of the Writing Test _____
C avoiding mistakes _____

From:	Jane Dilts
To:	
Date:	7 February
Subject:	RE: Information on B1 Business Preliminary Exam

(1) I'm glad to hear that you're going to take the B1 Business Preliminary Exam.
(2) In the exam, you must produce two pieces of writing: the first is an internal company communication and the second is a piece of business correspondence.
(3) The first might be a note, a message, a memo or an email of 30–40 words. The register (the language style) can be neutral or informal. There are written prompts (instructions) for this part of the Writing Test.
(4) The second piece of writing might be an email or a letter of 60–80 words. In this task, you will have to give information about a product, deal with requests, make or change reservations, apologise, complain, etc. This kind of communication is always with somebody outside the company and is written in reply to an email or letter from this person. The register is either neutral or formal.
(5) Remember to read your writing several times to check structure, content, grammar, vocabulary and spelling.
Good luck in the exam.
Best regards
Jane Dilts

3 Read the teacher's reply again and decide if the following features are connected with Part One or Part Two of the Writing Test. Tick ✔ as appropriate.

	Part One	Part Two
1 internal communication	☐	☐
2 business correspondence	☐	☐
3 30–40 words	☐	☐
4 60–80 words	☐	☐
5 note	☐	☐
6 letter	☐	☐
7 informal	☐	☐
8 formal	☐	☐
9 written prompts	☐	☐
10 reply	☐	☐

4 Correcting mistakes is an essential skill for writing. Read the memo below, which a student has written in the exam. Circle any mistakes and write the appropriate correction symbol above them.

Correction symbols:
Grammar	G	Spelling	Sp
Wrong Word	WW	Punctuation	P
Word Order	WO	This meaning is not clear	?

- You are going to attend a three-day training course.
- Write a **memo** to your boss:
  - saying that you will be out of the office
  - telling him when you are coming back
  - reminding him that one of your colleagues will deal with the new temp.
- **Write 30–40 words.**

MEMO

To:	Jeff Hutchinson
From:	
Date:	21 May
Subject:	Training Course

Hi Jeff

I'm going to a~~t~~nd a training course on selling techniques for tree day, so I'm not going to be in office.

I'll be back on Mondays, 27th May.

Remind that tomorrow a temp is start Deborah will show her what to do.

22   MODULE 2 EXAM SPOTLIGHT 23

Student's Book pages 22 and 23

EXAM FORMAT

Ask students to read the Exam Format information. Then ask the following questions to check comprehension:

1 *How long does the Writing Test last?*
(The text doesn't say how long the Writing Test alone lasts, just that the Reading and Writing Tests together last 1 hour and 30 minutes.)

2 *How many parts are there in the Writing Test?*
(Two parts.)

3 *In Part One, what type of text do you have to write and how many words should there be in the text?*
(A piece of internal communication of 30–40 words.)

4 *In Part Two, what type of text do you have to write and how many words should there be in the text?* (A piece of business correspondence of 60–80 words.)

5 *What is the total number of marks in the Writing Test?*
(30 marks.)

6 *Where must you write your answers?*
(On the Answer sheet.)

EXAM PRACTICE

1 Read the instructions with students. Tell them that they must answer all parts of the questions.

Ask students to write the email. Tell them not to copy the words in the question, but to use other words or phrases that mean the same.

Refer students to the Exam Success tip. Tell students that the *To*, *Date* and *Subject* information is not counted in the 30–40 words. However, the start / end (*Dear / Hi, Yours sincerely / Bye / See you*) are counted, as they demonstrate the correct level of formality.

Sample answer

Dear Ms Dilts

I'm writing to say that I'm getting ready for my B1 Business Preliminary exam. Could you tell me something about the Writing Test? And can you give me advice on how not to make mistakes?

Yours sincerely

Michela

2 Students work in pairs. Ask students to read the reply from Ms Dilts and to decide which paragraph is about:
A *Part One of the Writing Test*
B *Part Two of the Writing Test*
C *avoiding mistakes*.

Answers
A 3 B 4 C 5

3 Students work alone. Ask students to tick the appropriate boxes. Students check answers with their partner.

Answers
1 Part One
2 Part Two
3 Part One
4 Part Two
5 Part One
6 Part Two
7 Part One
8 Part Two
9 Part One
10 Part Two

4 Students work alone. Allow five minutes for this task. When they've finished, they should check their answers with their partner.

Point out that the memo contains two dates, written in two different ways: *21 May, 27th May*. Both are correct, but they shouldn't use both ways in the same piece of writing.

Answer

To: Jeff Hutchinson
From:
Date: 21 May
Subject: Training Course

Hi Jeff

Sp
I'm going to atend a training course on selling

Sp   *G*
techniques for tree day, so I'm not going to be

G
in office.

ww   *P*
I'll be back on Mondays, 27th May.

ww   *G*
Remind that tomorrow a temp is start Deborah
                                        P

will show her what to do.

Overview

3.1   Business topic: Company biography

READING   The man behind McDonald's

GRAMMAR   The past simple

READING   Company profiles

SPEAKING   Presenting your company

3.2   Business skills: Company performance

VOCABULARY   What companies do

WRITING   Press release

LISTENING   Company structure

VOCABULARY   Production, sales and share prices

READING   An agency built on proactive processes

3.3   Exam spotlight: Listening Test
            Introduction and Part One

Understanding the Listening Test format

Listening Test Part One

Useful language from Module 3

Wordlist

aircraft
announce
budget airline
business partner
commitment
contract
core business
decrease
delegate
delighted
design
device
distribute
dramatically
drop
entrepreneur
expand

fall
fleet
franchise
freelancer
gist
go public
go up
grow
hall
hardware
increase
level off
limited company (Ltd)
location
management
meet sb's needs

merge
negotiating
non-profit organisation
organic
partnership
performance
press release
provide
public limited company (plc)
purchasing manager
quarter
raw materials
remain steady
return
rise

self-employed
share
sharply
software
sole trader
sparkling water
staff
still water
successfully
supply
take over
takings
turnover
unique
validation
workforce
worldwide

Expressions

a dedicated service
a fast-growing market
a solid reputation
be keen on
by 40 per cent
consolidate one's leading position
current personal worth
double one's client base
give excellent returns to one's investors
go online
in this respect
meet client's needs
on schedule
take delivery
within budget

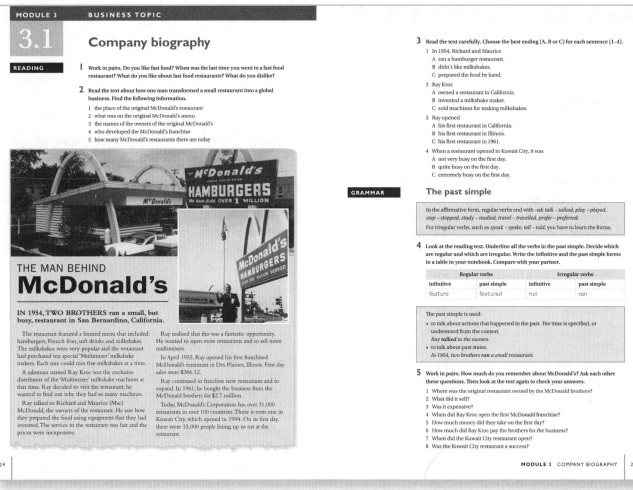

Student's Book pages 24 and 25

The man behind McDonald's

READING

1 As a lead-in, ask students to keep their books closed. Write the following letters on the board: *A D F F O O S T* (they're an anagram of *FAST FOOD*), and ask students how many words they can write from the letters in one minute. This can be done either on their own or as a class brainstorming. When the time is up, collect the students' contributions and ask them to open their books at page 24, where they'll discover the words *fast food* contained in the first question.

Ask students to work in pairs to do exercise 1. Then feed back to the whole class, asking the following questions:

Who likes fast food?

Who doesn't like fast food?

Who went to a fast food restaurant yesterday? Last week? Two weeks ago? Last month?

What do you like or not like about fast food restaurants?

Can you name some famous fast food restaurants?

2 Read the task with students. Point out that the word *information* is uncountable and that they have to find *five* pieces of information.

Allow five minutes for students to do this exercise. Tell them that they can underline the information they're looking for in the text. This is a good technique for finding specific information.

Answers
1 San Bernardino, California
2 hamburgers, French fries, soft drinks and milkshakes
3 Richard and Maurice (Mac) McDonald
4 Ray Kroc
5 over 31,000

3 Before starting exercise 3, ask students if they prefer to read a text silently or out loud. Point out that during the exam, students will have to read silently. Choose the reading style your students ask for. If they decide to read on their own, offer assistance with new words or any unclear points.

After checking their answers, ask students to read out loud the sentences or words that helped them to find the answers. Ask students to cross out any misleading information in the text that may make them choose the incorrect answer.

Answers
1 A   2 C   3 B   4 C

The past simple

4   Before doing exercise 4, present the past simple form on the board:

For regular verbs: use verb + -d or -ed, eg: *decide – decided*

For irregular verbs: write the present and past forms in two columns: eg: *run – ran*

Students do exercise 4 on their own. Then check answers in pairs.

You may want to point out the following before students feed back their answers to the class:

Pronunciation of regular verbs:
/t/ – stopped / passed / parked / washed
/ɪd/ – started / needed
/d/ – lived

Answers
Regular verbs

infinitive	past simple
feature	featured
include	included
decide	decided
want	wanted
talk	talked
prepare	prepared
realise	realised
open	opened
continue	continued

Irregular verbs

infinitive	past simple
run	ran
be	was / were
have	had
can	could
see	saw
buy	bought

Extension
The regular verbs in the text all use regular spelling. Ask students if they know any regular verbs which do not just take -ed in the past, and if they know any of the common patterns which these verbs follow. Write students' contributions on the board and fill any gaps.

For example:

live	→	live**d**
study	→	stud**ied**
play	→	play**ed**
stop	→	stop**ped**
prefer	→	prefer**red**
travel	→	travel**led** (BrE), travel**ed** (AmE)
panic	→	panic**ked**

5   Students work in pairs to do the exercise.

Answers
1 In San Bernardino, California.
2 Hamburgers, French fries, soft drinks and milkshakes.
3 No. It was very cheap.
4 In 1955.
5 $366.12.
6 He paid them $2.7 million.
7 It opened in 1994.
8 Yes, it was.

READING

Company profiles

1 Work in pairs. Write three things you know about each of these companies.

easyJet | lastminute.com | THE BODY SHOP

2 Complete the text with the correct form of the verbs. Which company in exercise 1 does this text describe?

> Anita Roddick and her husband Gordon got the idea for their business in 1970, when they
> (1) _____ (visit) a natural cosmetics store in San Francisco. Back in England, they
> (2) _____ (begin) producing their own naturally-inspired cosmetics and they (3) _____
> (open) their first shop in 1976. The products and the shop's philosophy (4) _____ (be)
> revolutionary for the time. The Roddicks (5) _____ (buy) the raw materials direct from the
> producers, and they (6) _____ (pay) their Community Trade suppliers a fair wage. Today, The
> Body Shop™ continues to bring ethical trade to the high street in more than 60 countries.

3 Complete the text with the correct form of the verbs in the box. Which company in exercise 1 does this text describe?

> be become begin not / have not / own sell not / sell take

> Stelios (1) _____ the first two aircraft he operated. He (2) _____ tickets through travel
> agencies and he (3) _____ any company employees. Everything was contracted from other
> companies. It was 1995, and it (4) _____ the beginning of a revolution in air travel. Just three years
> later, the company (5) _____ the first online air ticket, it (6) _____ services outside the UK and
> it (7) _____ delivery of its own fleet of planes. When it merged with another low-cost airline, Go,
> in 2002, it (8) _____ Europe's biggest budget airline.

4 Work in pairs. Use the prompts to write questions about lastminute.com™. Do you know the answers to any of these questions?

1 Brent Hoberman and Martha Lane Fox / the company (start)
  Where _____?
2 the website (sell)
  What _____?
3 the company (expand into)
  Which countries _____?
4 they / after six years (have)
  How many employees _____?
5 the company (go public)
  When _____?
6 Martha / the company (leave)
  When _____?

5 🎧 3.1 Listen and write the answers to the questions in exercise 4.

1 _____ 3 _____ 5 _____
2 _____ 4 _____ 6 _____

SPEAKING

Presenting your company

6 Decide whether these types of business organisations usually have one owner (O) or more than one owner (M).

1 a freelancer _____
2 a non-profit organisation _____
3 a public limited company (plc) _____
4 a sole trader _____
5 a limited company (Ltd) _____
6 a partnership _____
7 self-employed _____

7 Do you see yourself as a 'dot.com millionaire' or a celebrity entrepreneur? Work in pairs to design your own company, choosing one of the types of business organisation in exercise 6. Complete the first column of the table with your company biography.

	Your company biography	Your partner's company biography
Company name		
Type of company		
Product / Service offered		
Got idea for business in ... (when)		
First business activity (when / where)		
Expanded (where to / when)		
Notable successes		
Key dates / achievements		
Current operations		
Number of employees		
Current value of company		
Current personal worth		

8 Practise giving a spoken presentation about your company, using the notes you made in exercise 7.

9 Now present your company to a new partner. While you listen to the presentation, complete the second column of the table above with as much information as you can about this company. Ask follow-up or clarification questions as necessary.

10 Use your notes to write a short paragraph (60–80 words) about your company. You will not need to use all of the information. Choose the most relevant, interesting or unusual facts. Before you start, read the paragraphs about The Body Shop and easyJet™ again. Follow a similar organisation in your paragraph.

11 Work with your partner from exercise 7 again. Exchange your paragraphs and compare them. Did you choose the same information to write about?

Student's Book pages 26 and 27

Company profiles

READING

1 This exercise is a lead-in activity for exercise 2. It's important that students come up with some suggestions about these companies. Allow any ideas that they may have. If they can't find at least three things, ask questions to elicit some of the ideas below. *I know very little about this company* is also an acceptable answer.

Possible answers
The Body Shop™: They sell personal care products (eg soaps, shampoo, make-up). Their products are made from natural products and are not tested on animals. They started in the UK. They have shops all over the world.

easyJet™: They offer low-cost flights. The tickets are very cheap. They don't give you free drinks on board. You have to pay for the drinks.

lastminute.com™: You can buy a holiday online and get very good prices. Their website is user-friendly. You can book a flight or a hotel with a few clicks.

2 Do this exercise as a class or group exercise. Choose one student to read the text out loud; stop him or her when there is a gap, and ask the other students to give you the correct form of the verb.

Answers
The Body Shop
1 visited
2 began
3 opened
4 were
5 bought
6 paid

3 Ask students to work on their own. Point out that the plural of *aircraft* is *aircraft*.

Answers
easyJet
1 didn't own
2 didn't sell
3 didn't have
4 was
5 sold
6 began
7 took
8 became

4 Students work in pairs and write questions. If they don't know the answers, they can invent them. Comparing their answers with the listening will make the exercise more interesting and motivating.

Answers
1 Where did Brent Hoberman and Martha Lane Fox start the company?
2 What did the website sell?
3 Which countries did the company expand into?
4 How many employees did they have after six years?
5 When did the company go public?
6 When did Martha leave the company?

5 🎧 3.1 Play the recording for students to answer the questions in exercise 4.

3.1 Listening script
Our guest today on *Songs of my life* is the entrepreneur Martha Lane Fox, of the massively successful company lastminute.com. With her business partner, Brent Hoberman, Martha Lane Fox started lastminute.com in Brent's living room. The idea was simple – a website selling late flights and late hotel bookings. The company grew very quickly and expanded from the UK into France, Germany and Sweden. They bought other travel companies, and after six years they had 1,400 employees. Lastminute.com went public in 2000, and the shares in the company increased their value by 40 per cent in two days. Martha Lane Fox left the company in 2003. True to her entrepreneurial spirit, she wanted to start more new companies. Martha, it's a pleasure to have you here in the studio …

Answers
1 In Brent's living room.
2 Late flights and late hotel bookings.
3 France, Germany and Sweden.
4 1,400.
5 In 2000.
6 In 2003.

Presenting your company

SPEAKING

6 Do this exercise with the class. Elicit the answers *one owner* (*O*) or *more than one owner* (*M*). If students don't know the meanings of the input words, the definitions below might help:

Answers and definitions
1 O (a person who is self-employed and works for several businesses)
2 M (an organisation that does not try to make a profit)
3 M (a British company whose shares can be bought and sold by the public and whose debts are limited if it fails financially)
4 O (a person who trades by himself / herself without the use of a company structure or partners and bears full responsibility for the actions of his/her business)
5 M (a company whose owners have limited responsibility for the money that it owes)
6 M (a company that is owned by two or more people)
7 O (a person who doesn't work for an employer, but finds work for him/herself)

7 Students work in pairs and produce their own company biographies.

8 Students work in pairs. Each student gives his/her partner a spoken presentation, using the notes written in exercise 7. You may want to provide an example for the students to model.

Today I'd like to present my new company. Its name is LoseWeight.com Ltd.

We sell special shoes that make you lose weight when you wear them.

I got the idea for this business when …, etc.

Tell students that this presentation is only for practice, and that students should help each other.

9 Students change partners. In turns, they have to present their new company and listen to their partner's presentation. While they're listening, they make notes in the second column in exercise 7. Remind them to ask clarification questions, eg:

How do you spell 'LoseWeight'?

When exactly did you start?

Are you saying that you are a non-profit organisation?

10 Students use the notes from the first column in exercise 7 to produce a short paragraph of 60–80 words. Remind them that this is the length of the business correspondence they have to write in Part Two of the Writing Test. Students can write in the first person (*I, we*) or in the third person (*he, she, they*).

Ask some students to read out their paragraphs to the class. Students suggest improvements to the language and style of the paragraph.

Sample answer

> LoseWeight.com is a successful company that sells special shoes that make you lose weight by just wearing them. The idea came to a university student, Mark Zimmerman, when he added weight to his running shoes to burn more calories while jogging. He patented the idea in 2005 and started selling the shoes to his friends and relatives in Switzerland. The following year, he started taking orders from all over the world, thanks to the excellent website he set up.

11 Students exchange paragraphs with their original partner. Tell them they can underline in pencil any part of the text they think isn't clear or has mistakes. Refer them to the correction symbols on page 23. Their partner should try to correct any mistakes.

Photocopiable activity
See page 164.

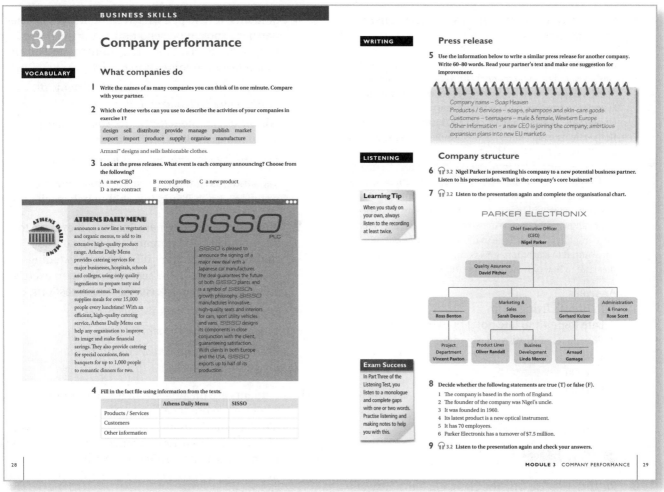

What companies do

VOCABULARY

1 As a lead-in, tell students to think of a company whose name begins with a certain letter, eg: *Think of a company whose name begins with the letter B.* The students should respond non-verbally when they've thought of one by either raising one hand, or by clicking their fingers or nodding their heads, or with any other movement that you think is appropriate for your class. Continue this exercise for about one minute, or at least until you've asked about five to nine letters. This will make them more productive when doing the task.

Students then write down as many companies as they can in one minute. They then work in pairs and compare their lists.

2 Students work in pairs and choose verbs to describe the activities of the companies they wrote in exercise 1.

3 Tell students that they have one minute to do this task. They'll realise that they don't have to read every word in the text to find the answers.

Answers

1 C (a new product – Athens Daily Menu)
2 D (a new contract – SISSO plc)

4 Students should work alone to do this task.

Answer

	Athens Daily Menu	SISSO plc
Products, services	meals, catering services (for special occasions)	seats and interiors for cars, sport utility vehicles and vans
Customers	major businesses, hospitals, schools and colleges	clients in Europe and the USA
Other information	15,000 meals every lunchtime	exports up to 50% of its production

Press release

WRITING

5 Tell students to write a similar press release for Soap Heaven. This shouldn't take more than 15 minutes. Students should get used to counting the number of words used in the writing tasks.

Sample answer

> Soap Heaven is pleased to announce that a new CEO is joining the company next year. Her name is Tanya Radcliffe and she has ambitious plans for expansion into new EU markets, especially Northern and Eastern Europe. The company is based in Portugal and produces natural soaps, shampoos and skin-care products that are very popular with teenagers, both male and female.

Company structure

LISTENING

6 🎧 3.2 Play the recording once for students to answer this gist question. Check their answer, then refer them to the Learning Tip about studying on your own.

Then refer students to the Exam Success tip about Part Three of the Listening Test. Remind students that during the exam they'll listen to the recording twice. During the first listening they should try to understand the general meaning and try to mark the correct answers. During the second listening, they should listen for the details and complete any questions that they've left unanswered. Also remind students that if they didn't hear a piece of information while listening, they should make an intelligent guess.

3.2 Listening script

Parker Electronix is based in Fleet, in the south of England. We are leaders in hardware and software solutions for satellite technology. My uncle, John Parker, founded the company in the 1960s. Our latest product is a new program for optical instruments for the European Space Agency. Our engineers are involved in all of the stages of a project, from planning to the final performance validation. The industrial department, supervised by Gerhard Kulzer, provides regular certified training for its staff. The R&D activities, supervised by Ross Benton, are essential for all future applications. We have a workforce of 60 employees and a turnover of $7.5 million. Now, let me introduce Arnaud Gamage, our contracts & purchasing manager. Arnaud will explain to you …

Answer
Hardware and software solutions for satellite technology.

7 🎧 3.2 Before listening for the second time, ask students to look at the organigram and try to remember what other departments were mentioned in the script. They could also try to guess what the missing departments might be.

Answers
R&D activities: Ross Benton

Industrial Department: Gerhard Kulzer

Contracts & purchasing: Arnaud Gamage

Alternative
As a pre-listening task, ask students to close their books. Tell them to try and remember as much as they can about the listening without taking notes. Sometimes students are concentrating so hard on writing down the words that they don't follow the overall meaning in a listening.

If you want your students to practise note taking during this listening task, you can suggest one of the following techniques, which you can use for any type of listening:

Listen to the recording and write:
- one key word for each topic that is mentioned
- all the numbers you hear
- all place names
- all people's names
- words you know / words you don't know

8 Students should answer the following questions from memory. They then check their answers in exercise 9.

9 🎧 3.2 As you play the recording again, ask the students to put up a hand when they hear the evidence for the correct answers. Stop the audio and elicit the correct answer.

Answers
1 False (Parker Electronix is based in Fleet, in the **south** of England.)
2 True
3 False (He founded the company in the **1960s**.)
4 False (Our latest product is a **new program for optical instruments**.)
5 False (We have a workforce of **60** employees.)
6 True

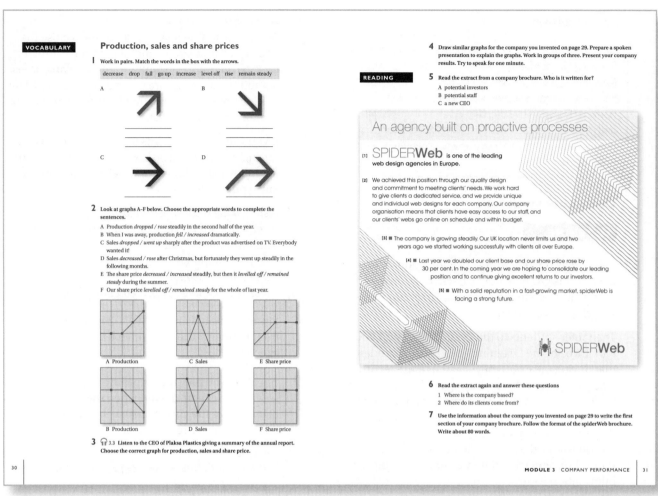

Production, sales and share prices

VOCABULARY

1 This activity introduces vocabulary to describe trends and graphs. With the students, match the first verb in the box with one of the arrows. Then ask students to complete the exercise in pairs.

Answers
A go up; increase; rise
B decrease; drop; fall
C remain steady
D level off

2 Ask students to look at graphs A–F. Ask them to say which verb or verbs in exercise 1 they could use to describe each graph, for example:
A *remain steady; increase / rise / go up*
Then students do exercise 2 and check their answers in pairs.

Answers
A rose
B fell
C went up
D decreased
E increased; levelled off
F remained steady

3 🎧 **3.3** Students listen to the recording and choose the correct graph to match each part of the CEO's summary.

3.3 Listening script
… and now I would like to turn to the final section of the report. As you can see, last year was an excellent year in production. The first two quarters were rather slow, but as a result of new orders from Asia, our production rose dramatically in the third and fourth quarter. This situation was reflected, of course, in our sales for last year. We started the year in a strong position, but in the second quarter worldwide sales fell sharply. This was a result of the high price of oil. However, as I mentioned earlier, new orders from Asia meant that sales went up to their previous level by the end of the year. Looking now at the share price, I am delighted to announce that last year was also an excellent year in this respect. The share price rose steadily for the first two quarters, and it remained steady at its maximum for the rest of the year. All in all, last year was a very positive year …

Answers
Production: A
Sales: D
Share prices: E

Photocopiable activity
See page 165.

4 Students work in groups of three. Each student draws three graphs showing the following trends: sales, production, share price. Each student has to present these graphs to the other two students, talking for one minute. After each presentation, each student should ask one follow-up question.

An agency built on proactive processes

READING

5 Students read the text. Then ask them to work on their own. Ask them to tick the correct answer and then put down their pens/pencils when they've finished. Remind them that they don't have to read the text in detail, just for the gist.

Answers
A potential investors

Ask students to underline the words in the text which helped them to choose the correct answer.

(**4**) Last year <u>we doubled our client base and our share price rose by 30 per cent.</u> In the coming year <u>we are hoping to consolidate our leading position and to continue giving excellent returns to our investors.</u>

6 Choose five students to read the five paragraphs in the text out loud. Then ask students to answer the questions.

Answers
1 The UK.
2 All over Europe.

7 Ask students to write the brochures for their invented company.

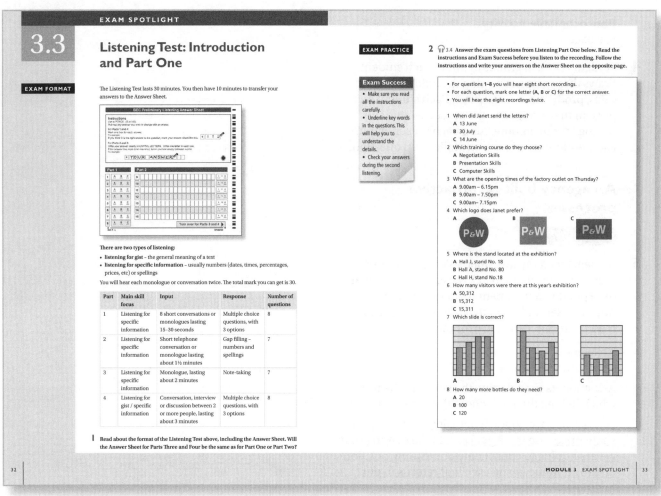

Student's Book pages 32 and 33

EXAM FORMAT

This page gives an overview of the Listening Test. Before starting, ask students some information they should be able to remember from page 12. For example:

In which part of the exam is the Listening Test?

How many marks can you get in the Listening Test?

How long does the Listening Test last?

How many parts are there in the Listening Test?

If the students can't answer some of the above questions, ask them to check the information on page 12. If you want to read more about this part of the exam, get a copy of the Cambridge English Business Handbook or download a copy from the Cambridge English Website. You can also hear some sample listening texts in MP3 format.

Draw attention to the picture of the Answer Sheet and tell students that while listening they can mark their answers on their question paper, but then they have to transfer their answers to their Answer Sheet.

Explain that there are two types of listening: listening for gist (the general meaning of a text) and listening for specific information (usually numbers or spellings). Reassure students that they will hear each recording twice.

| Ask students to read the overview, including the Answer Sheet, and answer the question.

Answer
No, it won't.

Listening Test: Part One

EXAM PRACTICE

2 🎧 **3.4** This listening task is similar to the Listening Test Part One. Draw students' attention to the first part of the grid on page 32.

Part	Main Skill focus	Input	Response	Number of questions
1	Listening for specific information	8 short conversations or monologues lasting 15–30 seconds	Multiple choice questions, with 3 options	8

Before playing the recording, read through the Exam Success tip with students.

Play the recording twice, with no pauses.

Give feedback. If some students made some mistakes, listen to the recording again pointing out where the correct answers are to be found. Ask students to read the audio script out loud in class. Try to keep male and female voices where possible.

3.4 Listening script

1

M Hello, Janet. Did you send those letters to our Italian suppliers?

F Yes, I sent them on 13th June. Let me check … No, sorry. I sent them on the 14th.

M Great, thanks.

2

M1 The new management have decided to invest in staff training.

M2 Oh, really? I knew nothing about that. What do they want us to do?

M1 They want us to improve our performance when presenting and negotiating, and make the most of our computer skills. Somebody has complained that our computers are out of date and so are our skills!

M2 Yes, I think they're right. Personally, I need to work on how to prepare my presentations.

M1 Me too. Let's start with presentation skills, then.

3

This is the answering machine for Benton Factory Outlet. We are open Monday to Wednesday from 9.00am to 6.15pm. On Thursday and Friday we are open from 9.00am to 7.15pm. We are closed on Saturday and Sunday.

4

F1 Here are the P&W logos the agency has just sent.

F2 Mm, let me see … I like the colours …

F1 What about the shapes?

F2 I'm not very keen on squares or rectangles.

F1 So, do you prefer this one?

F2 Yes, the circle is nice.

5

M1 Our booking for the Magic Children Expo has been confirmed.

M2 Excellent! Now we have to organise the stand. By the way, where exactly is the stand?

M1 Let me have a look. I've got the email here. It's number 18 in Hall J.

M2 Ah, that's the same hall as last year.

M1 Yes, but last year our stand was number 80.

6

M1 The exhibition went better than last year.

M2 Yeah, I'm really glad. It was a great success – especially for us.

M1 There were more people than last year. I've got the figures – yes, 15,312. That's a lot more than last year.

7

The sales were very good in December. Then we saw the usual decrease in January and February, and we recovered a bit in March.

8

F Hello, this is Jane Howell from Conference Room number 4.

M How can I help you, Ms Howell?

F We asked for 120 bottles of water, one for each delegate at our meeting, but there are only 100. Could you send us 20 more?

M Do you prefer sparkling or still water?

F Still, please.

M I'll send them to you immediately.

F Thanks a lot. Bye.

M Bye.

Answers

1 C   2 B   3 C   4 A   5 A   6 B   7 B   8 A

Overview

4.1   Business topic: International business

READING   **Opening the Silk Road once more**

LISTENING   **Listening: View on transportation**

SPEAKING   **Imported goods**

GRAMMAR   **Modal Verbs: *can/could* and *should***

READING   **The skill of effective teleconferencing**

4.2   Communication skills: Business communications

SPEAKING   **On the phone**

WRITING   **Dealing with complaints**

GRAMMAR   ***will* for offers and promises**

LISTENING   **Telephone messages**

4.3   Exam spotlight: Speaking Test Introduction and Part One

Understanding the Speaking Test format

Speaking Test: Part One

Giving personal details

Useful language from Module 4

Wordlist

act (v)
advice
agenda
agree
apologise
apology
available
background
ban (n + v)
blockade
budget figures
business conference
business2business (b2b)
caller
candidate
city
clothing
compete
competitor
compromise
consumer
container (large metal box)
convenient
copy (n)
could
creative
crisis
customer
customs
delivery

depend
disaster
discount
dispute (n)
distributor
dossier
effective
electrical goods
email address
embarrassing
empty
equipment
excuse (n)
export (n + v)
exporter
extension number
face-to-face
factory worker
file (n)
flat (adj)
freight forwarder
goods
Great!
hobby
ideal
import (n + v)
import ban
import control
import restriction
importer
informal
in-house

interview (n + v)
introduce (put into use)
item
journey
lose your job
loss
magazine
managing director
manufacturer
meeting
merchandising
message
mini-presentation
moderator
multinational
mute button
news
opinion
participant
participate
personal details
personnel
personnel manager
port
post office
press (v)
printer cartridge
producer
production manager
quantity

recommendation
reflect (show)
release
resign
retail trade
retailer
rival
schedule
scissors
season
send out
shipment
should
spokeswoman
stationery
stock (v)
suffer
supply (n + v)
tax form
teleconference
time difference
tip (advice)
topic
town
type (v)
video-conference
virtual meeting
warehouse
wholesaler
will

Expressions

accept an offer
express an opinion
flood the market
hit the headlines
I'm afraid
I'm sorry
in favour of
in time for
listen to music

make / receive a call
on the other hand
pass sth on to sb
reach an agreement
say sth back to sb
take a decision
take photos
the line is busy
who's calling?

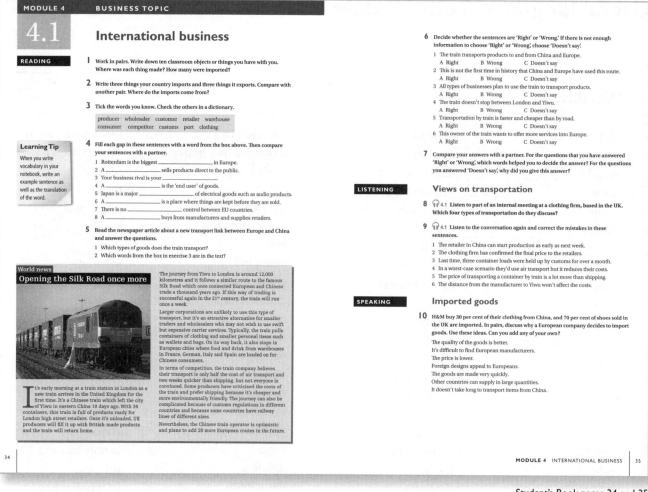

Student's Book pages 34 and 35

Opening the Silk Road once more

READING

1 Students work in pairs. Ask students to write down ten objects they have with them, where each object was made, and how many were imported. Allow four minutes for this.

Ask a few students to choose one of the objects they've written down, and say where the object was made. Then ask a few other students to say how many of their objects were imported.

2 Students write down three things that their country imports and three things it exports. Students compare their lists with another pair.

3 Ask students to work alone and tick the words in the box that they know. Students explain the meaning of the words they know to a partner. They can use a dictionary for the words they don't know.

4 Students work alone to do the exercise. Ask them to compare their answers with their partner.

Check answers. Then refer students to the Learning Tip.

Answers
1 port
2 retailer
3 competitor
4 consumer
5 producer
6 warehouse
7 customs
8 wholesaler

Extension
Ask students to produce sentences for the other two words from exercise 3. For example:

One of the best ways of increasing demand is to find new customers.

Protective clothing must be worn.

5 Ask students to read the questions before reading the text. Students should underline relevant information which answers the first question, as well as the words for question 2 as they find them. Check answers.

Answers
1 Products for London high street retailers, clothing, and smaller personal items such as wallets and bags, food and drink
2 retailer, wholesaler, clothing, warehouse, consumer, producer, customs

54

6 Ask students to read the questions in exercise 6. If they know the answer to the questions, they can underline the correct answer. Don't check answers at this stage as this will be done in exercise 7.

7 Ask students to explain their answers to a partner. They should underline the information in the text that shows that the statements are 'Right' or 'Wrong'. If there is no information that helps to answer the question, they should choose 'Doesn't say'. Choose individual students to give their answers and explain their choice.

Answers
1 A (*It's a Chinese train which left the city of Yiwu in eastern China … Once it's unloaded, UK producers will fill it up with British-made products and the train will return home.*)
2 A (*it follows a similar route to the famous Silk Road which once connected European and Chinese trade …*)
3 B (*Larger corporations are unlikely to use this type of transport …*)
4 B (*On its way back, it also stops in European cities …*)
5 C
6 A (*… plans to add 20 more European routes in the future.*)

8 🎧 4.1 Play the recording once. Then ask students which types of transportation the speakers had discussed. Play the recording again, then check with the class.

4.1 Listening script

A OK, so we've had plenty of interest in the new clothing range and a couple of large retailers are ready to place orders in time for their spring collections. I've already contacted our manufacturer in China and they can start production as early as next week!
B Wow! That is good.
A But it's still very tight with regards to delivery dates. And I still haven't confirmed the final prices with the retailers because we need to decide on transportation. Do you think shipping can deliver on time?
B Well, they always say they can do it in a month, but you remember last time?
A You mean when we had three container loads held up by customs for over a week?
B Exactly. It's safer to add on about ten days just in case.
A So a month and a half is more realistic. What's the alternative? By air?
B In a worst-case scenario we'd have to, but it really reduces our profits. Or we add that to the retail price …
A Yes, there's no way …
B … but I was going to say I may have found a good solution. There's a new train line from eastern China right into London. It's from a place called Yiwu and it takes about two and half weeks.
A Really? Can they guarantee that?
B Well, so far, their record has been very good. And the prices are very competitive. A little more than shipping but nothing like as high as air transport. Take a look at their quote for one container …

A Not bad. Who'd have thought we'd start using trains again!
B I know. Shall I contact them?
A Before you do that, you'd better check with our partners in China and see how far this place, what was it called …
B Yiwu.
A That's it. Yiwu. Find out how far it is from their location as that might affect the costs. Though I doubt it will be much different from road transport to the port.

Answers
Shipping, air, train, road

9 🎧 4.1 Ask students to read the sentences and correct any mistakes they see. Play the recording again. Ask students to check the sentences against what they hear, and make any further corrections. Students compare their answers with a partner.

Answers
1 The ~~retailer~~ <u>manufacturer</u> in China can start production as early as next week.
2 The clothing firm ~~has~~ <u>hasn't</u> confirmed the final price to the retailers.
3 Last time, three container loads were held up by customs for over a ~~month~~ <u>week.</u>
4 In a worst-case scenario they'd use air transport but it reduces their ~~costs~~<u>profits.</u>
5 The price of transporting a container by train is a ~~lot~~ <u>little</u> more than shipping.
6 The distance from the manufacturer to Yiwu ~~won't~~ <u>might</u> affect the costs.

Imported goods

SPEAKING

10 Read the information about the clothing company H&M™ with the students. Ask them to work in pairs to discuss the question, using the ideas listed, and to add any of their own to the list.

GRAMMAR

Modal verbs: *can/could* and *should*

Modal verbs have the same form for all subjects. The negative form ends with *n't* and the modal verb goes before the subject (*I, he,* etc) in questions.

- We use *can* to talk about present ability and possibility.
  I can speak English and Spanish. (ability)
  He can't finish the work before he goes home. (possibility)
- We use *could* to talk about future possibility and past ability.
  Our shops could be empty next week. (future)
  I couldn't speak to him yesterday. (past)
- We also use *Can/Could I/we* when asking for permission and making offers. We use *Can/Could you* in requests.
  Can I leave early this evening? (permission)
  How can I help you? (offer)
  Could you sign this form for me? (request)
- We use *should* to make recommendations, and to ask for and give advice.
  The European Union should protect European industry. (recommendation)
  You shouldn't be rude to customers. (advice)

1 Look at the words in brackets in the table above. Write the correct word next to each sentence below.

0 Can we use our dictionaries during the exam?   permission
1 Could you spell your surname, please? _____
2 Students should attend all their classes. _____
3 I can't do any of these questions. They're too hard. _____
4 You shouldn't stay up late the night before the exam. _____
5 She could be the best candidate for the job. _____
6 I couldn't speak to Mr Jones because he was in a meeting. _____
7 Can I show you what to do? _____
8 How fast can you type? _____

2 Complete the sentences with *can, can't, could* and *couldn't*.

1 You _____ smoke here. If you smoke, the alarm goes off.
2 I'm afraid Mrs Doriguez isn't available at the moment. _____ you come back later, please?
3 '_____ you read this dossier for tomorrow?' 'No, I'm sorry, I _____.'
4 Good morning, Johnson & Johnson. _____ I help you?
5 Mr Jensen is not in at the moment. _____ I take a message?
6 I _____ call you because my mobile phone battery was flat.

3 Work in pairs. Take turns as Student A and Student B in each of these situations.

Student A: Choose one of the problems below. Tell your partner about it.
Student B: Listen to your partner's problem and give him/her some advice.

- You have just sent an email full of spelling mistakes to an important client.
- Your colleague is often late for meetings with suppliers and it reflects badly on the company.
- Your boss can't keep his records organised and it gives you lots of extra work.
- You can't speak any other languages, but you want to be promoted.
- Your colleague is often away from his desk for long periods and you have to make excuses for him.
- You never remember clients' names and it is embarrassing.

READING

4 Do you prefer to communicate face-to-face or on the phone? Why?

5 Read an article about teleconferencing. What are the advantages and disadvantages compared to face-to-face communication?

THE SKILL OF EFFECTIVE TELECONFERENCING

For anyone who does international business, face-to-face meetings can be very useful – especially at the beginning of a new business relationship. However, such meetings often take up a sizeable chunk of time and costs can run high as a result of the flights, hotels, and meals. The alternative is teleconferencing which is a great way to connect people cheaply and it's much quicker than face-to-face meetings overseas.

It's true that teleconference meetings can often go wrong. People are sometimes late because they are calling in from different international time zones or because they have technical problems. But with proper planning and preparation – as with any meeting – you can usually avoid any difficulties.

The first thing to do is arrange a date and time that suits everyone and make sure everyone understands the local time. If you are based in London, don't plan the meeting at 9am with colleagues in South America because it's probably the middle of the night. Also, send out the agenda and any relevant information a few days in advance.

Teleconferencing can also get confusing if you have too many people attending, so limit it to about five people if possible. Like a normal meeting, you will need someone to lead the teleconference. This person needs to make sure everyone has a chance to speak and should also use other people's names a lot so everyone knows who's speaking. Afterwards, write the minutes – or summary – of the teleconference for everyone.

6 Read the text again and choose the correct ending (A, B or C) for each sentence (1–4).

1 Teleconferencing is ideal if
 A you want to work with people in other countries.
 B you don't want to bear the costs of face-to-face meetings.
 C you want meetings to be more effective.
2 Sometimes teleconferences go wrong because
 A people don't remember to telephone at the correct time.
 B a lot of employees prefer face-to-face communication.
 C people prepare and plan it like a normal meeting.
3 When arranging a date and time for the meeting,
 A think about where everyone is based.
 B only invite people in nearby countries.
 C remember that mornings are usually the best time.
4 When you lead a teleconference, it's a good idea to...
 A speak more than other people to avoid confusion.
 B invite lots of people so everyone knows what's happening.
 C say people's names when you want them to speak.

7 Match words from A and B to make collocations from the article.

	A	B
1	go	people
2	connect	a date
3	arrange	any difficulties
4	plan	wrong
5	send out	a meeting
6	have	the minutes
7	avoid	the agenda
8	write	technical problems

8 Write questions with collocations. Then ask your partner the questions.
How often do you have face-to-face meetings at work?

36

MODULE 4 INTERNATIONAL BUSINESS   37

Student's Book pages 36 and 37

Modal verbs: *can/could* and *should*

GRAMMAR

Before students do exercise 1, draw their attention to the information about modal verbs. Read the examples and uses with students.

1 Read the example with students. Ask students to complete exercise 1.

Answers
1 request
2 recommendation
3 ability
4 advice
5 future possibility
6 past possibility
7 offer
8 ability

2 Ask students to do exercise 2 alone. When they've finished, they should check their answers with a partner.

Answers
1 can't
2 Can/Could
3 Can, can't.
4 Can
5 Can
6 couldn't

3 Write on the board: *I want to earn more money.* Ask students to give you some advice.

Students work in pairs to practise the role play in exercise 3. Student A chooses a problem, Student B gives advice. Tell students to take turns.

Photocopiable activity
See page 166.

The skill of effective teleconferencing

READING

4 Ask students if they prefer to communicate face-to-face or on the phone. Then ask a follow-up question to find out if their preferences change depending on the person they're speaking to. Ask students to think about some of the things they like and dislike about teleconferencing.

5 Ask students to read the text. As they read, they should underline any ideas in the text that indicate the advantages and disadvantages of teleconferencing.

Answers
Advantages: cheaper, quicker
Disadvantages: technical problems, can be confusing with too many people

6 Ask students to read the sentences first, and then they should read the article again carefully. As they read the article, they can highlight any information that helps them to answer the questions.

Answers
1 B
2 A
3 A
4 C

7 Ask students which words from A go with words from B. Then ask them to read the article again, and find the collocations.

Answers
1 go wrong
2 connect people
3 arrange a date
4 plan a meeting
5 send out the agenda
6 have technical problems
7 avoid any difficulties
8 write the minutes

8 Give students five minutes to write some questions. In pairs, students then ask each other their questions.

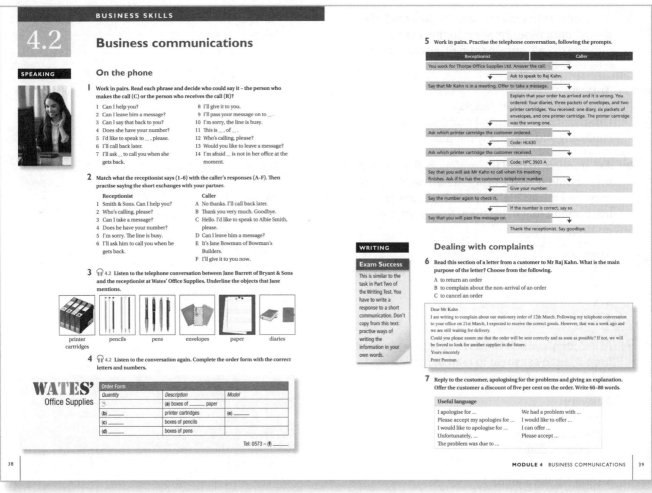

Student's Book pages 38 and 39

On the phone

SPEAKING

1 Tell students to imagine making a telephone call. Ask:

Who would say 'Can I help you?' Would it be the person who makes the call, or the person who receives the call?

Who would say 'Can I leave him a message?'

Ask students to complete the rest of the exercise individually. When they've finished, they can check their answers with a partner.

Answers

1 R   2 C   3 R   4 R   5 C   6 C   7 R
8 C   9 R   10 R   11 C   12 R   13 R   14 R

2 Ask students to match the sentences alone. Then they should practise saying the short exchanges with a partner.

Answers

1 C   2 E   3 A   4 F   5 D   6 B

3 🎧 **4.2** Tell students to look at the objects. Check that they know what they all are. Play the recording once. Then ask: *Which objects does Jane mention?*

4.2 Listening script

R = Receptionist   C = Customer

R Wates' Office Supplies Ltd, can I help you?
C Hello, I'd like to speak to Mariah Keaton, please?
R Who's calling, please?
C This is Jane Barrett, of Bryant & Sons.
R I'm afraid Ms Keaton is not in her office at the moment. Would you like to leave a message?
C Yes, I would. Our order has arrived, and you've sent the wrong items. We ordered three boxes of A4 paper, five printer cartridges, two boxes of pencils, and four boxes of pens. You sent us two boxes of A5 paper, the wrong printer cartridges, only one box of pencils, and no pens.
R I see. Which printer cartridges did you order?
C The code is HP92274A.
R And which did you receive?
C The code on the ones we received is FO26ND.
R OK, Ms Barrett, I'll ask Ms Keaton to call you when she gets back. Does she have your number?
C I think so. But I'll give it to you all the same. It's 0573 764812.
R Can I say that back to you? 0573 764812.
C That's right.
R I'll pass your message on to Ms Keaton.
C Thank you. Goodbye.

Answers

paper, printer cartridges, pencils, pens

4 🎧 4.2 Ask students to look at the order form. Ask them if they can remember any of the missing information. They can write the information in pencil on the order form.

Play the recording again. Tell students to check the answers they've written on their form, and to fill in any remaining gaps.

Answers
a) A4
b) 5
c) 2
d) 4
e) HP92274A
f) 764812

5 Students work in pairs using the prompts to practise a telephone conversation.

Ask students to sit back to back, so that they can't see each other's faces, to simulate the conditions of a real telephone conversation.

If students are in difficulty, ask them to turn to page 152 where they can read the listening script. When they've practised the conversation on page 152, they should try the prompted conversation again.

Ask two volunteers to come to the front of the class and perform the conversation.

Photocopiable activity
See page 167.

Dealing with complaints

WRITING

6 Ask students to read the three options. Tell them to read the letter quickly.

Answer
B to complain about the non-arrival of an order

7 Explain the activity to the class and ask them to reply to the customer's letter in exercise 6.

Refer students to the Exam Success tip. Tell students that it's important to do everything that is asked in the question, but they should not just copy from the text in the question. They should re-write the information in their own words.

Go through the Useful language section and ask students to write the reply. When they've finished, they should exchange their replies with a partner. If there are any mistakes, they should correct them. If they can, they should suggest improvements.

Sample answer

Dear Mr Paxman

I apologise for the fact that your order has not arrived yet. Unfortunately, this is a period of very high demand, and our usual supplier is causing us some problems. However, we now have all of the items you requested and we are ready to send your order. Because of this delay, I would like to offer you a 5% discount. Thank you for your patience.

Yours sincerely

Raj Kahn

(Student's Book reproduction, pages 40 and 41)

GRAMMAR

will for offers and promises

We often use *will* when we decide to do something - for example, in offers and promises.
I'll ask him to call you. (offer)
I'll do it later. (promise)

1 Complete the sentences with *I'll* and a suitable verb.

1 Mr Grey isn't in his office. _____ him you rang.
2 I know Carrie's extension number. _____ her for you.
3 _____ at these accounts today, I promise.
4 Those files look heavy. _____ them for you.
5 I pass the post office on my way home. _____ those letters for you.
6 I'm not usually late. _____ at work on time tomorrow!

2 Complete the conversation below with the sentences in the box.

I'll write the report tomorrow morning.	I'd like to check them again.
I'd like to speak to Natalia Marin, please.	I'll see you tomorrow.
I'll send them to you this afternoon.	Would you like to come?

Natalia Westlaine Pharmaceuticals.
Sven Hello. (1) _____
Natalia Speaking.
Sven Hi, Natalia. It's Sven. I need your budget figures for the report. Can you email them to me?
Natalia They're not ready yet, I'm afraid. (2) _____ Some of the figures aren't quite right.
Sven When do you think they'll be ready?
Natalia I'm working on them now. (3) _____ Is 4 o'clock all right?
Sven Yes, that's fine. (4) _____
Natalia Oh, by the way, Margareta is leaving next week. We're having a little party tomorrow afternoon. (5) _____
Sven Yes, I'd love to. What time?
Natalia Half past three.
Sven Great. (6) _____ Bye.

3 🎧 4.3 Listen to the conversation and check your answers.

4 Practise the conversation with a partner.

5 Work in pairs. Use the prompts below to practise conversations with your partner. Each exchange will involve making an offer, a promise or a request.

1 **Retailer:** The delivery of new LED TVs is late. Your special promotion starts tomorrow.
 Wholesaler: Promise to find out why there is a problem.
2 **Exporter:** You need prices and schedules for a shipment of electrical equipment to Mexico.
 Freight forwarder: Ask if the exporter wants the information by email or return call.
3 **Distributor:** You want to know when the merchandising products will be available.
 Manufacturer: Offer to find out and return the call.
4 **Wholesaler:** You want to know if your containers have arrived.
 Importer: Ask if the wholesaler wants to speak to the warehouse.

LISTENING

Telephone messages

6 🎧 4.4 Listen to extracts from four telephone conversations and tick the expressions you hear.

How do you spell that? ☐
Could you spell your name, please? ☐
M for Madrid. ☐
Did you say the 21st? ☐
Let me just check that. ☐
Could you repeat that, please? ☐

7 🎧 4.5 Listen to four telephone calls and correct two mistakes in each message.

1
REID WHELAN & BLAKE
Telephone Message
Message for: Ms Chandra
From : Joe Panetta
Caller's company: AC Associates
Tel./Email: 0632 157431
Message: Would you like to wait for the new brochure which is coming out in two weeks' time?

2
REID WHELAN & BLAKE
Telephone Message
Message for: Mrs Horbaczewski
From : Bob Davis
Caller's company:
Tel./Email: bd.davis@gmail.com
Message: Could you post Mr Davis a copy of his tax form for last year?

3
REID WHELAN & BLAKE
Telephone Message
Message for: Mrs Peters
From : Sigrid Junge
Caller's company: Hoffmann gmbh
Tel./Email:
Message: Can you see Ms Junge on the 16th? She can't fly to London on the 17th.

4
REID WHELAN & BLAKE
Telephone Message
Message for: Mr Dando
From : Martin Kramer
Caller's company:
Tel./Email:
Message: He hasn't accepted the first offer.

8 🎧 4.6 Listen to three short recordings. Choose the best answer (A, B or C) for each question.

1 When will the goods arrive?
 A on 3 February   B on 16 February   C on 19 February
2 Who does the caller want to speak to?
 A the personnel manager   B the production manager   C the managing director
3 What new time does the caller suggest for the meeting?
 A 1.00pm   B 2.30pm   C 4.30pm

40   MODULE 4 BUSINESS COMMUNICATIONS   41

Student's Book pages 40 and 41

---

will for offers and promises

GRAMMAR

1 **Possible answers**
1 I'll tell
2 I'll call/ring/phone
3 I'll look/take a look
4 I'll carry
5 I'll post
6 I'll be

2 Students complete the conversation.

3 🎧 4.3 Students listen and check their answers to exercise 2 (see underlining in script).

4.3 Listening script

N = Natalia   S = Sven

N Westlaine Pharmaceuticals.
S Hello. <u>I'd like to speak to Natalia Marin, please.</u>
N Speaking.
S Hi, Natalia. It's Sven. I need your budget figures for the report. Can you email them to me?
N They're not ready yet, I'm afraid. <u>I'd like to check them again.</u> Some of the figures aren't quite right.
S When do you think they'll be ready?
N I'm working on them now. <u>I'll send them to you this afternoon.</u> Is 4 o'clock all right?
S Yes, that's fine. <u>I'll write the report tomorrow morning.</u>
N Oh, by the way, Margareta is leaving next week. We're having a little party tomorrow afternoon. <u>Would you like to come?</u>

S Yes, I'd love to. What time?
N Half past three.
S Great. <u>I'll see you tomorrow.</u> Bye.

4 Ask students to practise the conversation in pairs.

5 Students work in pairs. They should practise each of the conversations once, taking turns to start.

Telephone messages

LISTENING

6 🎧 4.4 Students listen to the recording and tick the expressions they hear.

4.4 Listening script

1
M Good morning. Could I speak to Mr Aitken, please?
F I'm afraid he's not in the office today. Can I take a message?
M Just tell him Cailin called.
F Could you spell your name, please?
M Sure, it's C–A–I–L–I–N
F Thanks so much.

2
F And your address is?
M 27, Mendip Road.
F 27, Pendip Road.
M No, M for Madrid. Mendip.

3

M Hi, Sue. Can you call me back on 98 983 988?
F Let me just check that – 98 983 988?
M Yes. Can you call me back right now, please?

4

F And when is the delivery due?
M On the 23rd.
F Did you say the 21st?
M Sorry?
F Do you mean the 21st, 2–1, or the 23rd, 2–3?
M Oh I see. The 23rd, 2–3. The 23rd of June.

Answers

Tick expressions 2, 3, 4 and 5.

7 🎧 **4.5** Ask students to read the four telephone messages. Then they listen to the whole recording twice and identify the mistakes.

4.5 Listening script

1

R = Receptionist   **C** = Customer

R Reid, Whelan and Blake.
C Hello, I'd like to speak to Ms Chandra.
R I'm afraid she's not in today. Can I take a message?
C Yes, this is Joe Panetta, from AS Associates.
R I'm sorry, Panetta … is that P-A-N-E-double T-A?
C Yes, that's right.
R And you're from AS …
C Associates.
R Thank you. So what's the message, Mr Panetta?
C I'm calling about the brochure Ms Chandra wanted. Can you tell her that our new brochure is coming out in two weeks' time? Would she like to wait for that one rather than receive the old one now?
R I'm sorry, did you say two days or two weeks?
C Two weeks. Could you ask Ms Chandra to phone me and confirm which one she wants?
R Yes, of course. Does she have your number?
C I'll give it to you. It's 0632 158431.
R All right, Mr Panetta, I'll pass your message on to Ms Chandra.
C Thanks.
R You're welcome. Bye.

2

R Reid, Whelan and Blake.
C Hello, can I speak to Mr Horbaczewski?
R I'm afraid he's off sick. Would you like to leave a message?
C Yes, my name is Bob Davis.
R Could you spell your surname, please?
C Sure. D-A-V-I-S.
R And what is the message?
C I need a copy of my tax form for last year. Could you ask Mr Horbaczewski to email a copy to me, please?
R Certainly. Does he have your email address?
C I'm not sure. I'll give it to you anyway. It's B D dot Davis, at gmail dot com.
R All right, Mr Davis, I'll give your message to Mr Horbaczewski.
C Thank you very much.
R Not at all. Goodbye.

3

R Reid, Whelan and Blake.
C Hello, is Maria Peters in today?
R She is, yes, but she's in a meeting at the moment. Can I take a message?

C Yes, this is Sigrid Junge, from Hofmann GmbH.
R I'm sorry, could you spell your name, please?
C All right. Sigrid S-I-G-R-I-D, Junge J-U-N-G-E.
R And what was the name of the company?
C Hofmann, that's H-O-F-M-A-N-N, G-M-B-H
R Thank you. Now what is the message?
C I can't fly to London on 17th April. There are no places available. But I can come on the 18th. Could you ask Maria to confirm that she can see me on the 18th?
R Yes, of course. Does she have your number?
C Yes, she does.
R All right, Ms Junge, I'll give your message to Mrs Peters.
C Thanks.
R You're welcome. Goodbye.

4

R Reid, Whelan and Blake.
C Hello, I'd like to speak to Mr Dando.
R His line's engaged. Would you like to wait?
C Yes, please. …
R Hello, caller. I'm afraid the line is still busy.
C Can I leave a message?
R Certainly. What is the message?
C Could you tell him that I have accepted the first offer?
R You've accepted the first offer. OK. And could you give me your name, please?
C Oh, yes, of course. Martin Kraemer. That's K-R-A-E-M-E-R.
R Thank you. I'll give Mr Dando your message.
C Thank you.

Answers

Call 1: <u>AS</u> Associates; 0632 15<u>8</u>431.
Call 2: <u>Mr</u> Horbaczewski; <u>email</u> a copy.
Call 3: Ho<u>f</u>mann gmbh; on the <u>18</u>th.
Call 4: Kr<u>ae</u>mer; he <u>has</u> accepted the first offer.

8 🎧 **4.6** Ask students to read the questions. Then play all three recordings without stopping.

4.6 Listening script

1 **G** = Gabrielle   **R** = Roberto

G Hello, Roberto? It's Gabrielle. Can you tell me when the goods are arriving?
R Well, they're leaving on 16th February, and the journey takes three days. If everything goes well, you'll have them on the 19th.

2 **PO** = Personnel Officer   **C** = Caller

PO Good afternoon, Personnel.
C Oh, please excuse me, I think I must have the wrong extension. I wanted to speak to the production manager. Could you tell me her extension number, please?
PO Certainly, it's 2319. But she's not in her office at the moment. She's having a lunch meeting with the managing director.

3 **K** = Krystof   **B** = Berndt

K Krystof Grivas's office. I can't come to the phone at the moment. Please leave a message, and I'll get back to you as soon as I can.
B Yeah, Krystof, it's Berndt. The time is now 1 o'clock. Look, I won't be able to make our 2.30 meeting. Can we make it a bit later – 4.30 perhaps?

Answers

1 C   2 B   3 C

EXAM SPOTLIGHT

4.3 Speaking Test: Introduction and Part One

The Speaking Test lasts 12 minutes in total. It has three parts and you can get 30 marks. You do the Speaking Test with a partner.

Part One is an interview. This is a conversation between an examiner and each candidate. It lasts about two minutes in total. The topics for conversation could be: giving personal details, talking about your work or studies, describing your home, speaking about your hobbies, etc. You also have to give your personal opinions.

Part Two is a mini-presentation. Each candidate chooses one topic. You have one minute to organise your thoughts and one minute to present your ideas. At the end, the other candidate has to express his/her opinion of your ideas and you have to do the same. The topics for your presentation could be: choosing a course, booking a flight, selling a new product, etc. In total, this part lasts five minutes.

Part Three is a discussion. In this part of the test, the examiner presents a situation using pictures or a text. You then have a conversation with the other candidate, discussing ideas and making choices. The examiner asks you to explain your choices. The topics for discussion here could be: training, health and safety, business services, management skills, etc. The third part lasts five minutes in total.

1 Read about the Speaking Test above and decide if candidates do the following in Part One, Part Two or Part Three. Tick ✔ as appropriate. Some of the features are connected with more than one part of the test.

	One	Two	Three
1 You might look at pictures.	☐	☐	☐
2 You have time to prepare what to say.	☐	☐	☐
3 You talk about yourself.	☐	☐	☐
4 You choose what to talk about.	☐	☐	☐
5 You answer the examiner's questions.	☐	☐	☐
6 You discuss a situation with your partner.	☐	☐	☐
7 You talk for a minute about a subject.	☐	☐	☐
8 You comment on what your partner has said.	☐	☐	☐

EXAM PRACTICE

2 🎧 4.7 Listen to a recording of two candidates who are doing Part One of the Speaking Test. Write down the information about each candidate in this table.

Name	Christine (1) _____	João Cordeiro
City/Country	Brittany in (2) _____	(3) _____
Work and studies	Works for a multinational company in Paris. Finished school last year.	Works for an (4) _____ company. Attends an evening class in (5) _____
Reasons for liking job	Likes speaking English with colleagues and (6) _____	Likes working with (7) _____ people

Exam Success

Before the exam: practise speaking in small groups. During the exam: if you don't understand a question, ask the examiner to repeat it.

Spare time	Reading, listening to music, swimming and (8) _____	Taking photos, going to the cinema and visiting (9) _____
Opinions on towns and cities	Prefers (10) _____	Prefers big cities because it's exciting and there's a lot to do.

EXAM SKILL

3 Complete the examiner's questions from Part One of the Speaking Test in full.
1 What / name? *What's your name?*
2 How / spell / surname? _____
3 Where / from? _____
4 Do / work / study? _____
5 Do / like / job? _____
6 What / you / in / spare time? _____
7 Do / have / hobbies? _____
8 Do / think it's better / live in a small town / a big city? _____

4 🎧 4.7 Listen to the recording again. Check your answers in exercise 3.

5 Work in groups of three. Turn to the transcript of the recording on page 153 and read the conversation aloud.

EXAM PRACTICE

6 Prepare for Part One of the Speaking Test. Complete the first column of the table with your personal information. Then add an additional comment for each field, as in the examples.

	personal information	additional comment
your name	Phyllis Smith	It's difficult to spell.
your city and country	Rotterdam	It's a nice place to live.
your name		
your city and country		
your home		
your job		
your studies		
your hobbies		

7 Work in groups of three and practise similar conversations for Part One of the Speaking exam. Take turns to be the examiner and candidates. Use the questions in exercise 3 and include the information in exercise 6.

MODULE 4 EXAM SPOTLIGHT   43

42

Student's Book pages 42 and 43

EXAM FORMAT

1 Ask students to read the Exam Format section. Then they should answer the questions in exercise 1 before comparing their answers with a partner.

Answers
1 Three
2 Two
3 One
4 Two
5 One and Three
6 Three
7 Two
8 Two

2 🎧 4.7 Ask the students to look through the table to see the information needed. Play the recording once through and ask students to jot notes while they listen. Then play it again for them and ask them to write the answers.

4.7 Listening script
E = Examiner   C1 = Candidate 1   C2 = Candidate 2

E Good afternoon.
C1 and C2 Good afternoon.
E My name's Heather Barras and this is my colleague, Sharon Hutchinson. She will be listening to us. Now, could I have your mark sheets, please?
C1 Yes, here you are.
C2 Here you are.
E Thank you. Right. So, what's your name?
C1 My name is Christine Benferrhat.
E How do you spell your surname?
C1 It's B-E-N-F-E-R-R-H-A-T.
E And where are you from, Christine?
C1 I'm from Brittany, in France.
E And what's your name?
C2 My name's João Cordeiro and I'm from Portugal.
E João, do you work or study in Portugal?
C2 I work for an advertising company and I attend evening classes in English.
E And you, Christine, do you work or study in Brittany?
C1 I finished school last year. I have a new job near Paris. I work for a multinational company.
E And do you like your new job?
C1 Yes, I like it a lot. I like speaking English with my colleagues and our customers.
E And what about you, João? Do you like your work?
C2 Yes, I like it very much. I like working with creative people.
E OK. Christine, what do you do in your spare time?

C1 I don't have much spare time, but I like reading, listening to the music and I like swimming. When I go back to Brittany, I also like windsurfing.

E And you, João, do you have any hobbies?

C2 Yes, I like taking photos. I have a new digital camera and I like taking pictures of towns. I also like going to the cinema and I visit art exhibitions. There are a lot in Lisbon.

E Do you think it's better to live in a small town or a big city?

C2 I prefer big cities. It's exciting and there's a lot to do.

E Do you agree, Christine?

C1 No, I don't agree with him. I live near Paris, but that's because of my work. I would prefer to live in a smaller town, like my home town in Brittany. Maybe because I like the sea.

E Thank you. That's the end of Part One of the Speaking Test.

Answers
1 Benferrhat
2 France
3 Portugal
4 advertising
5 English
6 customers
7 creative
8 windsurfing
9 art exhibitions
10 smaller towns

3 Ask students to look at the words and write the examiner's questions in full.

Answers
2 How do you spell your surname?
3 Where are you from?
4 Do you work or study?
5 Do you like your job?
6 What do you do in your spare time?
7 Do you have any hobbies?
8 Do you think it's better to live in a small town or a big city?

4 Play the recording again. Check the answers for exercise 3 with the students.

5 Ask students to form groups of three. Tell them to turn to the transcript of the recording on page 153 and read the conversation aloud.

6 Ask students to write their personal information in the first column and one comment for each item in the second column, as in the examples.

7 Give students time to read the Exam Success tip on the previous page. Ask students to form new groups of three. They now have conversations based on the one in the transcript, but giving their own information. They should take turns being the examiner and the interviewees.

Extension
As extension practice for speaking, make photocopies of the questions on this page, and ask your students to practise interviewing each other when they have a few spare minutes during your lessons. This can also be used as a warmer or as a last activity before the end of lessons. Students should be encouraged to collect as many questions as possible.

How do you spell your surname?

Do you live in a village or a town?

Do you have any hobbies?

How do you spend your time when you are not working?

What is your favourite sport?

Can you explain why?

Do you like travelling?

Have you ever been abroad?

Do you have any brothers or sisters?

Do you have any pets?

How do you travel to work / to school?

Overview

5.1   Business topic: Career choices

READING   Escaping the rat race

VOCABULARY   Money expressions

GRAMMAR   The present perfect

LISTENING   Career changes

5.2   Business skills: Achievements and plans

READING   In-company communications

WRITING   Progress reports

SPEAKING   Talking about results

GRAMMAR   *going to* for future plans

LISTENING   Negotiating a bank loan

5.3   Exam spotlight: Reading Test Introduction and Parts One to Three

Practising Reading Test: Parts One to Three

Interpreting graphs

Useful language from Module 5

Wordlist

accommodation	earn an income	make enquiries	resign from
accountancy	earn money	make friends	retire
all in all	exhibition	make money	reward
bank loan	farmhouse	make progress	settle in
be in order	former	meet up	since
be off	give up	more than ever	slip
borrow	go bankrupt	office block	spend on sth
branch	grow up	on a small scale	stockbroker
business card	head office	paperwork	stress out
business park	HR	pay increase	take a holiday
business plan	huge	premises	take on staff
challenge	income	produce	trade in shares
competitive	keep up with	progress	trial
competitor	demand	progress report	unexpectedly
countryside	launch	publisher	utilities
debt	lend	rat race	work long hours
distribute	loan application	redundancy	
do sth different	make a loss	package	
E numbers	make a profit	removal company	

Expressions

Do you have any other income?
Have you ever borrowed money before?
Have you seen the news?
How much do you earn?
Where have you been?
Why do you want a loan?

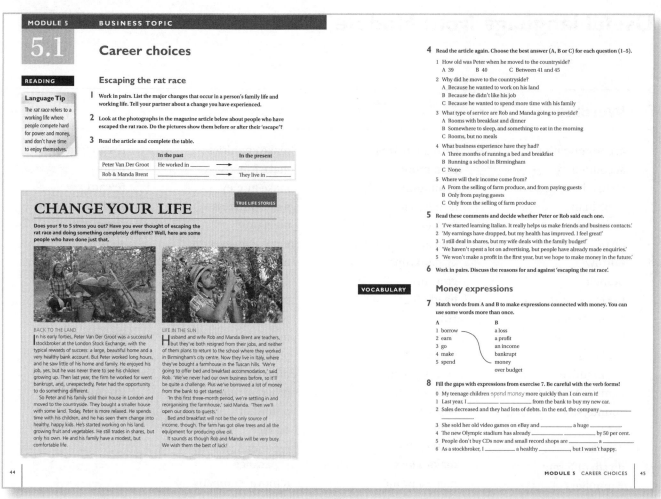

Student's Book pages 44 and 45

Escaping the rat race

READING

1 Before starting with the pairwork task, elicit experiences students have had by asking:
Think of one important change that you have recently experienced.
Or:
Think of one important choice you've recently made.
The students may come up with ideas such as:
I've changed my job.
I've got married.
I've chosen this language course.
I've decided to become a vegetarian.

When you've collected some interesting examples, ask students to work in pairs to do exercise 1.

2 Refer students to the Language Tip. It may be interesting to find out if there's a similar expression in the students' own languages. Then ask students to look at the photographs and answer the question, giving reasons for their answer.

Answer
The pictures show them after their 'escape'.

3 Students read the article and complete the table.

Answer

	In the past		In the present
Peter Van Der Groot	He worked in London as a stockbroker.	→	He lives in the countryside.
Rob & Manda Brent	They worked in Birmingham as teachers.	→	They live in Italy, in the Tuscan hills.

Alternative
Ask students to read the headings and the text out loud, with a different student reading each paragraph. This reading technique makes the students observe the structure of the paragraphs in a text. The different voices make the reading more pleasant and varied.

4 Students should read the article and do the task alone.

Ask students where they found the answers in the text.

Answers
1 C   2 C   3 B   4 C   5 A

5 Ask five students to read the five comments. Ask the rest of the class to decide whether Peter or Rob said each one.

Answers
1 Rob
2 Peter
3 Peter
4 Rob
5 Rob

6 Write the following on the board and elicit some reasons *for* and some *against*:

Escaping the rat race

pros   cons

Ask students to work alone and write some pros and cons of escaping the rat race. Here are some ideas:

Pros:
a quieter life / less stress
you can enjoy your free time
you have more time to spend with family and friends
you can do something you like

Cons:
you earn less money
you have to give up your career plans
you might give up work when you are at the top of your career

Then, in pairs, students discuss the pros and cons.

Money expressions

VOCABULARY

7 Write the word *Money* on the board and ask the students to invent some sentences with the word *Money*. They may be able to produce sentences like:
*I've **spent** all my **money**.*
*We **ran out of money** during our holiday.*
*I'd like to **change some money**.*
*I need to **borrow some money** from the bank.*
*She **earns a lot of money**.*
*I can **lend you some money**.*
*They **made a lot of money** by selling hamburgers.*
*I'm **saving money** to buy a new car.*
***Money loses its value**.*
*My little brother gets some **pocket money** every week.*

Point out any interesting collocations (in bold above); then students do exercise 7.

Answers
1 borrow money
2 earn an income / money
3 go bankrupt / over budget
4 make a loss / a profit / money
5 spend money

8 Ask students to fill the gaps with expressions from exercise 7.

Answers
1 borrowed money
2 went bankrupt
3 made, profit
4 gone over budget
5 making, loss
6 earned, income

GRAMMAR

The present perfect

We form the present perfect with *have/has* + the past participle of the verb.
They have (They've) resigned.
Past participles of regular verbs end with *-ed: talk – talked, hire – hired.*
For the past participle of irregular verbs, such as *speak – spoken, be – been, buy – bought,* you have to learn the forms.
Note that *go* uses two past participles in the present perfect.
He's gone to Rome. = He's in Rome now.
He's been to Rome. = He went to Rome and he came back.
We use the present perfect to talk about:
- something that has *recently* happened and that has a *consequence* or a visible result in the present.
  *I've just **bought** a new computer.*
- something that started in the past and continues in the present.
  *It's only 8.30 and I've already **answered** ten telephone calls this morning!*
- an action within a period of time which is not yet finished.
  *They **have been** colleagues since 2016.*
Note that we use the past simple to talk about a finished time and/or action.
I worked as a bank clerk from 2010 to 2015; then I left.

1 Look at the article on page 44 again. Underline all the verbs in the present perfect. How many are regular? How many are irregular?

2 Read about the changes in Petra Schein's life. Choose the correct options.

> **PETRA SCHEIN (1)** *has worked / worked* in human resources for Banque DeLux Online in Luxembourg since she left university. Four years ago, she **(2)** *has become / became* the HR manager of her branch when the former HR manager **(3)** *has retired / retired.* Last year, she **(4)** *has moved / moved* to the bank's head office. Since then, her responsibilities **(5)** *have increased / increased.* As a result, she has to spend more time at work.
>
> In her free time, Petra enjoys listening to music. She **(6)** *has wanted / wanted* to learn to play a musical instrument for a long time. Six months ago, she **(7)** *has bought / bought* a piano and this month she **(8)** *has started / started* taking lessons. But Petra doesn't have a lot of time to practise, so progress is slow.

3 Here are some time markers often used with the past simple (PS) or the present perfect (PP). Write PS or PP next to each one. Some can be used with both.

this week PP	last week ___	just ___	yesterday ___
today ___	... ever ... ? ___	when ___	since Friday ___
already ___	in 2007 ___	recently ___	three hours ago ___
not ... yet ___	for two days ___	never ___	How long ... ? ___

4 Put the time markers into the correct position in each sentence.
1 I have bought a guitar, but I don't know how to play it. (just)
2 Have you read any good books? (recently)
3 My friends want to go to the cinema, but I have seen the film. (already)
4 There's a great photography exhibition on in town. Have you seen it? (yet)
5 I've been here 20 minutes! Where have you been? (for)

5 Work in groups of three. Write five sentences about things you have or haven't done in your life. Include one false sentence. Read your sentences to the others. They try to identify the false sentence.
A: I've never eaten cheese.
B: I don't believe you. Haven't you ever eaten pizza?
A: Yes, but I take the cheese off.

LISTENING

Career changes

6 🎧 5.1 Petra Schein and Alex Bélanger meet at a conference. Listen to their conversation. What are their jobs?
Petra is a/an _____.
Alex was a/an _____; now he is a/an _____.

7 🎧 5.1 Listen to the conversation again. Decide whether sentences 1–4 are 'Right' or 'Wrong'. If there is not enough information to choose 'Right' or 'Wrong', choose 'Doesn't say'.
1 Petra and Alex have met before.
  A Right   B Wrong   C Doesn't say
2 Petra and Alex worked together three years ago.
  A Right   B Wrong   C Doesn't say
3 Alex takes pictures for magazines.
  A Right   B Wrong   C Doesn't say
4 Petra has moved to a different company.
  A Right   B Wrong   C Doesn't say

8 How has Alex's life changed in the last three years?

Student's Book pages 46 and 47

The present perfect

GRAMMAR

1 Ask students to read the information on the present perfect. Point out the difference between:
He's gone to Rome. = He's in Rome now.
He's been to Rome. = He went to Rome and he has come back.

Students look at the article on page 44 again and underline all the verbs in the present perfect. Make this task a competition. The student who's the first to find all the verbs and gives you the correct number of regular and irregular past participles is the winner.

Point out the use of the contracted forms and the uses of *ever* and *never* in the text.

Answers
Regular past participles: 3 (*he's started; they've both resigned; we've borrowed*)

Irregular past participles: 5 (*have you ever thought; people who have done; he has seen; they've bought; we've never had*)

2 Students either work alone or in pairs and choose the correct tense: past simple or present perfect. For some languages this grammar area is particularly challenging, so students will need plenty of help and practice with this.

While checking their answers, ask students to point out which time marker helped them to choose the correct option.

Answers
1 has worked (*since*)
2 became (*four years ago*)
3 retired (*when*)
4 moved (*Last year*)
5 have increased (*Since then*)
6 has wanted (*for a long time*)
7 bought (*Six months ago*)
8 has started (*this month*)

Photocopiable activity
See page 168.

3 Students could work in pairs. Some time markers can be used with either tense. This will depend on whether the speaker sees the time period of the action as being finished or still continuing. While checking answers, ask students to make a sentence to illustrate each tense (where both are possible), eg:

I've been very busy recently. / I met Paul recently.

I've never been to Asia before. / Shakespeare never left England.

How long have you been here? / How long did you stay with them?

I've been here for two days. / I stayed with them for two days.

Answers

this week – PP	last week – PS
just – PP	yesterday – PS
today – PP / PS	… ever …? – PP
when – PS	since Friday – PP
already – PP	in 2007 – PS
recently – PP / PS	three hours ago – PS
not … yet – PP	for two days – PS / PP
never – PP / PS	How long …? – PP/PS

4 Students work alone and put the time markers in the correct position in the sentences.

Answers

1 I have <u>just</u> bought a guitar …
2 Have you read any good books <u>recently</u>?
3 … but I have <u>already</u> seen the film.
4 Have you seen it <u>yet</u>?
5 I've been here <u>for</u> 20 minutes!

5 Write five sentences on the board about things you have or haven't done in your life. Include one false sentence. Students have to identify the false sentence by asking YES/NO questions or open questions.

Career changes

LISTENING

6 🎧 5.1 Ask students to look at the picture. Elicit a brief description of the people, setting, situations, etc. Elicit by asking *Wh-* questions.

Tell students that they're going to listen to a conversation between Petra and Alex and find out what their jobs are. Play the recording once.

5.1 Listening script

P = Petra   A = Alex

P Excuse me. Could you pass me a plate?
A Sure. … You're Petra Schein, aren't you?
P Yes, I am.
A I thought so. You probably won't remember me, but I came for an interview for an accountancy job with you about three years ago.
P Yes, Alex, isn't it? Bélanger.
A That's right.
P I seem to remember that one of your hobbies was photography. It was a real passion.
A You do have a good memory!
P So what happened? We offered you a job, but you went to work for one of our competitors – Deutsche Bank, I seem to remember.

A The conditions they gave me were better, I'm sorry to say.
P I can understand that. So, are you still working there?
A No, I've given up banking all together. I worked for Deutsche Bank for a little more than two years, but I didn't really like the job. There was too much competition among the employees, and I didn't really like that.
P Well, sometimes you have to be competitive if you want to make progress.
A I know, but it wasn't for me.
P So, what do you do now?
A I have become a professional photographer.
P You know, that doesn't surprise me. Are you in any particular sector?
A I take portrait photos. I've just bought a studio, and I'm creating a library of photos, which I'm going to publish on my website.
P You must give me your web address.
A Better than that, I can give you my business card. … And what about you? Are you still in human resources?
P Yes, I am. I've moved to the head office, and I'm the manager there. So now I'm even busier than ever …

Answers

Petra is a human resources manager.
Alex was an accountant; now he is a professional photographer.

7 🎧 5.1 Ask students to read the questions. Play the recording again and check the answers.

Ask students to read the listening script and underline the words that helped them to answer the questions.

Answers

1 A Right (*I came for an interview … with you about three years ago.*)
2 B Wrong (*We offered you a job, but you went to work with one of our competitors …*)
3 C Doesn't say
4 B Wrong (*I've moved to the head office …*)

8 Ask students how Alex's life has changed in the last three years.

Answer

He's given up banking all together, and he has become a professional photographer.

BUSINESS SKILLS

5.2 Achievements and plans

READING

In-company communications

1 Read this email and answer the following questions.
• Who is it to?   • Who is it from?   • What is the relationship between them?

```
From: Andres Martino
To: Elena Gonzalez
Subject: New cover designs
Date: 3 October
Hi Elena
I'm off to the Book Fair this afternoon, but I see that the new designs haven't arrived yet.
Please can you:
– call the design office; ask them to send you the three designs for the book covers –
this is urgent;
– write an email to the printers (Synapse) asking for price quotations for the three designs, in
full colour, and in black and white;
– send the three designs to the printers.
Can you email me a full progress report by 6pm, please?
Andres
```

Learning Tip
Read your writing twice to check for spelling, punctuation and grammar mistakes.

2 Read the email again and complete Elena's notes.

```
THINGS TO DO TODAY
1 call _____ and ask for _____
2 write to _____ and get _____
3 send _____
```

3 Work in pairs.
Student A: You are Elena Gonzalez. Refer to your notes in exercise 2. Then phone Octavio Flores, head of the design office.
Student B: Go to page 146.

WRITING

Progress reports

Exam Success
In Part One of the Writing Test, you have to include the information given in bullet points, and sometimes invent your own details. Check that you include all the relevant information.

4 Complete Elena's email to the printers.

```
From: _____   To: _____   Date: _____
Subject: Price quotation
Could you _____?
I attach _____ and tomorrow
Looking forward to _____
```

5 Write Elena's progress report to Andres. Write 30–40 words. Tell him:
• what you have done   • what you haven't done and why   • future actions.

READING

Talking about results

6 Work in pairs. Read this conversation between Berndt Reinhardt, the CEO of a publisher based in Cologne, Germany, and an ex-colleague, Franka. Fill each gap with the present perfect form of a suitable verb.

Franka   Hello. It's nice to see you again. You're looking well.
Berndt   Thanks! I am well. I (0) 've just come (just) back from the Turin Book Fair.
Franka   Ah! One of your favourite events. How did it go?
Berndt   Oh, the fair was quite a success. We had a lot of interest in a new series of science titles that we (1) _____. And I met up with some old friends. Do you remember Nuno, from Lisbon? Yes, all in all, it was very pleasant. And I do enjoy Italian food.
Franka   It's delicious, isn't it? Well then, Berndt, has this been a good year for you?
Berndt   Yes, it has. We (2) _____ really well in Western Europe – we (3) _____ more books than ever before. And we (4) _____ distributing in countries in Eastern Europe as well – for example, in Poland and Hungary. Poland is doing very well. The demand for our books (5) _____ almost as high as in Spain and Portugal.
Franka   That's great! I can see you (6) _____ very busy.
Berndt   Well, of course! You know me.
Franka   So what's next then? I'm sure you've got something new planned.
Berndt   Well, we're going to move the actual printing to Slovakia. We have a new contract with a printing company in Bratislava. They're going to take over about 80 per cent of our book printing next year. It's going to cut our costs considerably, I hope.
Franka   What a coincidence! I (7) _____ (just) to Bratislava.
Berndt   Well, I'm going to be there next month. I'm going to discuss the contract with the printers. And after that, I think I'm going to take a few days' holiday. It's been a very busy year.

7 🎧 5.2 Listen to the conversation and check your answers.

8 Use information from the conversation in exercise 6 to complete this news item in the magazine *Publishing Weekly*.

```
NEWS IN BRIEF
Berndt Reinhardt, (1) _____ of TGO Press,
has announced record profits for this year. TGO
Press have recently expanded into (2) _____
in a move which consolidates their strong
position in (3) _____. Reinhardt surprised
competitors at the Turin (4) _____,
presenting a series of (5) _____ books. Until
now, TGO has published fiction and poetry.
According to a source at Turin, TGO are
planning to (6) _____ their printing
operation to an (7) _____ European country
as well. TGO has certainly had a (8) _____
and successful time since Reinhardt took over
two years ago.
```

Student's Book pages 48 and 49

In-company communications

READING

1 As a lead-in, ask students to describe what items they'd normally find in an email. Elicit the following:
• Addressee(s)
• Sender
• Date
• Subject
• Opening salutation
• The message
• Closing salutation

Ask students to look at the email and answer the questions.

Answers
• Who is it to? **Elena Gonzalez**
• Who is it from? **Andres Martino**
• What is the relationship between them? **Elena is the PA to Andres.**

2 Ask students to read the email again and do exercise 2.

Answers
1 call the design office and ask for the three designs for the book covers.
2 write to the printers (Synapse) and get price quotations for the three designs (colour and black and white).
3 send the three designs to the printers.

3 Students work in pairs and do the role play.

Alternative
If you want to liven up the role play, you can give the students a characterisation. For example, Elena can be rude, polite, extremely polite, shy, very tired, very energetic, etc., whereas Octavio can be in a hurry, a very chatty person, rude, polite, tired, somebody who prefers work to holiday, somebody who likes/dislikes his job, etc. You can write the characterisation on a piece of paper and give it to the students, without showing them to their role play partner. If you choose the characterisation technique, ask a few pairs to act out their dialogue in front of the class and have the rest of the class guess or understand what type of person Elena or Octavio are.

Progress reports

4 When students have completed the email, ask one student to read his/her email out loud. Ask the rest of the class to point out any mistakes or to give different versions.

Remind students that it's good practice to read their writing at least twice, checking grammar mistakes first, then spelling and punctuation.

Sample answer

From: Elena Gonzalez
To: Synapse
Date: 3 October
Subject: Price quotation

Could you please send us a price quotation for three designs, for both full colour and black and white?

I attach two of the designs, and tomorrow I'll send the third one.

Looking forward to your reply.

Best regards

Elena Gonzalez

5 Ask students to write Elena's progress report.

Sample answer

Hi Andres

I called the design office and spoke to Octavio. Only two of the designs were ready. I've sent them to the printers and asked them for a price quotation. I'll send them the third one tomorrow afternoon.

Elena

Talking about results

6 Students work in pairs and, as they read the dialogue out loud, they fill in the gaps with the present perfect of a suitable verb. Don't check answers at this stage as this will be done in exercise 7.

7 🎧 5.2 Students listen and check their answers in exercise 6.

5.2 Listening script

F = Franka   B = Berndt

F Hello. It's nice to see you again. You're looking well.
B Thanks! I am well. I've just come back from the Turin Book Fair.
F Ah! One of your favourite events. How did it go?

B Oh, the fair was quite a success. We had a lot of interest in a new series of science titles that we've published. And I met up with some old friends. Do you remember Nuno, from Lisbon? Yes, all in all, it was very pleasant. And I do enjoy Italian food.
F It's delicious, isn't it? Well then, Berndt, has this been a good year for you?
B Yes, it has. We've done really well in Western Europe – we've sold more books than ever before. And we've started distributing in countries in Eastern Europe as well – for example, in Poland and Hungary. Poland is doing very well. The demand for our books has been almost as high as in Spain and Portugal.
F That's great! I can see you've been very busy.
B Well, of course! You know me.
F So what's next then? I'm sure you've got something new planned.
B Well, we're going to move the actual printing to Slovakia. We have a new contract with a printing company in Bratislava. They're going to take over about 80 per cent of our book printing next year. It's going to cut our costs considerably, I hope.
F What a coincidence! I've just been to Bratislava.
B Well, I'm going to be there next month. I'm going to discuss the contract with the printers. And after that, I think I'm going to take a few days' holiday. It's been a very busy year.

Answers
1 've published
2 've done
3 've sold
4 've started
5 has been
6 've been
7 've just been

8 Ask students to do exercise 8 on their own, using the information from the conversation in exercise 7. They then compare their answers with a partner.

Answers
1 CEO
2 Eastern European
3 Western Europe
4 Book Fair
5 science
6 move
7 Eastern
8 busy

GRAMMAR   *going to*

We use *going to* + infinitive to express future plans and intentions:

I'm going to take a holiday soon.

We can use *going to* + infinitive with or without a time expression.
We're **not** *going to* use that company again. They are very expensive.
She's going to look for a new job in the summer.

I Complete the dialogue with the correct form of the verbs in brackets.

A Have you seen the news? The company (1) _____
(go / move) out of the city centre to a new site.

B I know, they (2) _____ (go / build) a
new office block in the business park.

A That (3) _____ (go / be) difficult for a
lot of people to get to.

B Yes, and the building (4) _____
(not / go / be) as big as this one.

A What do you mean? (5) _____
(they / go / fire) people?

B I don't know. I've heard that they (6) _____
(go / offer) good redundancy packages.

A Really? What (7) _____ (you / go / do)?
(8) _____ (you / go / apply for) redundancy?

B Why not? I've been here for 15 years. I could get quite a lot of money.

A Oh …

2 Write sentences with *going to* using the prompts in brackets.

0 Our offices are too small. (look for / new office building)
We're going to look for a new office building.
1 His company is in financial difficulties. (look for / new job)
2 Our trials of the new product have been successful. (launch / in summer)
3 She has just had a pay increase. (buy / sports car)
4 The company has made record profits. (pay / staff / bonus)
5 He has seen an advertisement for a job he likes. (apply for / job)
6 She doesn't want to work for a company. (start / own business)

3 Read the notes you made at a recent meeting with your manager to discuss moving offices to new premises. Write down what you plan to do for each point.

arrange removal company
arrange new details on company stationery
make sure we keep the same phone numbers!
inform clients and suppliers
keep staff up-to-date with plans
arrange for new utilities contracts

LISTENING   **Negotiating a bank loan**

4 🎧 5.3 Jack and Jill Hopkins have applied for a bank loan to start a new business.
Listen to the meeting between Jack and the bank manager, and choose the best
answer (A, B or C) for each question (1–6).

1 What kind of business are Jack and Jill going to start?
  A making ice creams
  B selling fruit and vegetables
  C making fruit drinks
2 How many flavours have they got at the moment?
  A one: strawberry
  B two: strawberry and pear
  C three: pear, banana and mango
3 Why do they want a loan?
  A to make more flavours and increase the amount they make
  B to experiment with new flavours
  C to take on more staff to meet demand
4 Where are they going to sell their products?
  A in their own shops
  B in snack bars and similar outlets
  C in bars and restaurants
5 What are they going to change about the way they work?
  A They plan to change the bottles they use.
  B They are going to use a different production process.
  C They aren't going to change anything.
6 Who are they going to market their products to?
  A young families with children
  B young people
  C health clubs

5 🎧 5.3 Listen again and complete the bank manager's questions.

1 Have you already started making and _____ your _____ ?
2 Are you going to _____ your range?
3 How do you plan to _____ the _____ ?
4 Who do you think is going to be your main _____ ?

6 Work in groups of four, in two pairs.

Pair A: Prepare questions a bank might ask before lending money. Use the questions
in the Useful language box below and from exercise 5 to help you.
Pair B: Prepare ideas for a new business you want to start.

7 In your group of four, form two new pairs and act out the conversation.

Student A: You are the bank manager. Ask the questions you prepared in exercise 6.
Student B: You are the customer. Explain why you want to borrow money and answer
the questions your partner asks. What is the bank manager's decision?

Useful language

What do you do?	Have you ever borrowed money before?
Why do you want a loan?	Do you have any debts?
How much do you earn?	Do you have a credit card?
Do you have any other income?	How long have you been in business?

50   **UNIT 5** ACHIEVEMENTS AND PLANS   51

Student's Book pages 50 and 51

---

going to

GRAMMAR

I As a lead-in, ask students to look at the picture and ask them the following questions:

Is the man having a holiday now?

Has the man already planned a holiday?

Will he be on holiday next week?

Is he thinking of having a holiday?

Does the man intend to have a holiday?

Elicit students' answers and emphasise the idea of *intend* which is conveyed by *going to*.

Ask students to write a list of five things they're going to do soon; then ask them to produce full sentences orally. Alternatively, you can start a round of questions, eg: *Carlos, what are you going to do this evening?* Carlos replies; then he asks one other student a question with *going to*: *Martina, what are you going to do at the weekend?* One rule for this round of questions is that they can't use verbs or time markers already used by previous students.

Choose two students to read the dialogue between A and B. When they come to the gap, the rest of the class should give the answer.

Answers
1 is going to move
2 're going to build
3 's going to be
4 isn't going to be
5 Are they going to fire
6 're going to offer
7 are you going to do?
8 Are you going to apply for

2 Before writing the sentences, get the students to produce the correct sentences orally. Taking it in turns, students read each sentence silently, and then read the transformed sentences out loud.

Answers
1 He's going to look for a new job.
2 We're going to launch the new product / it in the summer.
3 She's going to buy a sports car.
4 It's going to pay the staff a bonus.
5 He's going to apply for the / a job.
6 She's going to start her own business.

3 Tell students not to just add *going to* to the points in the notes, but to add time markers and any other ideas as well.

Possible answers

Today, I'm going to phone the removal companies and arrange the date.

Tomorrow, I'm going to change the details on our company stationery. Then I'm going to send the file to the printers.

I'm going to phone the telephone company later to make sure that we keep the same telephone numbers.

Tomorrow morning, I'm going to send an email to all of our clients and suppliers informing them about the change of premises.

I'm going to send memos to all staff, to keep them updated.

Tomorrow, I'm going to call the utilities companies to arrange for new contracts.

Photocopiable activity
See page 169.

Negotiating a bank loan

LISTENING

4 🎧 5.3 Before starting the listening task, ask students if they know the word *loan*. Revise the money expressions containing *lend* and *borrow*. Ask them if they've ever asked for a loan from a bank, relatives, friends, etc. Collect students' ideas.

This task is similar to Listening Test, Part Four. Tell students that in the exam they'll have eight questions and they will hear the recording twice. Play the recording once. Ask students to read out to you the letters they've chosen. If some students made mistakes, play the recording again and give feedback.

5.3 Listening script
BM = Bank manager   **JH** = Jack Hopkins

BM OK, well, I've got all the paperwork here for your loan application. Everything seems to be in order. Let's just have a look at your business plan. Perhaps you could tell me about your ideas?
JH Yes, of course. We plan to make fruit drinks, from 100 per cent fruit – no extra sugar, or additives or E numbers. At the moment, we've only got a couple of flavours, strawberry and pear, but we want to expand our range to include more flavours.
BM You say that you've got some flavours. Have you already started making and selling your drinks?
JH Only on a small scale, but they're selling really well and we can't keep up with demand.
BM Right, so why exactly do you want a loan? Are you going to expand your range or increase your production?
JH Well, both, we hope.
BM And how do you plan to sell the drinks? Direct to the public?

JH No, we're going to sell through other companies. You know, in cafés, snack bars, at outlets in airports and railway stations. We've already had talks with the catering company that runs the 'Travel Snack' chain. They're going to stock our drinks in their main outlets.
BM And are you going to be able to expand quickly?
JH I think so, because we're going to keep everything simple. We plan to use the same basic plastic bottles that we've used until now, and we're going to use fruit that is easily available locally. Our production process is very simple too.
BM OK, what about your market? Who do you think is going to be your main market?
JH So far, most of our customers have been young people – you know, students, teenagers, people who are interested in drinking something healthy and natural. So we're going to try to consolidate that market. I don't think it's a good idea to change our strategy at the moment.
BM What kind of marketing have you done?
JH A friend of ours has designed a great website for us, and I think we're going to focus on the Internet for the moment.
BM OK, so let's look at these figures in more detail …

Answers
1 C   2 B   3 A   4 B   5 C   6 B

5 🎧 5.3 Play the recording once more. Students complete the questions.

Answers
1 selling, drinks
2 expand
3 sell, drinks
4 market

6/7 You may have some students that are creative and don't need much help with ideas. Some others will need a frame for their situation. You may want to suggest they choose English names, a town where the business is going to start up, a name for the bank, a name for the new products, etc.

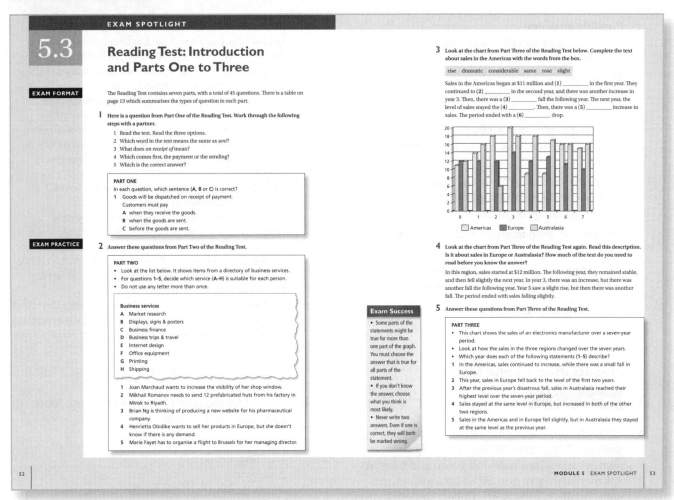

EXAM SPOTLIGHT

5.3 Reading Test: Introduction and Parts One to Three

EXAM FORMAT

The Reading Test contains seven parts, with a total of 45 questions. There is a table on page 13 which summarises the types of question in each part.

1 Here is a question from Part One of the Reading Test. Work through the following steps with a partner.

1 Read the text. Read the three options.
2 Which word in the text means the same as *sent*?
3 What does *on receipt of* mean?
4 Which comes first, the payment or the sending?
5 Which is the correct answer?

PART ONE
In each question, which sentence (**A, B** or **C**) is correct?
1 Goods will be dispatched on receipt of payment.
  Customers must pay
  A when they receive the goods.
  B when the goods are sent.
  C before the goods are sent.

EXAM PRACTICE

2 Answer these questions from Part Two of the Reading Test.

PART TWO
• Look at the list below. It shows items from a directory of business services.
• For questions 1–5, decide which service (A–H) is suitable for each person.
• Do not use any letter more than once.

Business services
A Market research
B Displays, signs & posters
C Business finance
D Business trips & travel
E Internet design
F Office equipment
G Printing
H Shipping

1 Joan Marchaud wants to increase the visibility of her shop window.
2 Mikhail Romanov needs to send 12 prefabricated huts from his factory in Minsk to Riyadh.
3 Brian Ng is thinking of producing a new website for his pharmaceutical company.
4 Henrietta Obidike wants to sell her products in Europe, but she doesn't know if there is any demand.
5 Marie Fayet has to organise a flight to Brussels for her managing director.

3 Look at the chart from Part Three of the Reading Test below. Complete the text about sales in the Americas with the words from the box.

rise   dramatic   considerable   same   rose   slight

Sales in the Americas began at $11 million and (**1**) _____ in the first year. They continued to (**2**) _____ in the second year, and there was another increase in year 3. Then, there was a (**3**) _____ fall the following year. The next year, the level of sales stayed the (**4**) _____. Then, there was a (**5**) _____ increase in sales. The period ended with a (**6**) _____ drop.

☐ Americas   ■ Europe   ☐ Australasia

4 Look at the chart from Part Three of the Reading Test again. Read this description. Is it about sales in Europe or Australasia? How much of the text do you need to read before you know the answer?

In this region, sales started at $12 million. The following year, they remained stable, and then fell slightly the next year. In year 3, there was an increase, but there was another fall the following year. Year 5 saw a slight rise, but then there was another fall. The period ended with sales falling slightly.

Exam Success
• Some parts of the statements might be true for more than one part of the graph. You must choose the answer that is true for all parts of the statement.
• If you don't know the answer, choose what you think is most likely.
• Never write two answers. Even if one is correct, they will both be marked wrong.

5 Answer these questions from Part Three of the Reading Test.

PART THREE
• This chart shows the sales of an electronics manufacturer over a seven-year period.
• Look at how the sales in the three regions changed over the seven years.
• Which year does each of the following statements (1–5) describe?
1 In the Americas, sales continued to increase, while there was a small fall in Europe.
2 This year, sales in Europe fell back to the level of the first two years.
3 After the previous year's disastrous fall, sales in Australasia reached their highest level over the seven-year period.
4 Sales stayed at the same level in Europe, but increased in both of the other two regions.
5 Sales in the Americas and in Europe fell slightly, but in Australasia they stayed at the same level as the previous year.

52 | MODULE 5 EXAM SPOTLIGHT 53

Student's Book pages 52 and 53

1 Ask students to read the information about the Reading Test. For more information and further practice of these types of question refer to the Cambridge *Business Handbook for teachers*, also available online at: www.cambridgeenglish.org

Here students start practising the type of questions they'll find in the exam. It's important that they become familiar with these types of questions, and that they acquire skills that will help them to make efficient use of their time during the exam.

Answers
2 dispatched
3 when they receive
4 payment
5 C

EXAM PRACTICE

2 Students should read the question on their own. Then ask them to explain what they have to do to a partner or to the class, before they do the matching task.

Students do this task individually, as if they were taking the exam. Ask them to time themselves, ie, the time they take to read the text and answer the questions. Tell students to write the starting and finishing time at the top of the page and keep a record of how long they take to do each exercise. By the end of the book, they'll have an idea of how to manage their time when they do the Reading and Writing parts.

Answers
1 B – Displays, signs & posters
2 H – Shipping
3 E – Internet design
4 A – Market research
5 D – Business trips & travel

Extension
Some students may find this exercise very easy, others will find it a bit more difficult. For students who finish earlier (the first three or five students), they can write a short sentence for the options that were not chosen above, ie:

C Business Finance (eg: Mr X wants to buy two new production units, but he doesn't have the funds.)

F Office Equipment (eg: Company Y has decided to buy new furniture and computers for the administration department.)

G Printing (eg: Ms Z wants to advertise her business services with a new brochure.)

3 Part Three of the Reading Test always contains one or more graphs. Students will have to acquire the skills to interpret graphs. The following exercises are devised to help students to read graphs more easily.

Students work alone. Ask them to complete the text, then to compare their answers with a partner.

Answers
1 rose
2 rise
3 dramatic
4 same
5 considerable
6 slight

4 Ask students to stop reading the text when they have the answer. Students should be able to answer after reading the following: *In this region, sales started at $12 million. The following year, they remained stable (…)*

Answer
Europe

Extension
You can ask students to write a similar description for the third region (Australasia). This can be set as an activity to be done in class or for homework.

5 Read through the Exam Success tips with the class. Then ask students to answer the questions for Part Three

Students do this task individually, as if they were taking the exam. Ask them to time themselves, ie, the time they take to read the text and answer the questions. Tell students to write the starting and finishing time at the top of the page and keep a record of how long they take to do each exercise. By the end of the book, they'll have an idea of how to manage their time when they do the Reading and Writing parts.

Answers
1 Year 2
2 Year 4
3 Year 3
4 Year 1
5 Year 7

Overview

6.1 Business topic: Business travel

LISTENING   **Flight problems**

GRAMMAR   **Reported speech**

READING   **Two tickets, no reimbursement**

6.2 Business skills: Travel arrangements

VOCABULARY   **Hotel amenities**

WRITING   **Booking enquiries**

LISTENING   **At the hotel**

LISTENING   **Arranging business travel**

SPEAKING   **Making a booking**

WRITING   **Changes to flight details**

6.3 Exam spotlight: Writing Test Introduction and Part One

Writing 30–40 words

Focusing on formal and informal style

Opening and closing an email

Useful language from Module 6

Wordlist

account	colleague	inspection	reasonable
action	common (usual)	instructions	receptionist
aeroplane	concierge service	Internet connection	refund (n + v)
air conditioning	confirmation	IT technician	reluctantly
air traffic controller	connecting flight	kind regards	return / single ticket
aircraft	consumer help	land (v)	seasonal
airplane (plane)	credit card	laptop	secretarial services
airport	customer services	late	security
alone	data	laundry	session
alteration	delay (n + v)	lie (v) (not say the	state-of-the-art
amenity	depart	truth)	steal
announcement	detail (n)	lounge	straight
arrangements	direct-dial telephone	luggage	strike
attend	disabled	luxury	stroll (v)
baggage handler	dish of the day	magazine editor	suitcase
best regards / wishes	dispute (n)	menu	take off (v)
board (v)	divert	miss (v)	timetable
boarding pass	economy class	multilingual	training course
book	ensure	online	transfer (v)
broadband access	excess charge	organic	translation services
buffet	facilities	otherwise	travel agent
business centre	first class	overbook	trip
business class	flight attendant	passenger	trouble-free
bye	fraud	passport	trousers
cancel	full / half board	pilot	unfair
cancellation	fully booked	plane	unreasonable
certification	healthy	porter	video projector
charge (money)	host (v)	printer	waiter
check-in clerk	human resources	protect	website
check-in desk	identity card	provisional	yours faithfully /
cleaner	immediate	purchase (v)	sincerely
client	in-flight magazine	quality control	
code	information desk	quote	

Expressions

be on time

by phone

How may I help you?

make a booking / an exception

over the limit

shake sb's hand

solve a problem

Student's Book pages 54 and 55

Flight problems

1 As a lead-in, ask students to keep their books closed and brainstorm all the people connected with travelling and all the documents connected with travelling.

When you've collected enough words, ask students to open their books. Explain the exercise to students, and ask them to work alone to do it. When they've finished, they can compare their answers with a partner.

Answers

People: passenger; pilot; air traffic controller; baggage handler; flight attendant

Documents: passport; boarding pass; identity card; return/single ticket

2 Do the exercise orally with the whole class. Choose students to read out the phrases and insert a word. If the student can't find the right word, the other students can suggest it.

Answers
1 journey
2 travel
3 trip (NB: 'journey' is also possible here, but 'journey' is the best answer for 1.)
4 return
5 luggage

Extension
Ask students to invent sentences that contain the other terms from exercise 1.

3 🎧 6.1 Ask students to read the task and the descriptions of the passengers. Play all recordings once, without stopping.

If students aren't able to identify the passengers, play the monologues individually, and ask students to repeat any phrases they remember.

Answers
Passenger 3 was very satisfied …
Passenger 1 missed his/her flight …
Passenger 4 was delayed because of a strike …
Passenger 2 was delayed because of bad weather …

6.1 Listening script

1 We got to the airport 30 minutes before the plane was due to take off, and we went straight to the check-in desk. First, the man at the desk said that the plane was already full because the flight was overbooked, so we couldn't get on.
But then he changed his story. He said there were empty seats on the plane, but we were late and the check-in desk was closed. So we missed our plane and we had to buy two tickets for another flight. You see, if the flight is overbooked, they give you a seat on a later one – but if you arrive late, you lose your money. I bet the man at the desk was lying.

2 I called the airline to ask if my flight was on time, and the man said that there might be a delay because of the snow. But when I arrived at the airport, there were no flights. The woman at the information desk told me to go back to my hotel and wait. She said they were going to close the airport, and she didn't know for how long.

3 I couldn't complain about anything. The airline sent a taxi to collect me from my hotel. At the airport, they took me straight to the desk to check my case in. I didn't have to wait. Then they let me sit in the First Class Lounge, even though I didn't have a first class ticket. The woman in the lounge said she would bring me some food from the buffet if I was hungry. Then, when it was time to go, they pushed my wheelchair all the way to my seat on the plane. And during the flight, they couldn't do enough for me.

4 There's one every week. If it's not the baggage handlers, it's the flight attendants, or even the pilots. The last time I travelled, it was the air traffic controllers. Oh, but they weren't stopping for the whole day, just for four hours, just long enough to cause absolute chaos. The announcement said there would be no cancellations that day, only delays.
But that meant that I missed my connecting flight in Frankfurt and had to fly out to Chile the following day.

4 🎧 6.1 Ask students to read the four questions. If they already know the answer, tell them to mark it. Play the recording again, stopping briefly between each speaker. Tell students to check the answers they've already marked, and to listen for the others.

Answers
1 B (*… we had to buy two tickets for another flight.*)
2 A (*… told me to go back to my hotel and wait.*)
3 A (*… they pushed my wheelchair …*)
4 B (*There's one every week.*)

5 In pairs, students tell each other about their worst flying experience. Allow a few minutes.

If any students have had a particularly unusual or funny experience, ask them to tell the class about it.

Reported speech

GRAMMAR

6 Read sentence 1. Ask students what the man's actual words were. Let students write the missing word in the space, then ask them to do the same for the other sentences.

Answers
1 is
2 Go, wait
3 're going, don't know
4 'll bring
5 will be

7 Read the instruction and the first example for direct speech: *am/is/are*: *It is late.* and for reported speech: *was/were*: *… it was late.* Then ask students to complete the table, and to read the box.

Answers

was/were	It was late.
Past simple	It left at 6am.
Past continuous	It was landing.
Past perfect	It had arrived.
Past perfect	It had taken off.
would	It would be early.
could	It could leave.

8 Ask students to look at the sentences in exercise 6 again. Ask them to find any examples where one pronoun is used in the reported speech and a different pronoun is used in direct speech. Do the same with possessive adjectives and time expressions.

Answers
2 She told me to go back to <u>my</u> hotel and wait.
 She said, 'Go back to <u>your</u> hotel and wait.'
3 She said <u>they</u> were going to close the airport, and <u>she</u> didn't know for how long.
 She said, '<u>We</u> are going to close the airport. <u>I</u> don't know for how long.'
4 The woman in the lounge said <u>she</u> would bring me some food.
 The woman in the lounge said, '<u>I</u>'ll bring you some food.'
5 'that day' – reported speech ➡ 'today' – direct speech

9 Ask students to read the table in exercise 7 again, and then to do the exercise alone. When they've finished, they can compare their answers with a partner.

Answers
1 luggage was over the limit.
2 would have to pay an excess charge of £45.
3 could be bad.
4 was going to take off at 15.55.
5 didn't eat meat.
6 would like the vegetarian menu.

Photocopiable activity
See page 170.

The reproduced Student's Book pages (56 and 57)

Two tickets, no reimbursement

1 Read this letter to a travel magazine. Has anything similar ever happened to you or anyone you know?

LETTERS TO THE EDITOR

Dear Editor

Last month I was on a business trip in Vietnam. I had a flight from the island of Phu Quoc to Ho Chi Minh City for my connecting flight back to Milan.

When I arrived at the airport, the representative at the check-in desk said the flight was cancelled and the next flight was in the morning. I said I had to catch my flight from Ho Chi Minh to Milan at midnight and I couldn't miss it. She didn't apologise and she said there was nothing she could do.

Luckily, there was a different airline check-in desk nearby and the person waved to me. She said they had a flight to Ho Chi Minh in one hour and there were seats. So, I bought another (much more expensive) ticket and ran to catch the plane. I arrived in time at Ho Chi Minh and I caught the connecting flight home.

Two days later, I called the first airline and explained what happened at Phu Quoc airport and that I wanted my money back. They said they couldn't do that because it was my decision to buy another ticket. I don't think I should have to pay twice for my airline ticket. Can you help me?

Mario Ricci, *Milan*

2 Read the letter again. Decide whether these sentences are 'Right' or 'Wrong'. If there is not enough information to choose 'Right' or 'Wrong', choose 'Doesn't say'.

1 The passenger's final destination was Ho Chi Minh City in Vietnam.
   A Right   B Wrong   C Doesn't say
2 At the airport, the first airline didn't have another flight until morning.
   A Right   B Wrong   C Doesn't say
3 The representative said she was sorry but couldn't do anything.
   A Right   B Wrong   C Doesn't say
4 The cost of the second ticket to Ho Chi Minh City was higher than the first.
   A Right   B Wrong   C Doesn't say
5 At Ho Chi Minh City airport, he complained again to another airline representative.
   A Right   B Wrong   C Doesn't say
6 The phone call to the airline customer service centre solved the problem.
   A Right   B Wrong   C Doesn't say

3 Compare your answers with a partner. For the questions that you have answered 'Right' or 'Wrong', which words helped you to decide the answer? For the questions you answered 'Doesn't say', why did you give this answer?

4 Work in pairs. Discuss what the magazine editor could do to help Mr Ricci.

5 This is the editor's reply. The paragraphs are in the wrong order. Put them into the correct order (1–5).

DEAR TRAVELLER

☐ I hope that our reply has been helpful and your next trip is free from problems.

☐ The terms and conditions on the airline's website reserves the right to cancel a flight for circumstances beyond its control. It must then offer the passenger a seat on the next available flight, which it did.

☐ The fact that you bought another ticket was your choice and so the first airline does not have to reimburse you for this. So, I'm afraid on this occasion the information you were given was correct.

☐ Dear Mario
Thank you for writing to us about your bad experience. It's clear that you have suffered from some poor customer service; however, based on your description, the airline has not actually broken any rules.

☐ Surprisingly, your economy ticket did not require the airline to offer you overnight hotel accommodation, though in our opinion, good customer care would mean trying to find passengers a suitable hotel for the night.

6 Check your answers.
1 Paragraph 1 introduces the reason for writing.
2 Paragraph 2 gives factual information about the situation.
3 Paragraph 3 explains the reason for the situation.
4 Paragraph 4 gives additional information and advice.
5 Paragraph 5 makes a concluding comment.

7 You are the customer services manager of the airline. Write a follow-up letter (60–80 words) to Mr Ricci telling him the following. Write five paragraphs as in exercise 6.
• The editor of the travel magazine contacted the airline about your complaint.
• The check-in staff have explained the details of the situation.
• The airline does not have to reimburse you for the ticket.
• On this occasion, they are happy to give a refund.
• They hope Mr Ricci will use the airline again.

Student's Book pages 56 and 57

Two tickets, no reimbursement

READING

1 Ask students to look at the title *Two tickets, no reimbursement,* and to predict what the letter is about. Collect suggestions.

Ask students to read the letter. When they've finished, ask them to describe what happened to Mr Ricci to a partner.

Find out if anything similar has happened to any of the students and tell them to describe what happened.

2 Ask students to read the questions and to mark the ones they can answer. Then ask them to read the letter again, and to find the words/phrases that give the answers to the questions. Don't check answers at this stage as this will be done in exercise 3.

3 Ask students to compare their answers with a partner, and to show which words/phrases gave the answers. Check the answers with the class, choosing individual students to answer, and to explain their answers.

Answers
1 B (*I had a flight … to Ho Chi Minh City for my connecting flight back to Milan.*)
2 A (*… and the next flight was in the morning.*)
3 B (*She didn't apologise …*)
4 A (*I bought another (much more expensive) ticket …*)
5 C
6 B (*I called the first airline … I wanted my money back … they said they couldn't do that …*)

4 Students work in pairs. Ask them to discuss what they think the magazine editor could do to help Mr Ricci.

5 In pairs, students take turns to read out the paragraphs of the letter. They then number the paragraphs in the correct order. Don't check answers at this stage as this will be done in exercise 6.

6 Before going through the correct order of the paragraphs, ask students to check that their answers agree with the description of each paragraph given here.

Answers
5 I hope that our reply has been helpful and your next trip is free from problems.

2 The terms and conditions on the airline's website reserves the right to cancel a flight for circumstances beyond its control. It must then offer the passenger a seat on the next available flight, which it did.

4 The fact that you bought another ticket was your choice and so the first airline does not have to reimburse you for this. So, I'm afraid on this occasion the information you were given was correct.

1 Dear Mario

Thank you for writing to us about your bad experience. It's clear that you have suffered from some poor customer service; however, based on your description, the airline has not actually broken any rules.

3 Surprisingly, your economy ticket did not require the airline to offer you overnight hotel accommodation, though in our opinion, good customer care would mean trying to find passengers a suitable hotel for the night.

7 Read the instructions with students. Ask them to write the follow-up letter. Remind them that they must answer all of the points, and that they must write 60–80 words.

Sample answer

> Dear Mr Ricci
>
> Our in-flight magazine editor has written to me about your complaint.
>
> I have spoken to the check-in staff, and they told me what they do in these situations. When flights are cancelled, we offer passengers a seat on the next flight, which would have been in the morning in your case.
>
> On this occasion, we will reimburse you for your first ticket. We look forward to seeing you on board one of our planes soon.
>
> Yours sincerely

Extension

When they've finished, tell students to exchange their letters with their partner. They should read through their partner's letter and try to identify any mistakes. If they can, they should suggest corrections. Choose two or three students to read out their letters.

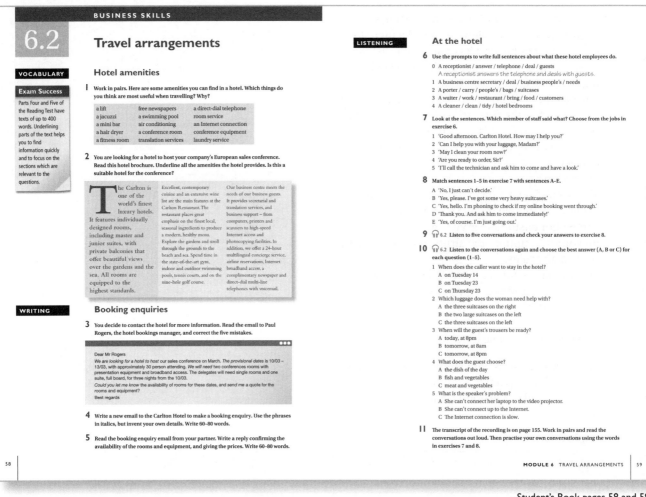

Student's Book pages 58 and 59

Hotel amenities

VOCABULARY

1 Explain any amenities that students don't understand before they do the task.

2 Read the Exam Success tip with students. Then ask them to read the hotel brochure and underline the amenities the hotel provides.

Answers
- Restaurant
- State-of-the-art gym
- Sports facilities: indoor and outdoor swimming pools, tennis courts, nine-hole golf course
- Secretarial and translation services
- Business support: computers, printers and scanners, high-speed Internet access and photocopying facilities
- 24-hour multilingual concierge service
- Airline reservations
- Internet broadband access
- Direct-dial multi-line telephones with voicemail

Yes, the hotel is suitable for the conference.

Booking enquiries

WRITING

3 **Answers**
1 ... ~~on~~ in March.
2 The provisional dates ~~is~~ are ...
3 ... with approximately 30 ~~person~~ people ...
4 for three nights from ~~the~~ 10/03.
5 ... the availability of ~~the~~ rooms ...

4 **Sample answer**

Dear Mr Rogers

We are looking for a hotel to host our marketing conference in June. The provisional dates are 23/06–26/06, with about 20 people attending. We will need one conference room with a computer for PowerPoint™ presentations. We won't need an Internet connection. We will need full-board, single-room accommodation for everyone attending, for three nights from 23/06.

Could you let me know the availability of the rooms, and send me a full quote for the rooms and equipment?

Yours sincerely

5 Students write a reply.

Sample answer

> Dear ...
>
> Thank you for your enquiry about hiring our hotel. We have 20 single rooms available for the dates you mentioned, and also one conference room. All of our conference rooms have computer presentation facilities with Internet access. The accommodation costs £95 per room per night, and the conference room costs £650 per day, including the cost of the equipment and the presence of a technician. Therefore, the total cost is £7,650.
>
> I look forward to hearing from you.
>
> Yours sincerely
> David Rogers

At the hotel

LISTENING

6 Students use the prompts to write full sentences, following the example.

Answers
1 A business centre secretary deals with business people's needs.
2 A porter carries people's bags and suitcases.
3 A waiter works in a restaurant and brings food to customers.
4 A cleaner cleans and tidies hotel bedrooms.

7 Students choose from the jobs in exercise 6 and say which hotel employee said which phrase.

Answers
1 receptionist   2 porter   3 cleaner
4 waiter   5 business centre secretary

8 Answers will be checked in exercise 9.

9 🎧 6.2 Students listen to five conversations and check their answers in 8.

6.2 Listening script
1
R = Receptionist   **G** = Guest

R Good afternoon. Carlton Hotel. How may I help you?
G Yes, hello. I'm phoning to check if my online booking went through. I haven't received any confirmation.
R When did you make your booking?
G Last Tuesday, the 14th.
R Could I have your name, please?
G Yes, it's Johanson.
R Let me see. Yes, Mr Johanson, we have a booking for you for Thursday, the 23rd, for one night.
G Good. Thank you.

2
P = Porter   **G** = Guest

P Can I help you with your luggage, Madam?
G Yes, please. I've got some very heavy suitcases. They're over there, on the right.
P Here you are, Madam. Which is your room?
G I'm sorry, these two big suitcases aren't mine. And this small one isn't mine either.
P They were the only suitcases on the right.
G Oh, I meant to say 'on the left'. One big suitcase and two small ones. I'm terribly sorry.
P No problem, Madam.

3
G = Guest   **C** = Cleaner

G Who's there?
C It's Alice, the cleaner. ... Good morning, Sir. May I clean your room now?
G Yes, of course. I'm going out now. Er ... the reception desk said I could give you my laundry. Is that right?
C Yes, that's right. Just leave your laundry in this bag.
G I need this pair of trousers cleaned. I'd like to wear them this evening. Do you think they will be ready by then?
C I'm sure we can manage that, Sir. What time this evening?
G I'll need them before 8 o'clock.
C That's no problem.
G Thank you very much.

4
W = Waiter   **G** = Guest

W Are you ready to order, Sir?
G No, I just can't decide. What would you recommend?
W Well, would you prefer meat or fish?
G I don't really want meat or fish today. I'd like some vegetables.
W Then maybe you would like to try our dish of the day. It's made with local organic vegetables.
G Yes, that sounds nice. And a glass of red wine, please.

5
S = Secretary   **CS** = Conference Speaker

S Hello. Business Centre. This is Christine speaking. How may I help you?
CS I'm in the main conference room and I've got a bit of a problem.
S What is the problem exactly?
CS Well, I've connected my computer to the video projector, and the Internet also seems to be working, but at this speed I won't be able to give my presentation. I need a faster connection.
S I'll call the technician and ask him to come and have a look.
CS Thank you. And ask him to come immediately. I'm getting nervous.
S I'll get him to come as soon as possible.

Answers
1 C   2 B   3 E   4 A   5 D

10 🎧 6.2 Students listen and complete the task.

Answers
1 C   2 C   3 A   4 A   5 C

11 Students practise reading the script, then practise their own conversations using words from exercises 7 and 8.

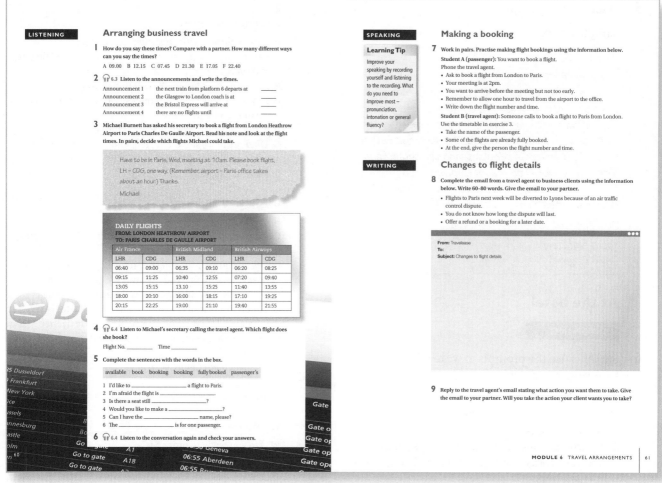

Student's Book pages 60 and 61

Arranging business travel

LISTENING

I Write a few ways of saying times on the board and elicit the different ways to read them. If you have a cardboard clock, you can move the clock hands. Students then do the exercise.

In pairs, students take turns to say the times in as many different ways as they can.

Answers

A 09.00: nine o' clock; nine am; oh nine hundred hours; nine in the morning

B 12.15: a quarter past twelve; twelve fifteen pm.

C 07.45: a quarter to eight; seven forty five am.

D 21.30: half past nine; twenty one thirty; nine thirty pm

E 17.05 five past five; seventeen oh five

F 22.40: twenty to eleven; twenty two forty; ten forty pm

2 🎧 **6.3** Ask students to listen to the announcements and to write the times.

6.3 Listening script

1 The next train to depart from platform six is the seven fifty-five to Manchester.

2 The eight fifteen Glasgow to London coach is now ready for boarding. Please make your way to the coach immediately.

3 Network Southwest apologises for the late arrival of the Bristol Express. This train will now arrive at twenty-three fifteen.

4 Due to a baggage handlers' dispute, all remaining flights today have been cancelled. There will be no flights until oh seven hundred hours tomorrow morning.

Answers

1 07.55   2 08.15   3 23.15   4 07.00

3 Ask students to read Michael Burnett's note and the flight times. In pairs, they decide which flight Michael could take.

Answers

Possible flights are: any on Tuesday evening, or Air France at 06:40, and British Airways at 06:20, on Wednesday morning.

4 🎧 **6.4** Tell students to listen to the telephone conversation between Michael's secretary and the travel agent. Which flight does she book?

6.4 Listening script

TA = Travel agent   **J** = Judith

TA Good morning. Langton Travel. Can I help you?

J Good morning. Yes. I'd like to book a flight to Paris Charles de Gaulle Airport, from London Heathrow, for tomorrow night.

TA For how many people?

J One adult. I see there's an Air France flight at 20.15.

TA Let me see, 20.15. Here we are, flight AF2271 ... I'm afraid the flight is fully booked ... but I see that there are still places on the 6 o'clock flight.

J No, that's too early.

TA Well, there's a British Airways flight at 19:40.

J No, that's also too early. I wanted a flight after 8pm.

TA Well, the British Airways flight is fully booked anyway. I'm afraid the Air France flight is the only one after 8 o'clock.

J What about Wednesday morning? He needs to land at Charles de Gaulle by 9am.

TA Both Air France and British Airways have flights arriving at, or before, 9am. The BA flight leaves at 6.20 and arrives at 8.25, whereas the Air France flight leaves later, but gets there at 9am exactly. Do you have any preference?

J Well, the British Airways flight gives him more time. Is there a seat still available on that one?

TA Yes, there is a seat available. Would you like to make a booking?

J Yes, please.

TA Can I have the passenger's name, please?

J Yes, it's Mr Michael, M–I–C–H–A–E–L, Burnett, B–U–R–N–E, double-T.

TA Do you have an account with us?

J Yes, the account code is LTBC 1784.

TA Thank you. OK, the booking is for one passenger on British Airways flight BA395 at 06.20.

J Let me take a note of that. Flight BA395, at 06.20.

TA That's right.

J Could you send an email to confirm the booking? My name is Judith Baird. You've got the address.

TA Yes, of course, Ms Baird.

J Thanks. Bye.

Answer
BA395, at 06:20.

5 Ask students to write the correct words in the space in each sentence. Don't check answers at this stage as this will be done in exercise 6.

6 🎧 6.4 Students listen and check their answers in exercise 5.

Answers
1 book
2 fully booked
3 available
4 booking
5 passenger's
6 booking

Making a booking

SPEAKING

7 Ask students to turn to page 155 and read the script of the conversation in exercise 4 in pairs. Then ask students to practise making flight bookings using the information given. Ask

students to sit back to back so that they aren't looking at each other. When they've finished, tell students to swap roles.

Read the Learning Tip with the students. Ask students what they think they need to improve most.

Changes to flight details

WRITING

8 Ask students to think about the style of the email (formal / informal) before they start writing.

When they've finished, students should exchange their email with their partner's.

Sample answer

> We have just heard that there is going to be a strike by air traffic controllers in Paris next week, so all flights to Paris will be diverted to Lyons. The strike could last only a short time, but there is no guarantee of this.
>
> Therefore, we can give you a refund on your ticket, or alternatively make a booking for a later date. Please let us know which option you would prefer.
>
> Yours sincerely

9 Students write a reply to the travel agent's email. They should write 30–40 words. When students have finished, ask some students to read out their travel agent's email and their business client's reply.

Sample answer

> From: JK Wilkins
> To: Travelease
> Subject: Re: Changes to flight details
>
> Thank you for your email about the strike in Paris next week. As I must go to Paris, I'll go by train. Therefore, I would be grateful for a refund on my ticket.
>
> Yours sincerely

Photocopiable activity
See page 171.

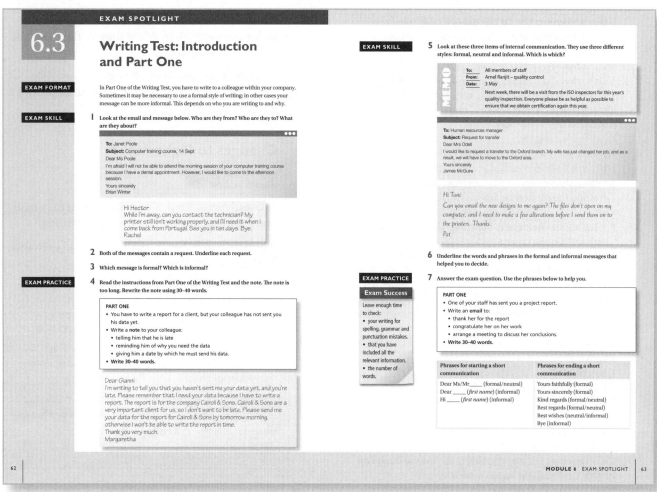

Student's Book pages 62 and 63

Writing Test: Introduction and Part One

EXAM SKILL

1 Remind students that in Part One of the Writing Test, they have to write a note, a message or an email to a colleague in their company. The style might be formal or informal, depending on who they're writing to.

Ask students first to read the email. Ask: *Who is it from? Who is it to? What is the email about?*

Ask students to suggest information about Brian Winter and Janet Poole. *Do they know each other? If so, how well? What makes you think that?*

Possible answers
The email is from Brian Winter to Janet Poole.

It's about the computer training course, which Brian can't attend in the morning.

The message is from Rachel to Hector. Rachel asks Hector to contact the technician because her printer isn't working.

2 Ask students to underline the request in each message.

Answers
1 ... I would like to come to the afternoon session.
2 ... can you contact the technician?

3 Students answer the questions.

Answers
The email is formal: (*Dear Ms Poole, I'm afraid, However, Yours sincerely, Brian Winter*)

The message is informal: (*Hi Hector, See you ..., Bye, Rachel*)
The use of contractions also indicates an informal style.

EXAM PRACTICE

4 The question here is in the style of the Part One question in the exam. Ask students to read the question and to explain what it asks them to do. Then ask students to read the note and explain what is wrong with it.

Ask students to rewrite the note using 30–40 words.

Sample answer

> Dear Gianni
>
> I haven't received your data yet, and it's getting late. I have to write the report for Cairoli & Sons, and I need the data for this. Please send it by tomorrow morning.
>
> Thanks.
>
> Margaretha

Sample answer

> Dear Emilia
>
> Thanks for your report. I found it very useful and interesting. It was well written and complete. I'd like to talk to you personally about your conclusions. Would next Thursday be convenient?
>
> Best wishes
> Mark

EXAM SKILL

5 Ask students to read the three messages. Ask them which one is formal, which is neutral, and which is informal and why.

Answers

Memo: neutral

Email: formal

Note: informal

6 Ask students to underline the words and phrases in the messages that helped them to decide which email is formal, which is neutral and which is informal.

Answers

Memo: contains facts, and is general, not personal

Email: *Dear Mrs Odell, I would like ..., ... to request ..., Yours sincerely, James McGuire*

Note: *Hi Toni, Thanks, Pat,* use of contractions

EXAM PRACTICE

7 Read the Exam Success tip with the students. Remind them that the Reading and Writing paper lasts one hour 30 minutes, so students must organise their time. For Part One of the Writing Test, they should try to complete the task in 10–15 minutes, which includes time to check their writing.

Ask students to read the question and to tell you what they have to do. Ask them if the question contains all necessary information, or do they have to invent something?

Before they start, students should think about the working relationship with the person they're writing to and whether the email should be formal, or informal.

Ask students to read the phrases, and then to write the email.

Students do this task individually, as if they were taking the exam. Ask them to time themselves, ie, the time they take to read the text and answer the questions. Tell students to write the starting and finishing time at the top of the page and keep a record of how long they take to do each exercise. By the end of the book, they'll have an idea of how to manage their time when they do the Reading and Writing parts.

Overview

7.1   Business topic: Products and services

READING   **Smart homes: the future is here**

GRAMMAR   **Comparatives and superlatives**

LISTENING   **Hotels of the future**

SPEAKING   **Customer service survey**

READING   **Choosing a business school**

7.2   Business skills: Orders and contracts

VOCABULARY   **Shapes and sizes**

LISTENING   **Making an order**

SPEAKING   **Service providers**

LISTENING   **Changing Internet service provider**

WRITING   **ISP contract**

7.3   Exam spotlight: Listening Test   Parts Two and Three

Taking a telephone message

Predicting information

Listening for synonyms

Useful language from Module 7

Wordlist

adjust
agree on
be made of
broadband
burglar
charge
circle
circular
cleanliness
clientele
comfort
convenient
courier company
curriculum
curricula (pl)
deep
depth
dial-up connection
diameter
domotics
edge
enable
facilities
fax

feel in control
filing cabinet
fire brigade
fit
form
graduate
height
high
homeowner
indeed
inflatable
ISP (Internet service provider)
landline
LCD (liquid crystal display)
lecturer
length
light setting
long
maintenance
money-saving
non-peak
occupied

oval
overall
party (group of people)
PDA (personal digital assistant)
pen drive
penalty charge
per annum
photocopier
provider
proximity
quotation
rate
rectangle
rectangular
reliable
remote control
round
running costs
scanner
semicircle
semicircular
service user

shape
size
skype
small business package
sophisticated
square
switch off
switch on
testimonials
triangle
triangular
tuition fee
turn off
turn on
typewriter
underwater
value for money
weigh
weight
wheel
wide
width

Expressions

For all other services, please hold.
If you are an existing customer, press 1.
It comes in a red wood finish.
On special offer.
That does indeed sound like a very exclusive hotel.
That's 74 by 50 by 65.
There's no charge for connecting calls.
What colours do they come in?

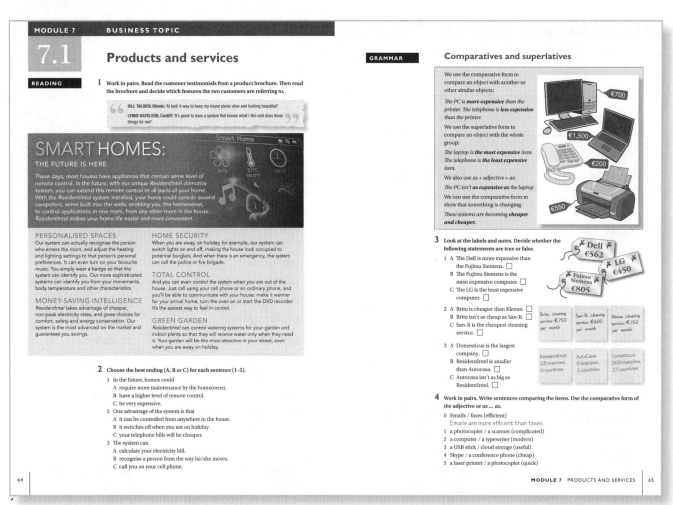

Smart homes: the future is here

READING

1 Pre-teach some of the vocabulary that's featured in the reading text. Students keep their books closed and guess the word that you're trying to define. For example:

A piece of equipment that's used to control something such as a television from a distance … (**remote control**)

Something that's easy to use, that's useful, or is near to where you are is … (**convenient**)

If there is a fire you call them … (**fire brigade**)

If you want to know the price of a product or a service you write or phone for a … (**quotation**)

While students are doing exercise 1, tell them to underline the words that were the objects of your definitions.

Answers
Bill is referring to *Green Garden.*
Lynne is referring to *Personalised Spaces.*

2 Tell students to do exercise 2 without looking at the text in exercise 1. Suggest covering it with a piece of paper. Tell them that they're allowed to have a quick look at the text only if they need to.

Answers
1 B
2 A
3 B

Comparatives and superlatives

GRAMMAR

Ask students to look at the pictures and cover the text. Then ask them the following questions:

Which product is the most expensive?

Which product is the least expensive?

Is the laptop more expensive than the PC?

Is the telephone less expensive than the printer?

After each question you can ask for the price.

Point out the different structures and write the patterns on the board.

comparatives	superlatives	expressions
more … than …*	the most …*	more and more …*
less … than …	the least …	
as … as …		

*Point out that we use these patterns for adjectives of more than two syllables. Otherwise, for one-syllable adjectives, we add -er and -est. You might want to point out some of the spelling rules which apply to one-syllable adjectives, eg for adjectives that end with -y, we drop the y and add -ier and -iest; some consonants are doubled (*big – bigger – biggest*).

3 Students do this exercise on their own and then check their answers in pairs. Ask them to point out which statements they didn't agree on.

Answers
1 A – false
   B – true
   C – true
2 A – false
   B – true
   C – true
3 A – true
   B – false
   C – true

4 Read the instructions and the example with the students. Then ask them to think of a sentence containing *as … as …* patterns. Collect some sentences (orally), then students do the exercise.

Possible answers
1 A photocopier isn't as complicated as a scanner.
   A scanner is more complicated than a photocopier. (It is user friendly.)
   A scanner isn't as complicated as a photocopier.
   A photocopier is more complicated than a scanner. (Its technology is simpler.)
2 A typewriter isn't as modern as a computer.
   A computer is more modern than a typewriter.
3 A USB stick isn't as useful as cloud storage.
   A USB stick is more useful than cloud storage.
4 A conference phone isn't as cheap as Skype.
   Skype is cheaper than a conference call.
5 A laser printer is as quick as a photocopier.

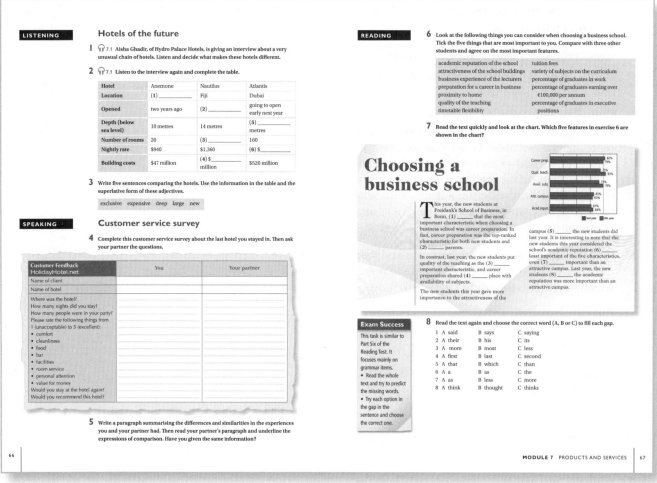

Student's Book pages 66 and 67

Hotels of the future

LISTENING

1 🎧 7.1 Ask students to look at the title. Brainstorm ideas on the theme *Hotels of the future*. Either keep the brainstorming free and accept all ideas, or you can provide some structure by putting the following categories on the board:

WHO

WHAT

HOW MANY

HOW MUCH

WHERE

HOW

WHEN

WHY

Starting from *WHO*, ask the following questions: *Who will open hotels? What will hotels be like? Where will hotels be built?* Get as many ideas as you can here. Then proceed with the listening.

7.1 Listening script

I = Interviewer **A** = Aisha

I Good evening. On this week's *Business Unusual*, I'm talking to Aisha Ghadir, the chief executive officer of Hydro Palace Hotels. Now, Ms Ghadir, from the name of your company, we can clearly understand that you are in the hotel business. But I believe there is something rather special about Hydro Palace Hotels.

A Well, we provide a luxury service for an exclusive clientele. But what is unusual about our hotels is the fact that they're underwater.

I When you say 'underwater', I assume you mean on the coast or at the water's edge?

A No, our hotels really are underwater – a true submarine holiday experience!

I Indeed! And not for the average family holiday budget, I suspect.

A Well, the hotels are not cheap to build, and maintenance and running costs are higher than for hotels on land. So, of course, if we want to make money, we have to charge more than normal hotels.

I So, how much does it cost to stay in one of your hotels?

A Well, let's consider the Anemone, which we opened two years ago in Florida, in the USA. One night costs $940 per person. There are 20 double rooms, so the hotel can accommodate up to a maximum of 40 guests.

I I see. I understand you've just opened a new hotel in Fiji.

A Yes, that's right, the Nautilus opened a month ago. One night there costs $1,360 per person. There are 78 double rooms, so the hotel can accommodate up to 156 guests. And there's a theatre with live shows every night.
I The hotels are both underwater. But exactly how far down are they?
A Well, the Anemone is 10 metres below the surface of the water, and the Nautilus is 14 metres below.
I And how much did the hotels cost to build?
A The Anemone cost $47 million and the Nautilus $190 million.
I And your next hotel? Where is that going to be?
A In Dubai. Building started 18 months ago. It's going to open early next year. This is a larger project than the other two; the Atlantis will have 160 double rooms, and it will be at a depth of 23 metres below the surface. The cost of construction is estimated at $520 million.
I So, how much will a night in the Atlantis cost?
A We expect to charge about $1,900 per person per night.
I Well, that does indeed sound like a very exclusive hotel. Thank you for coming to talk to us.

Answer
They're underwater.

2 🎧 **7.1** Before playing the recording for the second time, give students time to focus on what type of information is missing.

Answers
1 Florida, USA
2 a month ago
3 78
4 190
5 23
6 1,900

3 Students write their sentences individually, then they read them out loud to the class.

Possible answers
The Anemone is the least exclusive hotel.
The Atlantis is the most expensive hotel.
The Atlantis is the deepest hotel.
The Atlantis is the largest hotel.
The Atlantis is the newest hotel.

Customer service survey

SPEAKING

4 Ask students to fill in the first column and also to give reasons for their ratings to their partners.
eg: *My rating for the food is 3, because the coffee at breakfast was terrible. The food wasn't bad, but there was little variety. The brochure said 'great variety of local specialities,' but we only got international cuisine.*

5 Revise the concept of a paragraph with the students. They then do exercise 5.

Extension
Find out from students who has had the best or the worst hotel experience.

Photocopiable activity
See page 172.

Choosing a business school

READING

6 Tell your students to close their books. Ask them to brainstorm ideas on what is important when choosing a business school. After a few minutes, ask them to open their books and underline all the ideas they had during the brainstorming activity.

Then students do exercise 6. After ticking the five most important things, tell students that they should rate their choice from the most important (1) to the least important (5).

7 Ask students to go through the text quickly and not to read the text word by word. Wait until everybody has found the five features.

Answers
• Academic reputation of the school
• Attractiveness of the school building
• Preparation for a career in business
• Quality of the teaching
• Variety of subjects on the curriculum

8 Tell students to cover exercise 8. Ask one student to read the text out loud and pause at each gap. The rest of the class should say which words fit the gaps. Accept all possible answers. Then students fill in the gaps on their own.

Answers
1 A   2 A   3 B   4 C   5 C   6 C   7 B   8 B

Refer students to the Exam Success tip and point out that there are 12 questions in the Reading Test, Part Six.

7.2 Orders and contracts

BUSINESS SKILLS

VOCABULARY

Shapes and sizes

1 What is your favourite possession? Describe it to your partner without saying its name. Can your partner guess?

2 Complete the table. Use the noun or adjective which is related to the word in *italics*.

Noun	a *triangle*	a _____	a _____	an *oval*	a _____	a *semicircle*
Adjective	a _____ road sign	a *square* mirror	a *rectangular* swimming pool	an _____ table	a *circular* rug	a _____ seating arrangement

3 Match the questions (1–9) with the answers (A–J).

0 What's the length of an A4 sheet of paper?
1 What's the width of that orange box?
2 What's the height of that lamp?
3 What's the depth of that swimming pool?
4 What's the size of your LCD monitor?
5 What's the weight of that leather briefcase?
6 What's the price of that mobile phone?
7 What's the diameter of the wheel?
8 What colour is the screen?
9 What is that desk made of?

A It's 17in (inches).
B It's 2.5m deep.
C It's £200.
D It's 29.7cm long.
E It's 13cm wide.
F It's 2.5 kilos.
G It's 50cm in diameter.
H It's 1.8m high.
I It's blue.
J It's made of wood and metal.

4 Rewrite questions 1–7 in exercise 3 starting with *How*.

0 How long is an A4 sheet of paper?
1 _____
2 _____
3 _____
4 _____
5 _____
6 _____
7 _____

5 Work in groups of three.
Student A: Think of an object you use at work.
Students B and C: Ask questions to find out the object. You only have ten questions!

LISTENING

Learning Tip
Listen to English as much as you can in order to develop your listening skills. Use the Internet, DVDs and the radio (the BBC World Service, for example).

Making an order

6 🎧 7.2 Listen to the telephone conversation between a caller and a sales assistant in an office furniture shop. Answer the questions.

1 What does the customer want to buy? _____
2 What colour does he want? _____
3 Does he buy the item? _____

7 🎧 7.2 Listen to the telephone conversation again and complete the missing information.

Size of FC12W	Price
Height: (1) _____ cm Width: (2) _____ cm Depth: (3) _____ cm	FC12W: (5) £ _____ FC12M: (6) £ _____
Number of drawers	**Colours**
(4) _____	FC12W: (7) _____ wood finish FC12M: blue, (8) _____ or grey metal

8 Work in pairs. Look at these questions from the telephone conversation and decide whether the customer (C) or the assistant (A) asked each question. Then use the questions and the information in the table in exercise 7 to practise the conversation.

1 Good morning, Office Design. How can I help you? _____
2 And how high is your desk? _____
3 So you haven't got one in plastic? _____
4 How many drawers have they got? _____
5 How much do they cost? _____
6 And what colours do they come in? _____

9 Work in pairs.
Student A: Go to page 145.
Student B: You are going to organise a local public event and you would like to rent a children's inflatable toy. Look at the pictures below and call Inflatable World Ltd. (Student A) to ask for information about the size, weight and cost of the items.

Article Number	4832-CA (castle)
Size (metres)	Length: _____ Width: _____ Height: _____
Weight (kilograms)	_____
Prices (euros)	4-hour rental: _____ 8-hour rental: _____ 2-day rental: _____

Article Number	685–SL (slide)
Size (metres)	Length: _____ Width: _____ Height: _____
Weight (kilograms)	_____
Prices (euros)	4-hour rental: _____ 8-hour rental: _____ 2-day rental: _____

68 | MODULE 7 ORDERS AND CONTRACTS   69

Student's Book pages 68 and 69

Shapes and sizes

VOCABULARY

1 Ask a student to come to the board and draw some shapes. Ask the rest of the class to say the names of the shapes. As they do so, the student at the board should write the names inside the shapes, eg, *triangle, square, circle*, etc. Tell students to include shapes in the description of their favourite possession.

2 After students have finished exercise 2, ask them in which cases the noun and the adjective are the same (*square, oval*).

Answers
Nouns: square, rectangle, circle
Adjectives: triangular, oval, semicircular

3 Do this matching task with students.

Answers
1 E 2 H 3 B 4 A 5 F
6 C 7 G 8 I 9 J

4 Students do exercise 4 on their own. They can confer with partners only if they need some help.

Extension
As an extension to this exercise, you can ask students to think of alternative forms for questions 8: *What is the colour of the screen?* and 9: *What material is that desk made of?*

Answers
1 How wide is that orange box?
2 How high / tall is that lamp?
3 How deep is that swimming pool?
4 How big is your LCD monitor?
5 How much does that leather briefcase weigh?
  How heavy is that leather briefcase?
6 How much is that mobile phone?
  How much does that mobile phone cost?
7 How big is the wheel?

5 In this task students B and C have five questions each. If students B and C can't guess what the object is after ten questions, A should think of another object. The student who guesses what the object is first then has to think of a new object.

Making an order

6 🎧 7.2 Play the recording once. Tell students that they only have to answer three questions.

7.2 Listening script

SA = Shop assistant   **C** = Customer

SA Good morning, Office Design. How can I help you?
C Hello. I want to buy a filing cabinet that will fit under my desk.
SA I see. And how high is your desk?
C It's 74 centimetres.
SA That's very good. We've got two filing cabinets, the FC12W and the FC12M, which are both 74 centimetres high.
C No, no, they're too big. You see, it's 74 centimetres to the top of the desk. The filing cabinet can't be more than 69 centimetres high.
SA I'm sorry, we don't have anything that small.
C I see. Well how big is the FC12W?
SA I'm sorry?
C The FC12W. What are the dimensions?
SA Oh, yes. Er … well, as I said, it's 74 centimetres high, 50 centimetres wide, and 65 centimetres deep.
C That's 74 by 50 by 65. I see. And what about the FC12M?
SA It's the same size. The difference is that the FC12W is made of wood, and the FC12M is made of metal. W for wood, M for metal.
C I see. So you haven't got one in plastic?
SA Er … no. Only wood and metal.
C How many drawers have these cabinets got?
SA They've both got two drawers.
C I see. I wanted three drawers.
SA Well, these filing cabinets have only got two.
C I see. And how much do they cost?
SA The wooden cabinet costs £140. The metal one is cheaper at £90.
C And what colours do they come in?
SA The FC12W comes in a red wood finish, the FC12M in blue, black or grey paint.
C I see. No green, I suppose?
SA No, no green. You can always paint it if you want.
C Well, if I bought one FC12M, would you give me a discount because of the colour?
SA No, I'm afraid not. So do you want to buy one of the cabinets?
C Well, 74 centimetres is still too high, so they won't fit under my desk.

Answers

1 A filing cabinet (that fits under a desk).
2 Green.
3 No, he doesn't.

7 🎧 7.2 Tell students that this exercise is similar to Listening Test, Part Two. The only difference is that here, they have one more question to answer. Remind students that they only have to write a number or a word.

Answers

1 74   2 50   3 65   4 2   5 140   6 90
7 red   8 black

8 Students decide whether questions were asked by the customer or the assistant. They then use the questions and information in the table in exercise 7, as well as other information from the recording to practise the conversation. For example:

A Good morning, Office Design. How can I help you?

C Good morning. I'd like to buy a filing cabinet.

Answers

1 A   2 A   3 C   4 C   5 C   6 C

Extension

After students have practised the conversation, ask them to role-play the dialogue, reading from the listening script on page 156. Tell them that they should change some details such as the filing cabinet or the desk, size, price, colours, etc. This will make the reading more active and the students more involved.

9 Invite students to choose English names for their characters (the office manager and the organiser of the public event), and also to decide what type of public event it is going to be.

Answers

Article Number	4832-CA
Size (metres)	
Length:	5.5
Width:	5.5
Height:	5.5
Weight (kilograms)	140
Prices (euros)	
4-hour rental:	220
8-hour rental:	260
2-day rental:	340

Article Number	685-SL
Size (metres)	
Length:	20
Width:	4.5
Height:	6
Weight (kilograms)	450
Prices (euros)	
4-hour rental:	N/A
8-hour rental:	280
2-day rental:	360

Photocopiable activity
See page 173.

SPEAKING

Service providers

1 Read the newspaper articles and fill the gaps with the words in the box.

contracts · provider · landlines · service users · broadband · technical support

70 per cent of Internet (1) _____ say they are not satisfied with their Internet service (2) _____. The Consumer Protection Office received 24,210 complaints about telecommunications last year, of which 47 per cent related to the Internet, 36 per cent to mobile phones and the rest to (3) _____.

An increasing number of Internet service providers are offering faster and faster (4) _____ connections for a monthly charge. But we have found that, in reality, the speed and reliability is poor at certain times of day. In addition, (5) _____ is almost non-existent in many cases.

The Internet Users Association reports that the biggest problems are with cancelling (6) _____.

2 You are going to find out if your classmates' experiences with Internet service providers (ISP) is similar or different to those reported in the news stories. Work in pairs to write a questionnaire. Use the ideas in the left column of the questionnaire to help you.

	Questions	Person 1	Person 2	Person 3	Person 4
name of Internet service provider (ISP)?	What is the name of your Internet service provider?				
a speedy connection?	Do you have				
a reliable connection?					
technical support – opinion?					
monthly charge – opinion?					
overall opinion? (fast / easy to use / reliable / efficient / value for money)					

3 Ask several people the questions in your questionnaire. Then analyse the results of the questionnaire. Which company provides the best service? Report your conclusions to the class. Do you all agree?

LISTENING

Changing Internet service provider

4 7.3 Bryan Ross runs a small courier company. He currently pays between €100 and €200 each month for Internet and telephone services from NatNet. He is looking for a cheaper option. Listen to Bryan's telephone call to Maroon Communications and complete his notes.

MaroonBusinessOne package
What do I get?
- unlimited (1) _____
- mobiles & (2) _____
- 24-hour (5) _____
- no charge for (4) _____
- price of phone not included in package
  number of mobile lines (5) _____
  calls to technical support line (6) _____
  guaranteed broadband (7) _____
  broadband connection to (8) _____
How much?
- first three months (9) _____
- after that (10) _____
- contract lasts (11) _____

5 Compare your answers to exercise 4 with your partner. Do you think Bryan should change to the MaroonBusinessOne package? Why? / Why not?

WRITING

ISP contract

6 Put the sentences in this email from NatNet into the correct order (1–5). What is the purpose of the email?

_____ We look forward to your custom in the future.
_____ This request is now being processed.
_____ The contract will be cancelled at the end of the current billing period.
_____ You will be able to use your NatNet 24/7 until then.
_____ We have received a request to cancel contract number 738387.

7 Write an email from Maroon Communications to Bryan Ross to confirm his new contract with MaroonBusinessOne. Use the email in exercise 6 as a guide, and write about 40 words.

70

MODULE 7 ORDERS AND CONTRACTS 71

Student's Book pages 70 and 71

Service providers

SPEAKING

1 Ask students to look at the words in the box and explain them in their own words. Then students do exercise 1.

Answers
1 service users
2 provider
3 landlines
4 broadband
5 technical support
6 contracts

2 Students write their questions in the first column.

Possible answers
Do you have a speedy connection? Are you satisfied with the service?

Is your connection reliable?

Do they provide efficient technical support?

Do you think the monthly charge is good value for money?

3 Students use the questionnaire to carry out a survey of the class, and then decide which company provides the best or worst service in the country they are in.

Changing Internet service provider

LISTENING

4 7.3 Ask your students if they know how much they pay on average each month for Internet and telephone services. Ask them if they know of any cheaper offers that telephone companies are offering at the moment in their country. Then play the recording.

7.3 Listening script
RM = Recorded message   **D** = Dana
C = Customer

RM Welcome to Maroon Communications. If you are an existing customer, press 1. For information about mobile phones, press 2. For information about our Internet services, press 3. For information about our small business packages, press 4. For all other services, please hold.
D Good morning. Business services department, Dana speaking.
C Hello, I'd like some information about the small business packages you have.

D Certainly, Sir. Can I just ask you some questions?

C Yes, of course.

D Are you self-employed or do you have a business?

C I run a small company.

D Does your company have fewer than ten employees?

C Yes, it does.

D And which services are you interested in?

C Well, I need mobiles for my staff of six and an Internet connection for the office, basically.

D We have a special offer at the moment for small businesses. It's called MaroonBusinessOne and it gives you unlimited national calls on both mobiles and landlines, a 24-hour broadband connection, and no charge for connecting calls.

C And how many mobiles does that cover?

D The cost of the phones themselves is separate, but the MaroonBusinessOne service covers up to ten mobile phone lines.

C What about support and maintenance?

D With the MaroonBusinessOne package, all calls to the technical support line are free.

C No, sorry. I mean if there are problems with the phones themselves.

D The package is a service contract, so the equipment itself is not covered. We do guarantee the broadband connection 24 hours a day, however.

C And can I have more than one computer connected?

D The broadband connection is to your computer network or to a single computer. It doesn't matter which you have.

C OK, that's good. And how much does this package cost?

D The monthly charge is 75 euros for the first three months, on special offer, and then 120 euros after that.

C Right. And how long does the contract last?

D There is a penalty charge if you cancel the contract before two years.

C Well, I want to think about this.

D Certainly, Sir. And don't forget that you can find all of these details on our website.

C Yes, good idea. OK, thanks very much.

D Thank you for calling. Please stay on the line to answer our customer services feedback …

Answers
1 national calls
2 landlines
3 broadband connection
4 connecting calls
5 10
6 free
7 24 hours a day
8 network or single computer
9 €75 per month
10 €120
11 two years

5 After students have compared their answers, they should decide whether the MaroonBusinessOne package is a good offer.

Possible answer
Yes, because the customer will pay a fixed sum of €120 per month, instead of a sum between €100 and €200 per month.

ISP contract

WRITING

6 Students put the lines of this email in order.

Answer
The correct order is: 5-2-3-4-1
The purpose of this email is to confirm the cancellation of a contract.

7 Students write an email to confirm a new contract.

Sample answer

> Dear Mr Ross
>
> We have received your request to purchase our MaroonBusinessOne package. The contract will start as soon as we receive your signed copy of the contract, and you will be able to start using the new connection on the same day.
>
> Best regards
> Maroon Communications

7.3 Listening Test: Parts Two and Three

EXAM FORMAT

In Part Two of the Listening Test, you have to listen to a short telephone conversation or monologue that lasts about a minute and a half. There is a table on page 32 which summarises the types of question in each part.

EXAM SKILL

- Before the telephone conversation starts, you will hear some instructions. Listen to the instructions and read the form.
- Understand what the conversation is about. Who is calling? (a man or a woman?)
- After the instructions, you have ten seconds before the conversation starts. Read each line in order to see what kind of information you need to listen for.
- As you listen to the conversation, write down the possible answers. Sometimes you will have more than one answer for each question.
- During the second listening, cross out the incorrect information.
- After listening twice, you will have ten seconds to check your answers.

EXAM PRACTICE

1   Here is a typical task from Part Two of the Listening Test. Read the instructions. Predict what kind of information is needed for each question: what kinds of numbers or words will be heard? Do not listen to the recording at this stage.

Exam Success
- Before you listen, read all the instructions and the questions very carefully.
- In the pauses between listenings, check that your answers are clearly marked.
- Answer all the questions.

> **PART TWO**
> - Look at the form below.
> - Some information is missing.
> - You will hear a man telephoning a training company.
> - For each question (1–7), fill in the missing information in the numbered space using a **word, numbers** or **letters**.
> - You will hear the conversation twice.

> **Course booking**
>
> | | |
> |---|---|
> | Training course: | (1) .... skills |
> | Course code: | (2) .... |
> | Date: | (3) .... |
> | Number of participants: | (4) .... |
> | Name of company: | (5) .... Ltd |
> | Contact name: | (6) Charles .... |
> | Contact tel. number: | (7) 01536–... |

2   7.4 Listen to the conversation and write down the possible answers.

3   7.4 Listen again and cross out the incorrect information.

EXAM FORMAT

In Part Three of the Listening Test, you have to listen to a monologue that lasts about two minutes. There is a table on page 32 which summarises the types of question in each part.

EXAM SKILL

- Follow the same approach as in Part Two of the Listening Test.
- Try to predict what kinds of words you need to listen for.
- Note that you have 20 seconds to check your answers.

EXAM PRACTICE

4   7.5 Here is a typical task from Part Three of the Listening Test. Read the instructions, but do not listen to the recording at this stage.

> - Look at the notes about a company.
> - Some information is missing.
> - You will hear a presentation by the company's managing director.
> - For each question (1–7), fill in the missing information in the numbered space using one or two words.
> - You will hear the presentation twice.

> **Platt & Sons Ltd**
>
> | | |
> |---|---|
> | Products: | (1) .... |
> | Original line of business: | (2) making .... |
> | The first models were for: | (3) .... |
> | Main customers today: | (4) .... |
> | New product line available from: | (5) .... |
> | Future plans: to export to the EU, first to: | (6) .... and Germany |
> | Reports of financial difficulties are: | (7) .... |

EXAM SKILL

5   'Signal' words on the recording can help you identify the answers to the questions. These words can be synonyms (words with the same meaning), collocations (words that go together) or the actual words in the question. Work in pairs and match each group of 'signal' words below with the questions in the exam task above. Write the numbers.

Our customers now 4   We expect to bring out our _____
We intend to _____   He started off by producing _____
We manufacture _____   The machines made in 1958 _____
You might have seen _____

6   7.5 Now listen to the recording and fill in the missing information in the exam task. Did you notice the 'signal' words?

Student's Book pages 72 and 73

Listening Test: Part Two

EXAM FORMAT

Ask students to read the Exam Format.

EXAM SKILL

Ask students to read the information. If necessary, ask students to look back at page 32 to remind them about the Listening Test in general.

EXAM PRACTICE

1   Before playing the recording, read the instructions for the task with the students. Allow students time to read the exam instructions in the box. Then allow them time to analyse the type of information that is missing.

2   7.4 Play the recording without pausing. Students write down the possible answers.

7.4 Listening script

R = Receptionist   C = Customer

R Good morning, Webster Training. Can I help you?
C Yes, hello. I'd like to make a booking for one of your computer skills courses.
R Certainly, Sir. Which one are you interested in?
C Well, from your brochure, it's Course ECDL12M.
R Parts 1 and 2 of the European Computer Driving Licence, right?
C Yes, that's right.
R And when would you like to do the course?
C At the beginning of September, if that's possible.
R I'm afraid the first week of September is already booked. But I have spaces available on the course starting on Tuesday the 9th.
C That would be fine.
R And how many people are hoping to attend the course?
C There'll be eight in total.
R I'm afraid we can take a maximum of only six people per group.
C I see. Well, six then. We might have another group later on.
R That's fine. And what's the name of the company?
C Coxten Ltd. That's C–O–X–T–E–N.
R And are you the person I should call if I have any information or questions?
C Yes. My name's Charles Goff.
R G–O–U–G–H?

C No, it's G–O–double–F. And my telephone number is 01536 848497.
R All right, Mr. Goff. Thank you for your booking ...

Answers
1 computer
2 ECDL12M
3 Tuesday, 09/09
4 6
5 Coxten
6 Goff
7 848497

3 🎧 **7.4** Play the recording again for students to cross out the incorrect information.

Listening Test: Part Three

EXAM FORMAT

Ask students to read the Exam Format.

EXAM SKILL

Ask students to read the information and the Exam Success tip.

EXAM PRACTICE

4 Students read the instructions to the exam question and think about what they need to predict.

5 Read the information about 'signal' words with the class. Students then work in pairs to match each group of words with the questions in the exam task in exercise 4. They can write the numbers (1–7) that identify the pieces of information requested.

Answers
Our customers now – 4
We intend to – 6
We manufacture – 1
You might have seen – 7
We expect to bring out – 5
He started off by producing – 2
The machines made in 1958 – 3

6 🎧 **7.5** Now play the recording. Students do the exercise. Ask them if they noticed the 'signal' words.

Answers
1 exercise equipment
2 bikes
3 competitions
4 organisations, such as sports centres
5 early spring
6 France
7 not true

7.5 Listening script

All right. Hello, everyone. It's nice to see so many people. I'd like to welcome you this morning to this presentation of the company, Platt & Sons Ltd. My name is Barbara Platt, and I'm the managing director.

Now, as most of you will know, we manufacture exercise equipment. We have a full range, all made to the highest standards.

I'd like to say a little about how we began. The company was started in 1958, by my grandfather, Eugene Platt, who used to cycle competitively. Unfortunately, an accident put an end to his cycling career. That's when he started this company. He started off by producing bikes. The bikes he made in 1958 were competition models, but he soon started producing bicycles for recreational use.

In the early 1970s, we brought out our first cycling machine, which was very popular with the general public, and a bit later on, we developed a range of these machines.

In the 1980s, we started producing other equipment, such as rowing machines and multi-gyms. With these, we saw our clients change from mainly private individuals, who wanted equipment for home fitness, to organisations like sports centres, which now account for about 60 per cent of our sales. We also sell to a lot of hotels.

We've recently started working with a sports doctor to design some machines specifically for use in hospitals. We expect to bring these new products out in the early spring.

So far, we've focused on the domestic market, here in Britain, but we intend to start exporting, first to other countries in the European Union. France and Germany are possible candidates.

And last, but certainly not least, you might have seen the recent reports in the local press. You might have read that Platt & Sons is suffering financial difficulties, because we lost an important contract to one of our competitors. I can assure you that there is no truth in the reports. Of course, we were sorry to lose the contract, but we are healthier than we have ever been.

Extension

After listening, ask students to read the script and underline all the words that they don't understand. They could then ask their partner to explain the words if they can, then check in a dictionary.

Overview

8.1   Business topic: Manufacturing processes

READING   **Personalising your product with 3D printing**

GRAMMAR   **The passive**

VOCABULARY   **Supply and demand**

VOCABULARY   **Production philosophies**

READING   **Lean production philosophies**

8.2   Business skills: Problems and solutions

LISTENING   **Solving problems**

READING   **Use a Smart Lid**

GRAMMAR   ***when* and *if***

VOCABULARY   **Collocations with *problem***

SPEAKING   **We've got a problem**

8.3   Exam spotlight: Speaking Test
Parts Two and Three

Using prompts

Discussing a situation

Useful language from Module 8

Wordlist

additive
advertise
anti-virus program
apply
art
aspect
assembly line
automated
automatically
bacterium (pl bacteria)
barcode
be on site
brainstorm (v)
branded
burn
capacity
catastrophe
cause
ceramics
closed circuit television (CCTV)
coal
compatible
complaint
component
conference phones
crowded
deal with
dedicated
deface
defect (n)
delivery
demand
departure time

depressing
detect
develop
diesel
disagree
disposable
elimination
existing
explain
face (v)
factory
factory floor
fault
feature
financial return
fit (v)
foreign exchange department
frustrated
fuel
go off
graffiti
graffiti-free
graffiti-resistant
guide (n)
handmade
heat up
high-tech (also hi-tech)
imperfection
important
improvement
inefficient
in-flight service
innovative

interrupt
inventory
jet
just-in-time (JIT)
key feature
kiln
lean
lean production
lecture
licence (n, BrE), license (n, AmE)
license (v)
lid
lift
loading bay
local council
log on / off
maintenance
mechanism
melt
mistake
narrow
optical cell
order
outlet
output
overproduction
overtime
pager
petrol
philosophy
plant
plug in (v)
poka-yoke
pressure

prevent
process (n)
processing
produce
product
raw materials
reliable
response time
rope
satisfying
scanner
scenario
shipping company
smoke alarm
smoke detector
spray
standard
stick
stock
storage cost
successful
supply
surface
tank
technology
testimonial
treatment
ugly
under licence
vandal
voicemail
waiting time
warehouse
waste

Expressions

be in the right place at the right time
be off sick with flu
either ... or ...
go out of business
in a buyer's market

leave without giving notice
meet the standards
total quality management (TQM)
turn + colour (become)
under licence

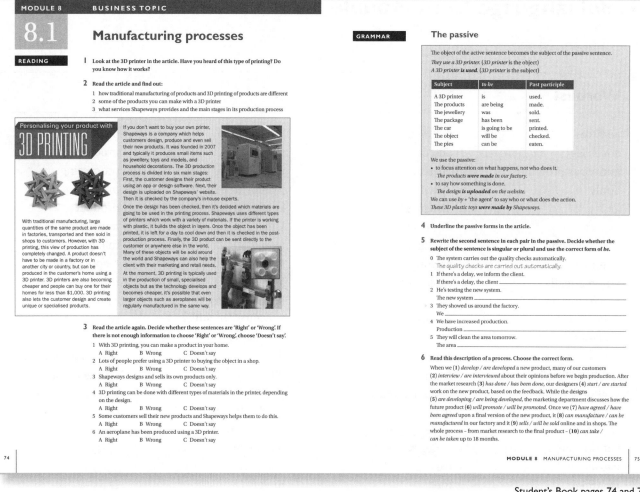

Personalising your product with 3D printing

READING

1   Ask students to look at the photographs. In pairs, students discuss what items can be 3D-printed.

2   Tell students to read the text carefully and underline the relevant pieces of information that they need to find.

Answers

1   With traditional manufacturing, large quantities of products are made in factories. With 3D printing, products are made at home.

2   3D printers can make items such as jewellery, toys and models, and household decorations.

3   Shapeways helps customers design, produce and sell. The main stages are designing, uploading, checking, choosing the materials, building in layers, sending (or delivery).

3   Ask students to read the statements first. Then ask them to read the article carefully. Tell them to underline the information that tells them whether the statements are right or wrong. Students can then compare their answers with a partner and discuss any answers that differ.

Answers

1   A (*… can be produced in the customer's home using a 3D printer.*)

2   C

3   B (*Shapeways is a company which helps customers design, produce and even sell their new products.*)

4   A (*… printers which work with a variety of materials.*)

5   A (*Shapeways can also help the client with their marketing and retail needs.*)

6   C

102

The passive

GRAMMAR

Write *PASSIVE* on the board. Ask students what the opposite of *passive* is (*active*). Then read through the information about the passive with students.

4 Ask students to underline the passive forms in the newspaper article.

Answers

With traditional manufacturing, <u>large quantities of the same product are made in factories</u>, transported and then sold in shops to customers. However, with 3D printing, this view of production has completely changed. <u>A product doesn't have to be made in a factory</u> or in another city or country, but <u>can be produced in the customer's home</u> using a 3D printer. 3D printers are also becoming cheaper and people can buy one for their homes for less than $1000. 3D printing also lets the customer design and create unique or specialised products.

If you don't want to buy your own printer, Shapeways is a company which helps customers design, produce and even sell their new products. <u>It was founded in 2007</u> and typically it produces small items such as jewellery, toys and models, and household decorations. The 3D production process is divided into six main stages: First, the customer designs their product using an app or design software. Next, <u>their design is uploaded</u> on Shapeways' website. <u>Then it is checked</u> by the company's in-house experts.

Once the design has been checked, then <u>it's decided</u> which materials <u>are going to be used</u> in the printing process. Shapeways uses different types of printers which work with a variety of materials. If the printer is working with plastic, it builds the object in layers. Once <u>the object has been printed</u>, <u>it is left</u> for a day to cool down and <u>then it is checked</u> in the post-production process. Finally, <u>the 3D product can be sent</u> directly to the customer or anywhere else in the world. <u>Many of these objects will be sold</u> around the world and Shapeways can also help the client with their marketing and retail needs.

At the moment, <u>3D printing is typically used</u> in the production of small, specialised objects but as the technology develops and becomes cheaper, it's possible that <u>even larger objects</u> such as aeroplanes <u>will be regularly manufactured</u> in the same way.

5 Read through the example together with the students. Ask them to do the exercise in pairs. Tell them to use the table at the top of the page as a reference.

Answers
1 is informed
2 is being tested
3 were shown around the factory
4 has been increased
5 will be cleaned tomorrow

6 Ask students to do the exercise on their own. When they've finished, ask them to work in pairs. They take it in turns to read a sentence, checking that they both have the same answer. If they differ, they should discuss their answers.

Answers
 1 develop
 2 are interviewed
 3 has been done
 4 start
 5 are being developed
 6 will be promoted
 7 have agreed
 8 can be manufactured
 9 will be sold
10 can take

Photocopiable activity
See page 174.

VOCABULARY

Supply and demand

1 Look at the words in the box. Tick the words that you already know and find the meaning of the others in a dictionary.

> automated   capacity   delivery   demand   handmade   order
> output   plant   produce   product   supply   warehouse

2 Choose the correct word in each sentence.

1 The phone manufacturer needs to build a new *plant / warehouse* to store their goods.
2 The company has received new *orders / deliveries* for their products from satisfied customers.
3 The existing factory cannot make enough to satisfy *supply / demand*.
4 The products are made using *an automated / a handmade* assembly line.
5 The factory is currently working at full *capacity / output*.
6 An international company could manufacture Chang Yue's *produce / products* under licence.

3 Complete the sentences with the six words that you did not use in exercise 2.

1 In a buyer's market, _____ exceeds demand.
2 Plans are being discussed for a new engineering _____.
3 Paul got his idea for the new business when he bought a _____ toy in a market in Bolivia.
4 Fresh dairy _____ is available from farm shops throughout the country.
5 We must increase our _____ in order to meet all the orders that we have received.
6 _____ to customers in the north are made on Wednesdays and Fridays.

VOCABULARY

Production philosophies

4 Match the words in column A with their definitions in column B.

A		B	
1	raw materials	A	a detailed list of items
2	production processes	B	the area where production takes place
3	factory floor	C	the cost of keeping goods in a warehouse
4	storage costs	D	the time from getting an order to producing the goods
5	waste	E	things which help to make something better
6	improvements	F	the actions taken to manufacture something
7	defects	G	inefficient or unnecessary use of substances, time, energy and money
8	inventory	H	goods, materials or components in the warehouse
9	response time	I	imperfections or faults
10	stock	J	the basic supplies or resources used to produce goods

5 Work in pairs. Which of the words (1–10) above are places? Which are physical items, and which one is a financial item?

6 What do you know about the concept of 'lean production'? Work in groups of three and compare your ideas.

READING

Lean production philosophies

7 Read this article taken from a business management journal. Underline the words from column A in exercise 4.

Lean production

New ways of doing business often happen when companies have problems. This was true for the car company Toyota™ in the 1950s after the Second World War. Its production processes were slow and inefficient, so it looked for new ideas. At that time, the Ford Motor Company™ was the most successful car company, so Toyota studied the system of mass production at Ford. Toyota learnt that Ford could produce a lot of cars but that they also produced a lot of waste. Toyota, on the other hand, planned to increase production rates while keeping waste levels low. Eventually, they came up with a system called 'lean production'. This system eliminated waste and encouraged improvements in productivity.

For Toyota, there were seven types of waste: overproduction was one of them, and it happened when Ford predicted high car sales but didn't manage to sell all the cars ultimately. There was also expensive inventory waste where extra raw materials occupied space in warehouses, leading to higher storage costs. A long response time was to be expected due to the slow movement of materials and goods around factories, and this was a waste of time.

Inefficient motions that led to people or machines expending unnecessary effort or time, such as having to bend down to pick up an item from the factory floor when a conveyor belt could deliver items to waist height, were another form of waste. Transportation became the fifth area of waste when products had to be transported from one factory to another. Ford also liked to add special features to cars, but Toyota realised customers didn't always want them. Such wastes in overprocessing resulted in extra cost but not extra profit. Finally, Ford's mass production resulted in lots of faults and defects, and their system of quality control was not cost-effective.

Toyota introduced a system of 'lean production' where you produced more cars but without paying more for labour or raw materials. It used a just-in-time (JIT) system where new stock only arrived when it was needed. The company also introduced quality control at every stage of the process to reduce the number of faulty products. Nowadays, lean production is used in most types of manufacturing to prevent waste and overproduction.

Exam Success

Prepare for Part Five of the Reading Test by reading longer texts (300–400 words) and identifying:
• the main idea of each paragraph.
• the purpose of the text (to give an opinion, etc).
• factual information.

8 Read the article again and answer the following questions.

1 Why did Toyota need a new way of producing its cars?
2 What problem did Toyota discover about the Ford Motor Company and its production process?
3 What were the seven types of waste?
4 What was Toyota's main idea behind the system of 'lean production'?
5 What was the name of a system used to control the delivery of stock and raw materials?

9 Work in groups of three. Decide how lean production could be applied in your company. Next, join another group and compare your ideas.

• What types of waste are there?
• How could you use the system of 'lean production' to prevent this waste?

Student's Book pages 76 and 77

Supply and demand

VOCABULARY

1 Ask students to read the words in the box and tick the ones they already know. Tell them to write down a definition for each word. They can use a dictionary for the words they don't know. Then choose a few students to give their definitions of words, which the rest of the class must identify.

2 Allow students a few minutes to do the exercise alone.

Point out that *produce* is also a noun which means food or materials obtained through farming, eg: *agricultural produce, dairy produce.*

Answers
1 warehouse
2 orders
3 demand
4 an automated
5 capacity
6 products

3 Ask students to look again at the words in the box in exercise 1, and to read the words not used in exercise 2 out loud (*plant, deliveries, supply, handmade, output, produce*). Tell them to use these words to complete the sentences in this exercise.

Answers
1 supply
2 plant
3 handmade
4 produce
5 output
6 Deliveries

Production philosophies

VOCABULARY

4 Students match the words with their definitions.

Answers
1 J   2 F   3 B   4 C   5 G
6 E   7 I   8 A   9 D   10 H

Alternative
Students work in pairs. One student covers column B and reads the items in column A. The other student covers column A and reads the definitions in column B. (NB: Student B will take a little longer to read his/her definitions.) Student A chooses one item from his/her column, eg *improvements* and Student B must read the corresponding definition (*things which help to make something better*). Then Student B reads one of the definitions, and Student A finds the corresponding item.

5 In pairs, students identify which words in exercise 4 are places, physical items, or financial items.

Answers
places: loading bay, factory floor
physical items: raw materials, waste, inventory, stock
financial item: storage costs

6 Ask students to close their books. Divide the class into groups of three. Write *lean production* on the board. Ask students if they know anything about this concept of *lean production*. If they don't know the term, ask them what they think *lean* might mean.

READING

7 Ask students to open their books and read the text quickly for the words in exercise 4.

Answers
Paragraph 1: waste; production processes; improvements
Paragraph 2: raw materials; storage costs; inventory; response time
Paragraph 3: defects; factory floor;
Paragraph 4: stock

8 First, read the Exam Success tip with students. Then ask students to read the questions. They then read the text more carefully, underlining the answers to the questions. When they've finished, they should compare their answers with a partner.

Answers
1 Because its production processes were slow and inefficient.
2 Ford produced a lot of waste.
3 Overproduction, expensive inventory, slow movement, unnecessary effort and time, transportation, overprocessing, faults and defects.
4 To produce more cars without paying more for labour and raw materials.
5 Just-in-time (JIT).

9 Students work in groups of three. Ask them to decide how to apply lean production in their company (they could use a company where they have worked in the past, or invent a fictional company). Allow them ten minutes to discuss their ideas.

Students should discuss the types of waste that they notice in their companies, and think of ways to prevent them.

Then put students into new groups and tell them to compare their ideas. Finally, ask individual students to present their ideas to the class.

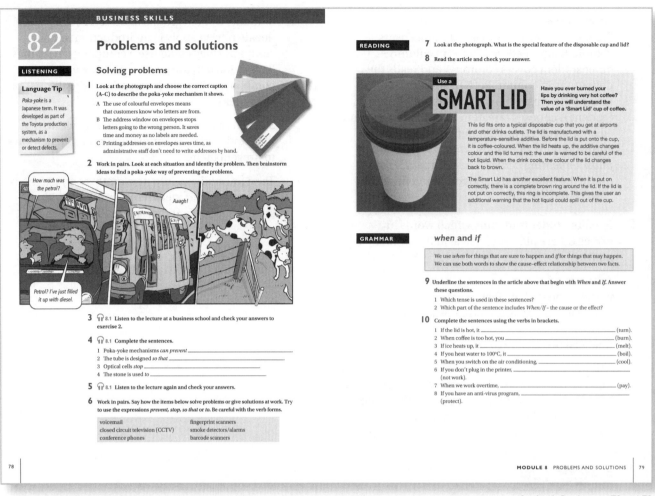

Student's Book pages 78 and 79

Solving problems

LISTENING

1 Ask students to look at the photo. Explain that this is an example of poka-yoke. Read the Language Tip with students. Ask students what it is in the photo that can prevent mistakes. Write their ideas on the board.

Then ask students to read the three captions, and to choose the correct one for the photo.

Answer
B

2 In pairs, students look at the three situations and identify what the problem is, then brainstorm poka-yoke ways of preventing the problems.

When most students have found some solutions to each situation, choose a few students to describe their ideas. Don't check answers at this stage as this will be done in exercise 3.

Answers
1 Somebody has filled the car with the wrong fuel.
2 Somebody has got stuck in the doors of a bus.
3 The cows are escaping, because the gate was left open.

3 🎧 8.1 Play the recording once.

Tell students to discuss the actual solutions with their partner. Then choose three students to describe the solutions to the class.

8.1 Listening script
Good morning. We're continuing the theme of Total Quality Management this morning, and in this lecture I'm going to look at the concept of the poka-yoke mechanism.

Let's think firstly about things going wrong – about mistakes, in other words. Mistakes happen in organisations for many reasons, but we need to realise that almost all of them can be prevented. The secret, really, is people making the effort to identify when problems happen and to do something about them. This is where the use of poka-yoke mechanisms can prevent a mistake from becoming a catastrophe.

Let me illustrate with some everyday examples that you probably haven't thought about before. How many of you have ever filled up your car with diesel instead of petrol? I can see you shaking your heads, of course. You are thinking that the tube for the diesel is too big to fit into your petrol tank, which is correct. The tube is designed so that it only fits the right tank. So that's an example of poka-yoke, and it's a very simple idea. But what about putting the narrow petrol tube into your diesel car? Another poka-yoke mechanism, which actually measures the diameter of the tube, keeps the opening to the diesel tank closed in this case.

Staying with transport ... A friend of mine once had a terrible experience when she tried to get off a crowded bus. The driver closed the doors without checking, and drove off! These days, modern buses use optical cells, like the ones you see in lift doors. These optical cells stop the doors from closing when people are getting off the bus.

Poka-yoke devices don't have to be high-tech though. What about those big stones you see on a rope on gates in the countryside? You don't need to worry about closing the gate behind you: the stone is used to make the gate close automatically.

Now let's move back to organisations and the kinds of mistakes that can be prevented in the production process ...

Answers
1 The tube for diesel is too big to fit in the hole of a petrol car; the diesel car has a mechanism that measures the diameter of the tube.
2 Optical cells stop the doors from closing when people are getting off the bus.
3 A big stone makes the gate close automatically.

4 🎧 8.1 These sentences are taken from the lecture. Ask students to complete the sentences and then compare their answers with their partner. Don't check answers at this stage, as this will be done in exercise 5.

5 🎧 8.1 Students listen and check their answers in exercise 4.

Answers
1 Poka-yoke mechanisms *can prevent* a mistake from becoming a catastrophe.
2 The tube is designed *so that* it only fits the right tank.
3 Optical cells *stop* the doors from closing when people are getting off the bus.
4 The stone is used *to* make the gate close automatically.

6 Students work in pairs. Ask them to take it in turns to explain how one of the items solves a problem or gives a solution at work. If the listener has something to add, he/she can do so. Students should try to use the expressions *prevent, stop, so that* and *to*.

Possible answers
Voicemail is a telephone answering system created so that you can receive telephone messages even when you can't answer the phone.
Closed circuit television (CCTV) is used to watch different parts of a large building to protect it against thieves.
Conference phones are used so that you can call a number of people in different parts of the world, and everyone can take part in the same conversation.

Fingerprint scanners are used to identify people for security purposes; for instance, at airport passport control.
Smoke detectors / alarms are used to inform the fire brigade when there is a fire, and to prevent it from causing a lot of damage.
Barcode scanners are used to keep track of the goods that are sold by a shop, to prevent the shop from running out.

Use a Smart Lid

READING

7 Ask students to look at the photograph and think about an answer to the question. Elicit ideas from the class. Don't check answers at this stage as this will be done in exercise 8.

8 Ask students to read the text and to check their answers. Were any of the students correct? Ask them if they know of any similar poka-yoke mechanisms.

Answers
The lid changes colour, from brown to red, when the liquid inside the cup is hot.

If the lid is on the cup correctly, there is a brown ring around the lid. If the lid is not on correctly, the ring is incomplete.

when and *if*

GRAMMAR

9 Read the information about *when* and *if* in the box. Then ask students to read the text again, and underline the sentences that begin with *when* and *if*. They then answer the two questions.

Answers
1 Present simple tense
2 The cause

10 Read the first sentence with the class and elicit the answer from students. Ask them to complete the exercise alone. When they've finished, they can compare their answers with a partner.

Possible answers
1 turns red
2 burn yourself
3 melts
4 boils
5 the room cools down
6 it doesn't work
7 the company pays us extra
8 it protects your computer against infection

VOCABULARY

Collocations with *problem*

1 There are a number of verbs that collocate with the noun *problem*. Complete the sentences with the correct verbs from the box. You can use more than one verb in some of the sentences.

avoid   cause   deal with   detect   explain   have   solve

1 As a production manager, I try to _____ problems as soon as possible. I have to meet my production targets!
2 The new machinery we installed is _____ some problems. I don't think it is compatible with the old system.
3 Jan, can you help me? I'm _____ a problem logging onto the computer system.
4 Well, I'm sure I'll be able to help you if you _____ the problem clearly.
5 I think it's a good idea to try out the new system at the weekend. That way we can _____ any problems with our customers.
6 I enjoy working in customer services – it's true that we _____ problems all day, but it's very satisfying when we can _____ someone's problem.

SPEAKING

We've got a problem

2 At Txoklat, a biscuit company, David, the production manager, and Angela, the plant manager, are discussing a problem. Read what David says. Then complete the conversation with the sentences in the box.

OK, I'll contact Head Office immediately.	Is it serious?
Oh no! Have you stopped production?	Oh, what's wrong, exactly?
Yes, I'll do that, too.	Hi, David. Is something wrong?

Angela   (1) _____
David   Yes, I think we've got a problem with our Txoko-cake line.
Angela   (2) _____
David   Yes, I'm afraid it is.
Angela   (3) _____
David   Some kind of bacteria has been found in one of the machines.
Angela   (4) _____
David   Yes, of course. We're trying to find the cause of the problem right now.
Angela   (5) _____
David   Could you tell the laboratory as well, please? They could help us.
Angela   (6) _____

3 🎧 8.2 Listen to the conversation and check your answers.

4 **Work in pairs.**
Student A: Go to page 145.
Student B: First, choose one of the problems below and explain the problem to Student A. Then listen to Student A's problem and make suggestions. Use the expressions from exercise 2.

1 Your computers keep crashing. No information is lost, but this wastes time and your staff are feeling very frustrated.
2 Half of your staff are off sick with flu. It's the end of the month and the accounts need to be done.
3 The electricity supply keeps going off. It is only off for a few minutes each time, but everyone's work is interrupted – and this costs money.

5 **Work in groups of three. Look at the case study. Then read your role cards and follow the instructions.**
Student A: You are the production manager.
Student B: You are the maintenance manager.
Student C: You are the purchasing manager.

Learning Tip
Improve your speaking confidence by:
• practising conversations with different partners.
• learning useful expressions, eg for agreeing and disagreeing, and giving and asking for opinions.

Language Tip
A *kiln* is an oven for baking clay or other ceramics.

CASE STUDY — Ceramic plc
Your company makes ceramics. In the last month, production has been stopped five times. The problem is in the kiln where the products are heated. The high temperature needed is not being reached and consequently the ceramics are of poor quality. The production manager has called a meeting to discuss the problem and to find a solution.

ROLE CARD A — Production manager
The constant interruptions in production are costing the company a lot of money. The finished products do not meet industry quality standards, and production targets were not met for last month. The only recent change in the production process was the change in the type of fuel used. You want to go back to the old fuel supplier.

ROLE CARD B — Maintenance manager
You think the problem is either with the quality of the raw materials for the ceramics or with the fuel. You want action to be taken soon because your maintenance workers are spending too long cleaning the kiln. There is other programmed work to be done as well.

ROLE CARD C — Purchasing manager
You are responsible for buying the fuel (coal) for the production process. You got an excellent price on coal from the Far East. You signed a contract for two years. The quality of the coal was guaranteed. You think the kiln is not being maintained properly.

6 Write a memo to the plant manager to report on the conclusions of the meeting. Write 60–80 words.

Student's Book pages 80 and 81

Collocations with *problem*

VOCABULARY

1 Ask students to close their books. Elicit with the word *problem* any verbs that combine, eg *solve a problem*. Write them up on the board. Ask students to give full sentences.

Ask them to open their books and do exercise 1.

Answers
1 detect
2 causing
3 having
4 explain
5 avoid
6 deal with, solve

We've got a problem

SPEAKING

2 Ask students to read the sentences in the box. In pairs, students decide which of the sentences go where in the conversation. Don't check answers at this stage as this will be done in exercise 3.

Extension
When they have finished, they can practise reading the conversation.

3 🎧 8.2 Students listen and check their answers in exercise 2.

8.2 Listening script
A = Angela   D = David

A Hi, David. Is something wrong?
D Yes, I think we've got a problem with our Txoko-cake line.
A Is it serious?
D Yes, I'm afraid it is.
A Oh, what's wrong, exactly?
D Some kind of bacteria has been found in one of the machines.
A Oh no! Have you stopped production?
D Yes, of course. We're trying to find the cause of the problem right now.
A OK, I'll contact Head Office immediately.
D Could you tell the laboratory as well, please? They could help us.
A Yes, I'll do that, too.

Answers
1 Hi, David. Is something wrong?
2 Is it serious?
3 Oh, what's wrong, exactly?
4 Oh no! Have you stopped production?
5 OK, I'll contact Head Office immediately.
6 Yes, I'll do that, too.

4 Students work in pairs. Tell Student A to go to page 145. Students should mimic the conversation in exercise 2. Student A starts by saying *Hi ..., is something wrong?*, then Student B continues with *Yes, I think we've got a problem with ...*, choosing one of the problems in the list.

Ask students to swap roles and talk about the other problems.

Choose a pair of students to present one of their conversations to the class. To make it more entertaining, they could be melodramatic about the situation.

5 Read the Learning Tip with students first. Then tell students to form groups of three, with people they don't normally talk to. Each group should decide who is Student A, who is Student B, and who is Student C.

Read the case study for 'Ceramic plc' together with students. Allow time for students to read their instructions. Then ask students to have a discussion about what you should do to solve this problem. Allow ten minutes for students to conclude their discussions.

6 Ask students to write a memo to the plant manager reporting their conclusions. They should write 60–80 words.

Photocopiable activity
See page 175.

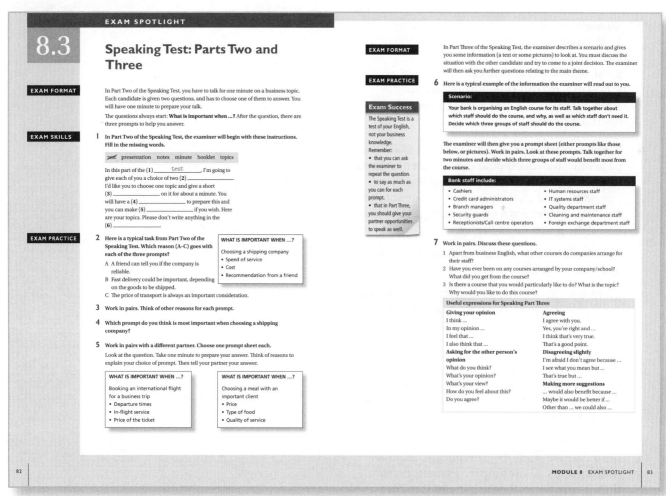

Student's Book pages 82 and 83

Speaking Test: Part Two

EXAM FORMAT

Ask students to read the Exam Format.

Write *Speaking Test: Part Two* on the board. Then write *What is important when …?* Ask students to complete the question. Elicit suggestions. When there are a few suggestions on the board, ask students to choose one. Ask them to suggest items that are important for that question and to explain why they've suggested that item.

EXAM SKILLS

I Read the words in the box and fill in the missing words in the passage. Check answers with the class.

Answers
2 topics
3 presentation
4 minute
5 notes
6 booklet

EXAM PRACTICE

2 Read the instructions. Then ask students to read the question and answer the question. Ask them if there are any other factors that are important when choosing a shipping company.

Answers
Speed of service – B
Cost – C
Recommendation from a friend – A

3 Students work in pairs. Allow four minutes for students to think of other reasons for the prompts in exercise 1.

Answers
Other reasons: types of packing, customs, discounts, extra costs

Extension

When students have a few reasons for each prompt, tell them to write down one word for each reason on a piece of paper: the word should help them to remember the reason. In turns, they choose one of the words from their piece of paper and explain to their partner the reason and what prompt it relates to.

4   Tell students to decide which prompt from exercise 1, and from the ones they've thought of, is most important when choosing a shipping company. There is no correct answer, but it might be interesting to find out how many students choose each prompt. Ask students to put their hand up if they've chosen *Speed of service*, etc.

5   Ask students to work with a different partner. The first question is for Student A, but both students should read it. The preparation time is only one minute, so students have to think of the reasons quickly. Writing one word to remind them of the reason, instead of a sentence, will save time.

Student A prepares his/her answer, and then tells Student B his/her answer. Student B should listen. When Student A has finished, Student B should give his/her answer to the same question, and explain the answer. He/she can choose the same prompt as Student A.

Speaking Test: Part Three

EXAM FORMAT

Tell students to close their books. Read the Exam Format to students. Then refer students to the Exam Success tip. Explain that they should have a real conversation. They should listen to their partner and respond to what he/she says.

EXAM PRACTICE

6   Students work in pairs: Student A and Student B. Ask Student A to open his/her book and to read the scenario to Student B. Ask Student B: *What different jobs and positions are there in a bank?* Then ask: *Which ones would benefit from the course?* Ask Student Bs to open their books. Tell students to look at the list of bank staff. They have two minutes to discuss which three groups of staff would benefit most from the English course. It isn't important that they come to a final decision, but that they both participate. When they've finished, have a class discussion on which staff groups would benefit most. Students must present their reasons why.

7   Students should work with the same partners. Ask them to read the questions and discuss them; then open the discussion up to the whole class.

Overview

9.1   Business topic: The future

READING	Developing driverless cars
GRAMMAR	The future: *will* for predictions
GRAMMAR	The first conditional
READING	Strategies for the future
LISTENING	A strategy meeting

9.2   Business skills: Meetings

READING	Tropical storm hits Poland
LISTENING	Crisis meeting
GRAMMAR	*will* + time clauses
SPEAKING	Brainstorming
LISTENING	Crisis strategy
VOCABULARY	Collocations with *meeting*
WRITING	Letter of apology

9.3   Exam spotlight: Reading Test
Parts Four and Five

Predicting the content of an article from the title

Scanning and analysing a text

Focusing on key words

Reading for specific information

Useful language from Module 9

Wordlist

advise	crisis meeting	lamb chops	smoothly
after-school care	cut off	life-threatening	solar panel
allegation	damage	low cost	spill
although	dead	malpractice	stabilise
army	departmental	media	steak tartare
assess	meeting	middle	start up
assessment	disrupt	management	state-of-the-art
assurance	dozen	occupant	storm
aware	draw up a plan	party	subcontractor
be evacuated	emergency team	PEST(LE) analysis	subsidiary
blow over	exchange rate	podcast	sweep across
board (meeting)	exhaust emission	pollute	take time off
briefing	fight back	poultry	tank
bring down	fuel	prototype	tasteless
chair (v)	guarantee	rail link	telecommuting
chairperson	high-speed trains	research	tram
collapse	hurricane	restore	trivial
collateral	hybrid	run a meeting	viable option
crane	incident	run on (fuel)	
crisis	joint venture	salmonella	

Expressions

appoint a spokesperson	It sounds good to me.
arrange a meeting	miss a meeting
assess the damage	over to you
attend a meeting	set priorities
Can you take the minutes?	stay within emission targets
collect information	take a look at
financial malpractice	The next item on the agenda is …
fix the roof	the wind dropped
go bankrupt	things go from bad to worse
handle a crisis	work flexible hours
hold a meeting	

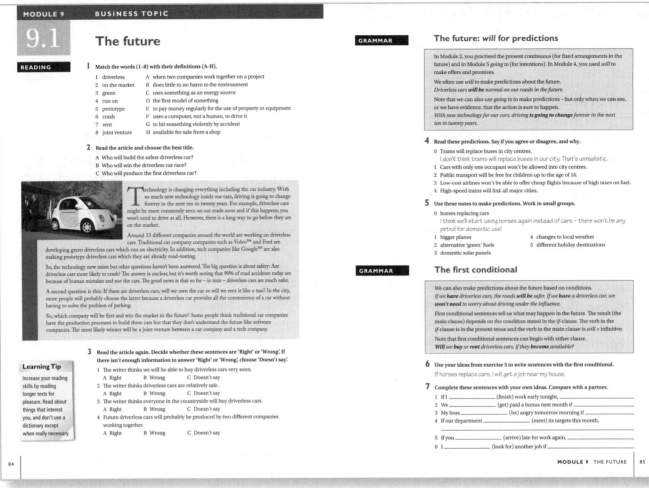

Student's Book pages 84 and 85

Developing Driverless Cars

READING

1 Ask students if they know anything about driverless cars. Ask them if they've read any articles or have seen any special reports on TV about them. Introduce the idea of driverless cars and ask them if they would be interested in taking a ride in one. Elicit ideas and experiences. Students then do the matching exercise.

Alternative

Divide the class into two groups. The students in the first group read the words 1–8 out loud. The students in the second group provide answers from A–H.

Answers
1 F   2 H   3 B   4 C   5 D   6 G   7 E   8 A

2 Remind students that they have to read quickly. Tell them to stop reading when they think they've got the answer. Collect students' answers, but don't check them yet. Tell students to continue reading to find out if they were right or wrong.

After checking the answer, point out that the topic of an article is often to be found at the beginning, usually in the first paragraph.

Answer
B

3 Tell students to underline all the words in the text which helped them understand the correct answers. Remind them that the 'Doesn't say' option may be true or false in the real world, but here students must concentrate on what the text says. For example, sentence 2 may be true in the real world, but if the text doesn't say that, the correct answer is 'Doesn't say'.

Answers
1 B (*… there is a long way to go before they are on the market.*)
2 A (*… so far – in tests – driverless cars are much safer.*)
3 C
4 A (*The most likely winner will be a joint venture between a car company and a tech company.*)

The future: *will* for predictions

GRAMMAR

Revise the present continuous used for fixed arrangements in the future, *going to* used for intentions and *will* used to make promises and offers with students. Ask them to write a sentence for each of these uses. Then ask students to produce sentences that are true for them.

Introduce the new use of *will* and *going to* to make predictions and read the information in the box.

4 Read the example with students and point out the correct use of *I don't think this will happen*. Tell students that you don't usually say *I think this will not happen* in English. Also point out that in the Speaking Test, candidates are often asked to agree or disagree on a topic.

5 As this is a speaking exercise, tell students to produce sentences orally. If they want to write some sentences down, they can do so for homework. To simulate natural conversation, tell students that they have to establish eye contact with the other students in their group.

The first conditional

GRAMMAR

Introduce the first conditional with a simple example. Write on the board:

If it rains, I'll stay at home

I'll go for a walk, if it's sunny

Ask students which action in the sentences happens first (*if it rains – if it's sunny*) and which happens next (*I'll stay at home – I'll go for a walk*). Tell students that the verb in the *if*-clause (the condition) must be in the present. The verb in the main clause (the consequence) must be in the future.

Point out that the first conditional is used to make predictions and hypotheses that are likely to happen. Then read the information about the first conditional with students.

6 Students write sentences with the first conditional, using their ideas from exercise 5.

Possible answers
1 If bigger planes start flying over our district, we'll start a protest against the airport management.
2 If we don't find alternative 'green' fuels, we'll run out of oil in a few years.
3 If we install domestic solar panels, we'll save a lot of money in the future.
4 If we keep cutting down trees in big forests, we'll experience more and more changes to local weather.
5 If there is no more fuel, people will have to find different holiday destinations closer to home.

7 Students write their own ideas and compare with a partner. Then check possible answers with the whole class, making sure that students have used the correct tense in both parts of the sentence.

Answers
1 finish, *will* + infinitive
2 'll get, present
3 will be, present
4 meets, *will* + infinitive
5 arrive, *will* + infinitive
6 'll look for, present

Photocopiable activity
See page 176.

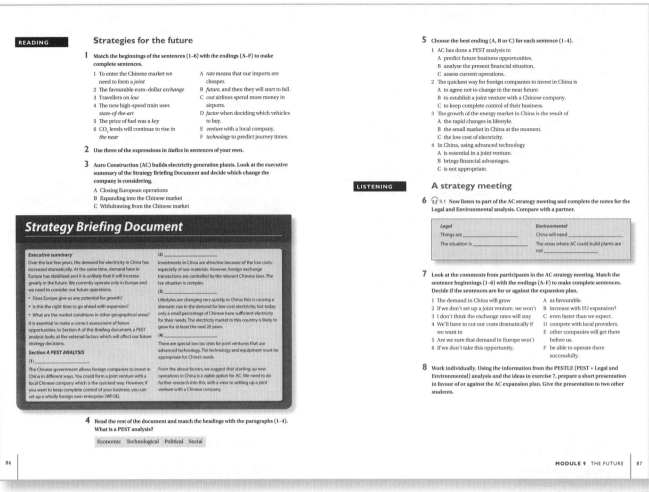

Student's Book pages 86 and 87

Strategies for the future

READING

1 You can introduce this topic by presenting the ideas of *future expansion, future markets, future economy*, etc. Check how familiar students are with these themes. A brainstorming activity is a good tool to elicit students' ideas.

Give a few minutes to do exercise 1. Then choose students to read the complete sentences out loud.

Answers
1 E 2 A 3 C 4 F 5 D 6 B

2 Students can work in pairs or individually to write three sentences using the expressions in exercise 1.

3 Students do exercise 3. They only have to read the first paragraph to do the exercise.

Answer
B

4 Ask four students to read one paragraph each from the PEST analysis secion of the document in exercise 3. Ask four other students to suggest an appropriate heading for each paragraph and ask the rest of the class to determine whether the choice of the headings is correct or not. Then ask the students to read out loud which parts in the text confirm that the choice of the headings is correct.

Ask students if they can explain what a PEST analysis is and if they understand what the letters P.E.S.T. stand for.

Extension
Write *PEST* on the board and ask students if they have a positive or negative feeling regarding this word. Collect ideas. Then ask them to rearrange the letters in PEST to make a more positive word. (Answer: STEP)

Answers
1 Political
2 Economic
3 Social
4 Technological

A PEST analysis is an analysis of the environmental factors that affect all businesses and organisations. PEST is an acronym for the Political, Economic, Social and Technological factors of the external environment. As *PEST* can have a negative connotation, the letters are sometimes rearranged to construct the more optimistic term of *STEP* analysis.

5 Students work alone and do exercise 5, which is similar to Reading Test, Part Five. Remind them that in the exam they'll have a text of about 300–400 words and six multiple choice questions like these.

Answers
1 A   2 B   3 A   4 B

A strategy meeting

LISTENING

6 🎧 9.1 Tell students that a variation of the PEST analysis is the more complete version PESTLE analysis, where the last two letters of the acronym stand for Legal and Environmental.

Play recording 9.1 once, or twice if necessary.

9.1 Listening script
S1 = Speaker 1   **S2** = Speaker 2

S1 OK, so now that we've looked at the political, economic, social and technological analyses, I'd like to briefly complete the analysis by looking at the legal and environmental aspects.
S2 Yes, I imagine the legal situation is very complex.
S1 Well, you know, the legal factors were not so complicated until recently. The problem is that things are changing all the time in China. You know they recently changed the law on private property, and nobody can really predict what those changes are going to mean. So the whole thing is very difficult to comment on. It's a very unpredictable situation.
S2 I see. Well I think we will need to look at that in more detail. I'm a bit worried about the implications there. And what about the environmental considerations?
S1 Well, obviously we need to do an Environmental Impact Assessment. The Chinese government are strict about corporate social responsibility, especially for joint ventures. So we will need to give them assurances and guarantees that we will stay within the emission targets. On the other hand, the areas where we could build plants are not environmentally protected, so that isn't going to be a problem initially.
S2 Great, something positive at last. By the way, what's the Chinese position with regard to the Kyoto protocol?

Answers
changing all the time
unpredictable
assurances and guarantees
environmentally protected

7 Give a few minutes to do exercise 7. Then ask students to read their sentences out loud in turns and add whether they think the sentence is for or against the expansion plan. For each item, find out if anybody has a different answer.

Answers
1 C (for)
2 F (against)
3 A (against)
4 D (against)
5 B (against)
6 E (for)

8 Students prepare their presentations in favour of or against the AC expansion plan. They then form groups of three and take it in turns to give their presentations to the other two students.

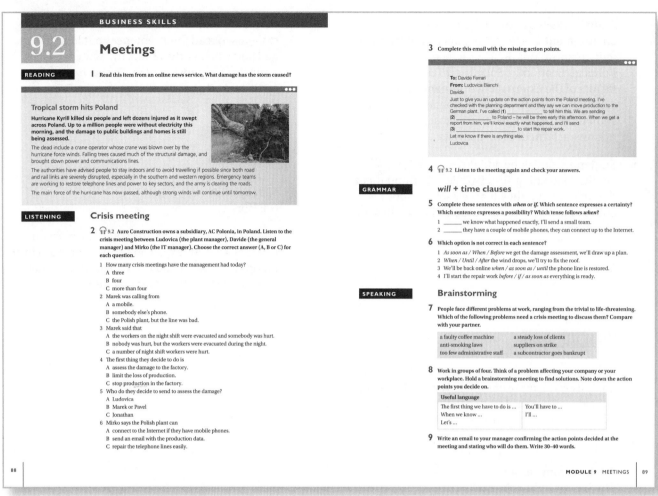

Student's Book pages 88 and 89

Tropical storm hits Poland

READING

1 Choose one student to read the news item out loud, while the rest of the class read it silently. Suggest that the student reads the item in the style of a newsreader. Students then answer the question.

Finally, ask students to read the news item again and check any unknown words.

Answer
The storm killed six people, injured several dozen, left up to a million people without electricity, damaged public buildings and homes.

Crisis meeting

LISTENING

2 9.2 Tell students to read the questions first. Then play the recording once. Ask students for their answers. If they all answered correctly, move on to the next exercise, otherwise allow a second listening. Point out that this exercise is similar to Listening Test, Part Four, but in the exam there will only be five questions.

9.2 Listening script

L = Ludovica   **D** = Davide   **M** = Mirko

L This is the fourth emergency meeting today. Is there anything that's not an emergency in this company?

D Look, I'm sorry about this, but it's a real problem. I just got a call from Marek, and …

M Who is Marek?

L He's our Polish plant manager.

D … and they've been hit by a hurricane.

M In Poland? I didn't know they had hurricanes in Poland!

D No, I know. Anyway, the roof has blown off, and the electricity and telephones are down. Marek was calling from his mobile, but he said it took hours to get through and the communication was pretty bad!

M Was anybody hurt?

D Apparently not. But the workers on the night shift were evacuated.

L Any damage to the machinery?

D I have no idea. Marek sounded pretty worried. It will take some time to assess the damage.

M No electricity or phones – so, no Internet. They're completely cut off.

L They do have a generator. If it works, we can at least turn the system on.

D Wait, let's set priorities: the first thing we have to do is to limit the loss of production. Can we move production to one of our other plants?

L I'll check with the planning department.

D Good! Then they'll need somebody to help them with damage assessment – they don't have the experience for this. Ludovica, I'm afraid you'll have to help them. Call Marek on his mobile. Then send Jonathan over there as soon as possible.

L When we know what happened exactly, I'll send a small team to start the repair work and to co-ordinate the local maintenance people.

D Excellent! Now, the Internet ... Mirko, what can we do until the electricity and telephone lines are repaired?

M Well, if they have a couple of mobile phones with computer connections, they will be able to connect up to the Internet.

L Then they can send us the production data we haven't got yet, and we can send them a couple of emails.

D Great! Let's get started.

Answers
1 B   2 A   3 B   4 B   5 C   6 A

3 Students do the task on their own. If they need some help, they can confer with a partner. Don't check answers at this stage as this will be done in exercise 4.

4 🎧 9.2 Students listen again and check their answers in exercise 3.

Alternative
If you've already played the recording twice, tell students to listen and read the script on page 158 of the Student's Book.

Answers
1 Marek
2 Jonathan
3 a small team

will + time clauses

GRAMMAR

5 Write *IF* and *WHEN* on the board. Elicit at least two sentences containing *if*, *when* and a *will* future from the students and write a couple of interesting ones on the board. If sentences containing mistakes are produced, tell students to find the mistakes and correct them.

Students do exercise 5.

Answers
1 When (certainty)
2 If (possibility)
WHEN / IF + PRESENT

6 Ask students to cross out the wrong option.

Answers
1 Before
2 Until
3 until
4 before

Extension
Ask students to produce two sentences containing *before* and *until*, eg:
I'll let you know before I go on holiday.
I'll have to stay at the station until the strike ends.

Brainstorming

SPEAKING

7 Explain the degrees of seriousness from trivial (not serious) to life-threatening (very serious). You could also consider the difference between long-term problems and urgent situations or emergencies. Then ask students to decide which problem needs a crisis meeting.

Possible answers
Too few administrative staff.
Suppliers on strike.
A subcontractor goes bankrupt.

8 Tell students that during a real brainstorming session, people sit round a table and discuss as many ideas as possible in order to find a solution to a problem. Each idea is recorded, either written or digitally recorded; only later, the same team or a different one chooses the best solution.

For this exercise students may have to think of a company they have had experience with in the past if they are not currently working. Alternatively, you may wish to offer a selection of fictional companies for students to choose from. The photocopiable activity on page 177 also offers an alternative activity suitable for pre-work students.

9 Ask students to write their email to one of the other people in their group. In each group, each student should write and receive one email. Ask students to correct the email they receive.

Photocopiable activity
See page 177.

LISTENING

Crisis strategy

1 Complete the sentences about business crises using the words in the box.

> fight　collapsed　damaged　cost　hit

1　Share prices _____ last night following the US political crisis.
2　The retail sector was _____ hard when interest rates went up again this month.
3　Enron's reputation was _____ after the allegations of financial malpractice.
4　The salmonella incident _____ the poultry industry millions in lost sales.
5　UK banks will _____ back after online fraud chaos.

2 Companies need a strategy to deal with a crisis. Put the four steps (a–d) of a typical crisis communication plan in order.

a　Decide who will be responsible for handling the crisis.
b　Decide who will be the point of contact between your crisis team and the media.
c　Collect information and make sure you know the relevant facts.
d　Identify who you need to communicate with: your customers, the media, etc.

3 🎧 9.3　Listen to a podcast by Ellis Whims, a PR expert, and check your answers to exercise 2.

4 🎧 9.3　Listen again and complete the missing information.

1　Every organisation needs a _____
2　A crisis plan enables a company to handle a crisis quickly and _____
3　First, collect information about the _____
4　Second, appoint a _____ to handle the crisis.
5　Third, appoint a _____ to be the contact between the crisis team and the media.
6　Fourth, identify your key _____: your customers, employees, salespeople and the media.

Exam Success

This exercise is similar to Part Three of the Listening Test. Before you listen, remember to read all the information, and try to predict what is missing.

5 Do you know what to do in a crisis? Can you remember the advice that Ellis Whims gave?
Student A: Close your book and tell Student B what steps to follow.
Student B: Listen to your partner and check the information.

90

VOCABULARY

Collocations with *meeting*

6 Put each word into the correct group (1–3).

> attend　arrange　agenda　action points　board　chair　crisis
> chairperson　departmental　hold　minutes　miss　run　team

1　types of meeting　　　　board
2　verbs connected to meetings　　　attend
3　nouns connected to meetings　　　agenda

7 Write a word in each gap.
1　Can you take the _____, please?
2　How many people usually _____ the meetings?
3　Can we move on to the next item on the _____?
4　Where's Olga? She will _____ the meeting if she doesn't get here soon.
5　Can we _____ a different time for the next meeting?

8 One of your important customers and his client suffered food poisoning at your restaurant recently. You have seen this letter of complaint in a specialist catering magazine. Your business partner has just informed you that this bad review and an Internet blog are affecting business and bookings are down 50 per cent. Hold a meeting with your business partner and decide what to do. Use the strategy from exercises 2–4 to make a crisis communications plan. Use the Useful language on page 89 to help you.

and after waiting at our table for about thirty minutes, our waiter finally returned to take our order. We both ordered fish soup, which was tasteless and far too hot, as we discovered when the waiter spilled most of it over both the table and ourselves. The main courses, of steak tartare and lamb chops, were not very good either. The only good thing about the meal was the top quality fresh cream desserts and perfect coffee. After the terrible service and poor food, we were happy to leave and forget all about the experience. But later that evening, I'm afraid things went from bad to worse

WRITING

Letter of apology

9 One of your action points from the meeting is to write to the customer. Read the letter of complaint again and write a letter of apology from the restaurant management, including the information below. Write about 60–80 words.

• apologise for the poor service
• apologise for the food poisoning incident
• accept full responsibility
• offer a complimentary dinner for two

MODULE 9 MEETINGS　91

Student's Book pages 90 and 91

Crisis strategy

LISTENING

1 Tell students to keep their books closed. Tell them to think of some bad news which may affect a company. Brainstorm ideas and write key words on the board. Help with unknown words if necessary. Then tell students to open the books and compare the bad news on the board with the sentences in exercise 1. Find out if any problem mentioned by the students is also contained in the sentences. As they compare the items, they complete the sentences.

Answers
1 collapsed　2 hit　3 damaged　4 cost
5 fight

2 Draw students' attention to the four points. Tell them to decide whether this is the correct order for a crisis-facing strategy or if the steps should be changed. Accept students' answers and ask them to give reasons for their choices, but don't confirm the correct answers at this stage as this will be done in exercise 3.

3 🎧 9.3 Students listen and check their answers in exercise 2.

9.3 Listening script
A = Announcer　　**E** = Ellis Whims

A Welcome to our Monday podcast for 5th March. Today our guest speaker is Ellis Whims, a PR expert, and she's going to talk about crisis management. Ellis, over to you.
E A business crisis can take many forms. Unhappy customers can, unfortunately, give a lot of trouble. Do you remember the recent headlines about the woman who said she found a human finger in her food at a MegaBurger restaurant? MegaBurger estimate that this situation cost them $2.5 million in lost sales. And the story of the finger was actually false!

So if the unthinkable happens to you and your company, what do you do? How do you respond? Every organisation needs a crisis plan to enable it to handle a crisis quickly and effectively.

The most important part of crisis management is preventing a crisis in the first place. Take a hard look at your company and examine potential problems. An experienced public relations professional will help you to create your Crisis Communications Plan. This contains four steps:

First, collect information about the situation – make sure you know the relevant facts.

Second, appoint a crisis team – these people will be responsible for handling the crisis itself.

Third, appoint a spokesperson – this person will typically serve as the point of contact between your crisis team and the media.

Fourth, identify your key audiences – your customers, employees, salespeople and the media.

If the worst should happen, don't panic. Take a deep breath and collect your crisis team. Examine the situation quickly and decide on the appropriate action, as well as the message you want to send to your customers, your employees, and the public in general.

The most important actions in a crisis are: acting quickly to resolve the situation, telling the truth, being available for the press, showing confidence and compassion, communicating changes in the situation as quickly as you can.

You've probably seen that when a customer experiences a problem and you resolve it for them quickly, that customer becomes more loyal than they were before the problem. The same phenomenon is true in a crisis. Communicating quickly and effectively to your key audiences can actually strengthen your brand image in their eyes.

A Thank you, Ellis. Thanks for listening, podcasters. Don't miss our talk next week, same day, same time.

Answers
c, a, b, d

4 🎧 9.3 Read the Exam Success tip with students and add that in the exam they'll have to write one or two words in the gaps.

Then play the recording again.

Answers

1 crisis plan	4 (crisis) team
2 effectively	5 spokesperson
3 situation	6 audiences

5 Tell students that this is going to be a kind of a competition. The aim is to judge who remembers most of the advice and the correct sequence. To do this, Student B will be the 'judge'. Student B can keep her or his book open, but it should be hidden from Student A.

Collocations with *meeting*

VOCABULARY

6 Write the word *MEETINGS* on the board and draw three columns. Write *Types; Verbs; Nouns* as the headings for the columns.

Elicit from students: different types of meeting, verbs that collocate with *meeting*, and nouns that collocate with or are related to meetings.

Then students do exercise 6 alone.

Answers
1 board, crisis, departmental, team
2 attend, arrange, chair, hold, miss, run
3 agenda, action points, chair, chairperson, minutes

7 Students fill in the gaps with the correct words.

Answers
1 minutes   2 attend   3 agenda
4 miss   5 arrange

8 Ask one student to read the customer's letter. Give some characterisation and emphasis (the customer was very sick and when he wrote the letter, he was very angry).

Then students work in pairs or small groups to make a crisis communication plan. They should remember the following points:

1 Collect information about the situation and make sure you know the relevant facts: Who bought the food? Who supplied it? Did the food poisoning originate in your restaurant?

2 Decide who will be responsible for handling the crisis: you, the manager, your business partner.

3 Appoint a spokesperson who will be the point of contact between the crisis team and the media: yourself, your business partner, your lawyer, etc.

4 Identify your key audiences: customers and competitors in this case. Choose the best way to address your audience: a press release, an apology letter, new publicity, etc.

Letter of apology

WRITING

9 Students write an apology letter. Remind them that this task is similar to Writing, Part Two.

Sample answer

> Dear Mr Weakes
>
> I'm writing to apologise for the poor service you received in our restaurant last week, and for the food poisoning you suffered.
>
> We would like to point out that an inspection by the local authority confirmed that hygiene standards in our kitchens are very high, and that all our food is delivered fresh every day and is of the best quality.
>
> However, we accept full responsibility and would like to offer a complimentary dinner for two.
>
> Yours sincerely
>
> The Manager
> Kingfisher Restaurant

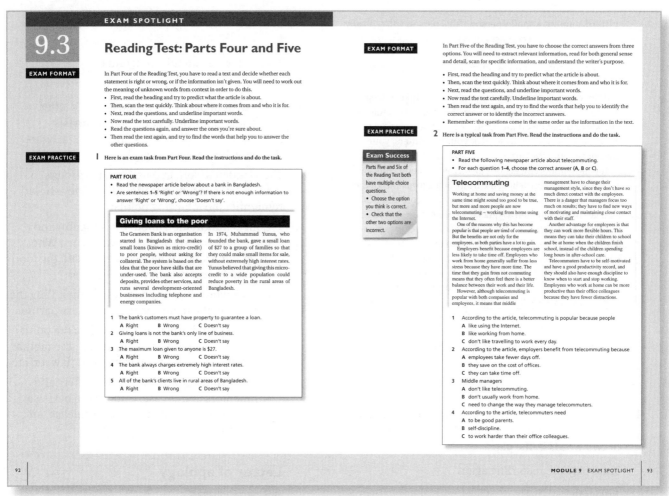

Reading Test: Part Four

EXAM FORMAT

Read the opening description of this part of the exam with the students. Remind students what is meant by 'Right', 'Wrong', 'Doesn't say'. ('Right': the text contains information that confirms this statement. 'Wrong': the text contains information that contradicts this statement. 'Doesn't say': even if you know that the statement is true or false, the text does not contain any information that either confirms or contradicts this statement.)

EXAM PRACTICE

1 Students do this task individually, as if they were taking the exam. Ask them to time themselves, ie, the time they take to read the text and answer the questions. Tell students to write the starting and finishing time at the top of the page and keep a record of how long they take to do each exercise. By the end of the book, they'll have an idea of how to manage their time when they do the Reading and Writing parts.

Ask students if Part Four of the Reading Test contains more or fewer than five questions. (More: Reading Part Four has got seven questions.)

Always ask students to underline in the text the parts that helped them to find the correct answers.

Once students have completed the exam task, check the answers with them. For each question, discuss which are the key words in the sentence, and identify the part of the text which gives the answer.

Answers
1 B (... *without asking for collateral*)
2 A (*The bank also accepts deposits, provides other services ...*)
3 C
4 B (... *without extremely high interest rates ...*)
5 C

Reading Test: Part Five

Read the information about Part Five of the
Reading Text with the class.

Ask students to read the information and the
Exam Success tip.

EXAM PRACTICE

2 Students do the Reading Test Part Five task on
their own, as if they were taking the exam. Ask
them to time themselves, ie, the time they take to
read the text and answer the questions, as with
Reading Test Part Four.

Ask students if they'll have more or fewer than
four questions in the exam. (More: Reading Part
Five has got six questions.)

Answers
1 C (*... people are tired of commuting.*)
2 A (*... employees are less likely to take time off.*)
3 C (*... middle management have to change their
    management style ...*)
4 B (*... they should also have enough discipline ...*)

Overview

10.1 Business topic: Career development

READING	Business skills portfolio
GRAMMAR	Relative clauses
LISTENING	Leadership qualities
VOCABULARY	Describing people
READING	Don't just manage, lead!

10.2 Business skills: Organising a conference

VOCABULARY	Collocations
LISTENING	What's still to do?
LISTENING	The conference budget
SPEAKING	Small talk
LISTENING	Offers and invitations
WRITING	Replying to an invitation

10.3 Exam spotlight: Writing Test Part Two

Structuring business correspondence

Responding to a letter of complaint

Useful language from Module 10

Wordlist

accept
acknowledge
actually
admire
admit (allow in)
alcohol
alternative
ambitious
approximately
assist
associate (adj)
auxiliary
be focused
be missing
borrow
boss
break
caffeine
cancel
casual
catering
chamber of
   commerce
charismatic
clear
clever
commercial
communicate
conclusion
conference
conference pack
confident
connect
contribute
count on sb
culture

decline
dress code
drop out
dynamic
encourage
enrolment
enterprise
entrepreneurial
expansion
expertise
faulty
feedback
finalise
fish
flexibility
flu (influenza)
foster (v)
front
get in touch
growth
habit
head office
host
huge
improve
in-company
initiative (new
   action)
IQ (intelligence
   quotient)
IT developer
keynote
lack
leadership
lecturer
lecture theatre

meditation
memorise
microphone
mind gymnastics
motivate
move on
networking
outcome
participate in
patient (adj)
perhaps
planner
politics
portfolio
praise (n + v)
preferential
prioritise
priority
productive
profit
profitability
programme
promote
punctuality
push (v)
quotation
quote (n + v)
really (very much)
recommend
refer
refund
repair
replace
replacement
resolve (v)
responsibility

right / left-handed
route
salmon
screen
self-confidence
seminar
sequence
set off
shopping list
shower
slight
small talk
smart-casual
sound system
stranger
strategic planning
strengthen
suit (set of clothes)
summarise
taboo
task
the Press
thoroughly
tie (clothing)
tuna
umbrella
vegetarian
venture
vice versa
video beamer
wonder (question)
   (v)
workplace
workshop
worry
yoga

Expressions

as soon as possible (ASAP)
at the last minute
be / go over budget
bring sb up-to-date
corporate hospitality
from as little as €...
I'd be delighted to.

I'd like to join you.
I'll be around.
internationally recognised
It's a two-day event.
make decisions
Make yourself comfortable.
Please, take a seat.

ready to go to print
Shall we set off?
stick with sth
The fee is 3% up on last year.
throw sth away
under control
value for money

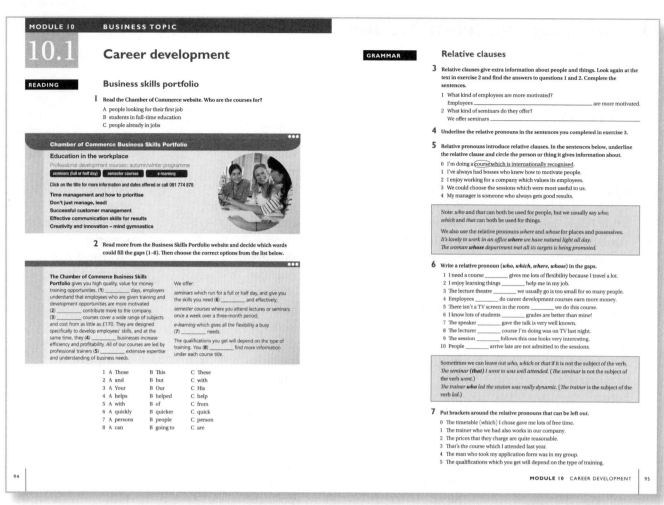

Student's Book pages 94 and 95

Business skills portfolio

READING

I   Students read the web page quickly and answer the question.

Answer
C people already in jobs (*Education in the workplace*)

Alternative
Before students answer the question, ask them to read the web page for 15 seconds and find out as much information as possible. When 15 seconds are up, tell students to close their books. Elicit the information shown:

• *Which organisation produced the website?* (the Chamber of Commerce)
• *What is it about?* (the Business Skills Portfolio / education in the workplace)
• *What types of courses are described?* (There are three types of courses: seminars, semester courses, e-learning.)

• *What are the topics of the courses?* (The courses cover: time management, leadership, customer management, effective communication, creativity and innovation.)

Tell students to open their books and read the web page again and find out if there is any information they did not remember. They then answer the question.

2   Ask students to read the text, and to choose one word from the three options to write in each space.

Answers
1 C   2 A   3 B   4 C   5 A   6 A   7 C   8 A

Relative clauses

GRAMMAR

3   Tell students to read the text in exercise 2 again and complete the sentences, which have been taken from the text.

Answers
1 who are given training and development opportunities
2 which run for a full or half day.

4 Ask students to underline the relative pronouns in the sentences they've written in exercise 3.

Answers
1 <u>who</u>
2 <u>which</u>

5 Go through the instructions and the example sentence with the class. Ask students to do the exercise alone. When they've finished, tell them to compare their answers with their partner.

Then read the information about *who, that, which* and *where* with students.

Answers
1 (bosses) who knew how to motivate people.
2 (company) which values its employees.
3 (sessions) which were most useful to us.
4 (someone) who always gets good results.

6 Ask students to work alone to do this exercise. When they've finished, tell them to compare their answers with their partner.

Read the information about leaving out relative pronouns with the students.

Answers
 1 which
 2 which
 3 where
 4 who
 5 where
 6 whose
 7 who
 8 whose
 9 which
10 who

7 Explain to students what they have to do, and read the example sentence. Then ask students to put brackets around the relative pronouns that can be left out.

Answers
1 The trainer (who) ...
2 The prices (that) ...
3 That's the course (which) ...
4 The man who took my application form was in my group.
5 The qualifications (which) ...

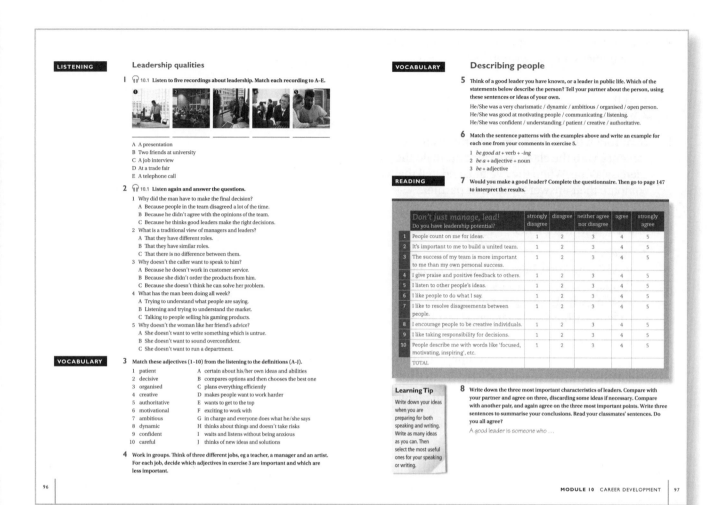

Student's Book pages 96 and 97

Leadership qualities

1 🎧 **10.1** Ask students to suggest situations in which they might need to be careful to give a good impression of themselves. Ask them to explain why. Then ask students to look at the five pictures. Tell them that they are going to listen to five short conversations about people in leadership roles.

Ask students to read the descriptions of the five conversations. They should listen to the whole recording, and make a mental note of any information they hear.

Play the recording once, without stopping. Ask students to discuss with a partner which pictures match recordings 1–5. Then play the recording again and ask students to write down their answers. Provide feedback to the class.

10.1 Listening script

1

Woman: Can you tell me about a moment in your current job when you've had to show leadership qualities?

Man: Well, err. Once I had to manage a team of five people on a project. It was a difficult project and so people often disagreed. I always thought it was important to listen and be patient, but in the end – when no-one could agree – I had to be decisive and make the final decision. I think being confident enough to make the decision is important in leadership.

2

In my talk, I'd like to compare what it is to be a manager and a leader. Let's begin by looking at managers. Traditionally, a manager makes systems run well. They are careful and organised. The classic idea of the leader, on the other hand, is someone who thinks more globally, takes risks and plans for the future. They also have to be creative and motivational. However, this division between managers and leader is an old view. Modern managers also have to lead …

3

Man: Hello, can I help you?

Woman: Yes, can I speak to the person in charge of customer services, please? It's about a problem with your latest delivery.

Man: I can help you with that.

Woman: Are you the manager?

Man: No, I'm afraid my manager is out of the office, but I can take a message or perhaps I can deal with it?

Woman: I really need to speak to the person in authority …

4

Takemura: How do you do? My name's Mr Takemura.

Jeff Kelly: Nice to meet you. My name's Jeff Kelly. I'm the owner of a small tech start-up. We specialise in video gaming.

Takemura: Ah, interesting. How long have you been here?

Jeff Kelly: Since it started. I've mainly been listening and understanding how things work here in this part of the world.

Takemura: I see. And are you presenting your products this week? Do you have a stand?

Jeff Kelly: No, I don't but I can show you some of our work now if you are interested.

Takemura: Certainly, please go ahead …

5

Woman: Hey, can you help me with something?

Man: Sure, what is it?

Woman: I'm filling in this application for a job. I've never done it before. They want me to write a personal statement and describe where I see myself in five years' time.

Man: So where do you see yourself?

Woman: I suppose I'd like to be running my own department.

Man: OK, so you could start with something like, er … 'I'm an ambitious and dynamic person who is good at motivating others.'

Woman: Good at motivating others? Doesn't that sound like I'm showing off?

Man: Well, if you want to lead people, you need to be authoritative but you also need to show …

Answers

1 E (a telephone call)
2 A (a presentation)
3 C (a job interview)
4 D (a trade fair meeting)
5 B (two friends at university)

2 🎧 10.1 Students listen to the recording again and answer the questions. Provide feedback to the class and ask students to justify any answers that are different from their own.

Answers

1 A (Because people in the team disagreed a lot of the time)
2 A (That they have different roles)
3 C (Because she doesn't think he can solve her problem)
4 B (Listening and trying to understand the market)
5 B (She doesn't want to sound overconfident.)

VOCABULARY

3 Ask students to suggest words or phrases that are associated with *leadership*. Ask the students what qualities are important for leaders and why. Ask students to match the right adjectives to their definitions.

Answers

1 I
2 B
3 C
4 J
5 G
6 D
7 E
8 F
9 A
10 H

4 Ask students to form groups of three. Each of them should think of a job, and decide which adjectives in exercise 3 are important for the job, and which are less important. Students should then discuss with one another to see if their opinions match. After the discussion, ask for volunteers to tell the class the job they chose, and explain why they think the three adjectives that they chose are the most important for it.

Describing people

VOCABULARY

5 Ask students to name some political, religious and business leaders. Write the names of these leaders on the board. Students work in pairs. Ask them to choose a leader, either one already mentioned, or another leader that they can think of. Tell them to describe the leader to their partner, using the words and phrases given, or using their own words. They can refer to the person by name. Allow students a few minutes to do this.

Extension

Ask for a volunteer to describe a leader, but without naming him/her. The other students should try to guess the person from the description.

6 Students match the three sentence patterns with the examples in exercise 5. They then write an example for each of the sentence patterns using the words from exercise 5, and read out their examples to the class.

Don't just manage, lead!

READING

7 Ask students to do the questionnaire on their own. When they've done it, they should add up their scores. Tell them to turn to page 147 to read the interpretation and ask them if they agree with it.

Then read the Learning Tip with students.

8 Ask students to write down important characteristics of leaders, then choose the three most important ones. Students then compare their choices with a partner and agree on the three most important characteristics. They then compare with another pair.

Finally, students write three sentences and swap their sentences with someone they haven't paired up with, and compare their decisions.

Photocopiable activity
See page 178.

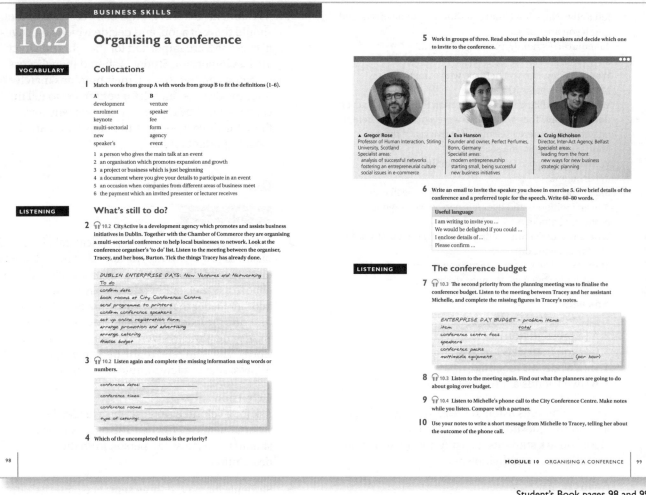

Collocations

VOCABULARY

I **Answers**

1 keynote speaker
2 development agency
3 new venture
4 enrolment form
5 multi-sectorial event
6 speaker's fee

What's still to do?

LISTENING

2 🎧 **10.2** Play the recording once without stopping.

10.2 Listening script

B = Burton   **T** = Tracey

B Tracey, can you bring me up-to-date on how the Dublin Enterprise conference is going?

T Yes, everything is going well and there are only a few things to be finalised. The theme, as you know, is starting up and networking for small businesses, and we are aiming it at local business people.

B So it's basically an opportunity for businesses to get together and see what they can offer each other.

T Yes, that's one way of looking at it. We're hoping that it will strengthen the connections between local entrepreneurs and help to create and develop new ventures.

B Have we confirmed the date as May the 4th?

T Yes, the dates are confirmed, but actually it's May the 3rd and 4th. It's a two-day event, running continuously from half past nine until half past five both days.

B And it's at the City Conference Centre again?

T Yes, everything is booked there. We've got the main room and four smaller rooms.

B Do we have a copy of the programme ready to go to print?

T Well, that's one of the things which I mentioned, which still needs to be finalised. All the workshop leaders are in place, but we have a slight problem with the keynote speaker. Our original speaker has cancelled and we are still in the process of choosing an alternative speaker.

B I wonder, do we really need a speaker at an event like this?

T I think we do. It provides a focus to the whole two days, and last year's talk was a huge success.

B So, that needs to be finalised as soon as possible, doesn't it?

T Yes, it's the first thing on my list for after this meeting, don't worry!

B OK, what else?

T Well, again sticking with things which worked well last year, we're doing online enrolment via the website, and the event is being promoted on our website and all our associate websites, as well as in the press.

B Are we repeating the lunch? We had that Michelin chef last time, didn't we?

130

T No, I think that was for the Marketing Week, wasn't it? We're using the Conference Centre facilities, and providing hot and cold snacks all through the day.
B Well, it sounds as if it's all under control. Shall we leave it there for now?
T Actually, there was one last point. We're having some problems with the budget. The Conference Centre fee has gone up quite a lot since last year and that means we're having to try and make cuts in other areas. I'll have to ask Michelle to look at the figures again …

Answers
Tick the following: confirm date, book rooms, set up online registration form, arrange promotion and advertising, arrange catering

3 🎧 **10.2** Students complete the information.

Answers
3rd–4th May; 9.30am–5.30pm; five rooms; hot and cold snacks

4 **Answer**
Priority: choose keynote speaker

5 Students should think about the theme of the conference when deciding.

6 **Sample answer**

> Dear Ms Hanson
>
> I am writing to invite you to speak at a conference in Dublin on 3rd–4th May. The theme is *Starting up and networking for small businesses*, and the target is local business people.
>
> We would be delighted if you could give the keynote speech on the 3rd. Please confirm that you are available for this event. I enclose details of the other events at the conference.
>
> Yours sincerely

The conference budget

LISTENING

7 🎧 **10.3** Students listen and complete the notes.

10.3 Listening script
M = Michelle   **T** = Tracey

M I still think we're going to be over budget.
T Let's see where the main problems are … It's the Conference Centre fees that are the problem. The main conference room is €300 a day, so that's €600 for the two days. Extra rooms – they're €140 each. We've got four extra rooms, haven't we, so that's eight times €140, which is … €1,120.
M Giving a total of €1,720.
T This seems much more expensive than last year. Have you got last year's figures with you?
M No, but I remember that we only paid them about €1,500 last time. Do you want me to get in touch with them again?
T Good idea! Let's look at the other problem items. The speaker … €2,000 seems a lot! Who's coming?

M I think Eva Hanson has accepted. We had to find someone at the last minute because the original speaker dropped out.
T Oh, I saw her speak last month in Copenhagen. She's very good, actually.
M She's only staying for one night, so that keeps the hotel bill down a bit.
T OK. How did you calculate the cost of the conference packs?
M Well, last year, we had 300 participants. So I calculated for 350 this year. 350 times 2.5 is 875.
T It's quite a lot, isn't it? Can't we get that figure down a bit?
M I doubt it. We've already got a fairly big discount from the printers.
T Then, yes, that sounds fine. What's this cost for the multimedia equipment … €20 per hour?
M Yeah, I checked that with the Centre. All of the rooms have got standard equipment – computer, video beamer, microphones and sound system. And this is all included in the price of the rooms. But if we want an Internet connection, it will cost €20 per hour.
T I think we can do without the Internet. What do you think?
M I'll have to check and get back to you.
T Yes, do that. It's not a large sum, but we need to get these totals down somehow.
M As you said, it's the Conference Centre fees that have pushed us over budget.
T Yes, give them a ring and let me know what they say to you, OK?

Answers
centre fees €1,720; speakers €2,000; packs €875; equipment €20 per hour

8 🎧 **10.3** Students listen again and answer the question.

Answer
Enquire about a reduction in conference centre fees, and if Internet is needed.

9 🎧 **10.4** Students listen and take notes.

10.4 Listening script
B = Bill   **M** = Michelle

B Bill Duffy, City Conference Centre.
M Bill, hi. It's Michelle here from CityActive.
B Hello! How are you? Nice to talk to you again. What can I do for you?
M Look, I wonder if I could check the quote you gave us for our Enterprise Days conference? It seems a lot higher than last year.
B What did we quote you?
M 300 for the main room and 140 for each additional room.
B Just a minute … Oh, I'm sorry! You've been quoted the commercial rates instead of the preferential rates. The preferential rates are only three per cent up on last year's.
M Well, that's good news. Can you email them to me?
B No problem. I'll send them right now. Sorry once again about that.
M Oh, these things happen. Thanks. And see you in a couple of weeks at the conference?
B Yes, I'll be around. Bye.

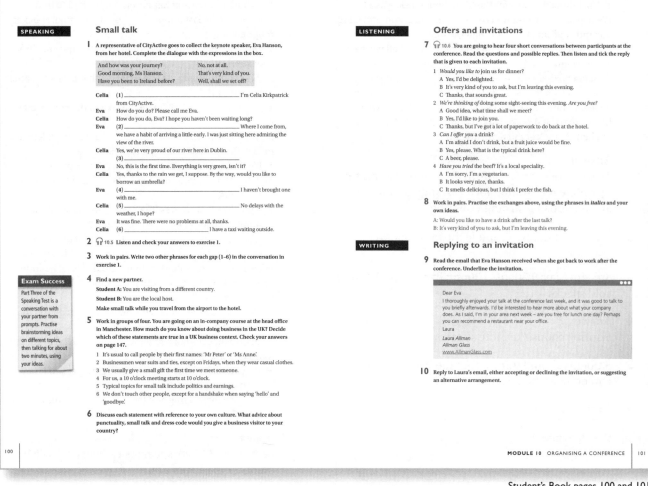

Student's Book pages 100 and 101

Small talk

SPEAKING

1 Tell students to read the phrases in the box. Then ask them to write the phrases in the correct places in the dialogue. Don't check answers at this stage as this will be done in exercise 2.

2 🎧 **10.5** Play the recording once, without stopping. Students listen and check their answers in exercise 1. The answers are underlined in the script.

10.5 Listening script
C = Celia   E = Eva

C Good morning, Ms Hanson. I'm Celia Kirkpatrick from CityActive.

E How do you do? Please call me Eva.

C How do you do, Eva. I hope you haven't been waiting long?

E No, not at all. Where I come from, we have a habit of arriving a little early. I was just sitting here admiring the view of the river.

C Yes, we're very proud of our river here in Dublin. Have you been to Ireland before?

E No, this is the first time. Everything is very green, isn't it?

C Yes, thanks to the rain we get, I suppose. By the way, would you like to borrow an umbrella?

E That's very kind of you. I haven't brought one with me.

C And how was your journey? No delays with the weather, I hope?

E It was fine. There were no problems at all, thanks.

C Well, shall we set off? I have a taxi waiting outside.

Extension
When they've finished, ask them to practise the dialogue with a partner.

3 Students work in pairs. For each space in the conversation, they should write two other phrases.

Possible answers
1 Hello, Ms Hanson. / Hello, is that Ms Hanson?
2 No, not long. / No, I haven't. Don't worry.
3 Have you visited Dublin before? / Have you ever been to Dublin before?
4 Yes, thank you. / Yes, please.
5 Did you have a good journey? / How was the flight / journey?
6 Let's go. / If you're ready, we can go. / Shall we set off?

4 Students change partners. They practise small talk, using the phrases from exercise 3.

132

5 Students form groups of four. Ask them to decide which of the statements are true. Then tell them to turn to page 147 to check their answers.

Answers
1 False
2 False
3 False
4 True
5 False
6 True

6 Allow five minutes for students to talk about what is normal behaviour in their culture/s.

Offers and invitations

LISTENING

7 🎧 10.6 Ask students to read the questions. Then play the recording once, without stopping. Students tick the reply that they hear for each invitation.

10.6 Listening script
1
M = Male   **F** = Female
M1 Well, it's been a really productive day, hasn't it?
M2 Yes, it has. I've made some very promising contacts.
M1 Would you like to join us for dinner?
M2 Yes, I'd be delighted.
M1 Great. I'll see you in the hotel reception at about 8 o'clock then.
2
F1 Have you been to Dublin before?
F2 Yes, I was here a couple of years ago, actually.
F1 We're thinking of doing some sight-seeing this evening. Are you free?
F2 Thanks, but I've got a lot of paperwork to do back at the hotel.
F1 Oh, I know what you mean. I'm hoping to do some work on the plane home tomorrow.
3
M Please, take a seat and make yourself comfortable.
F Thanks.
M Can I offer you a drink?
F A beer, please.
M OK, a nice cold beer coming up.
4
M I'm not sure what to order. There's a great selection.
F Have you tried the beef? It's a local speciality.
M I'm sorry, I'm a vegetarian.
F Oh, I had no idea. Well, they do some excellent vegetarian dishes here.

Answers
1 A   2 C   3 C   4 A

8 Ask students to invent their own exchanges, using the phrases in italics.

Replying to an invitation

WRITING

9 Ask students to read the email from Laura Allman and underline the invitation.

Answer
… are you free for lunch one day?

10 Ask students to reply to Laura's email, choosing whether to accept or decline the invitation. If they choose to decline it, encourage them to suggest an alternative arrangement.

Sample answer

> Dear Laura
>
> Thank you for your email. I am free on Wednesday and I would be delighted to have lunch with you then. There's a nice French restaurant just around the corner. If you like, we can go there.
>
> Eva

Photocopiable activity
See page 179.

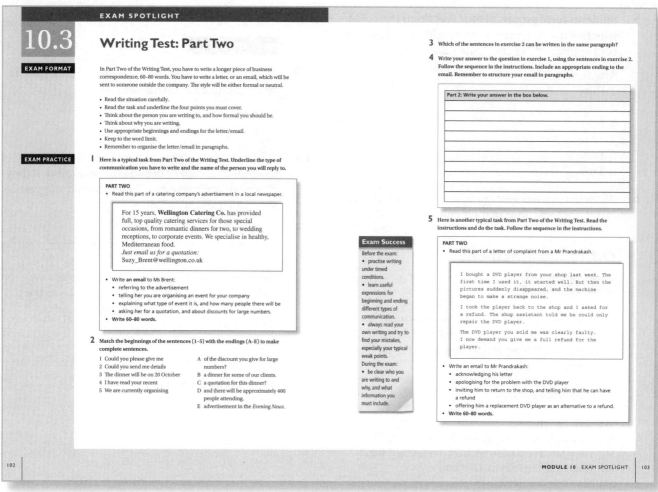

Student's Book pages 102 and 103

Writing Test: Part Two

EXAM FORMAT

Read the opening description of this part of the exam with the students.

Extension

Write the numbers 1–7 vertically down the left-hand side of the board. Ask students to take a piece of paper and copy the numbers. Beside each number, they should write one key word that helps them to remember the instruction in the Exam Format notes.

Then ask them to close their books, and only look at the seven words on their sheet of paper. In pairs, they should take turns to explain the seven instructions.

Ask students which words they wrote beside the numbers. Choose one word for each instruction, then ask a few students to explain the instructions to the whole class.

EXAM PRACTICE

1 Ask students to read the task and follow the instructions.

Answers
an email, Ms Brent.

2 Students match the phrases. Then ask them to check their answers with a partner.

Answers
1 C 2 A 3 D 4 E 5 B

3 Ask students to look back at exercise 2 and find sentences which you could write in the same paragraph.

Answers
Sentence 1 and sentence 2.
Sentence 5 and sentence 3.

4 Ask students to write the email using the sentences from exercise 2.

Sample answer

> Dear Ms Brent
>
> I have read your recent advertisement in the *Evening News*.
>
> We are currently organising a dinner for some of our clients. The dinner will be on 20 October, and there will be approximately 400 people attending.
>
> Could you please give me a quotation for this dinner? Could you send me details of the discount you give for large numbers?
>
> Yours sincerely
> David Loader

5 Read the Exam Success tip with students.

Ask students to read the task, and to write the email. (This could be set for homework.)

Students do this task individually, as if they were taking the exam. Ask them to time themselves, ie, the time they take to read the text and answer the questions. Tell students to write the starting and finishing time at the top of the page and keep a record of how long they take to do each exercise. By the end of the book, they'll have an idea of how to manage their time when they do the Reading and Writing parts.

When students have finished, ask them to swap their emails with a partner, who should correct it and suggest any improvements. Allow time for students to make changes, then choose students to read out their emails.

Sample answer

> Dear Mr Prandrakash
>
> Thank you for your letter about the DVD player you bought from our shop.
>
> I am very sorry that it does not work properly, and we will of course be pleased to give you a full refund for the machine if you bring it back to the shop.
>
> Alternatively, we can replace the player with another of the same model.
>
> Yours sincerely
> Maureen Price

Overview

11.1   Business topic: Health and safety

VOCABULARY	**Signs**
LISTENING	**A factory tour**
GRAMMAR	**Modal verbs:** *must(n't)* **and** *(don't) have to*
READING	**Why is it dangerous?**
VOCABULARY	**In your break**
VOCABULARY	*go, play* **and** *do*

11.2   Business skills: Reporting accidents

GRAMMAR	**The past simple and past continuous**
LISTENING	**After the accident**
READING	**Theme park safety**
SPEAKING	**Safety suggestions**
WRITING	**Information leaflet**

11.3   Exam spotlight: Listening Test Part Four

Predicting the content of an interview

Listening for synonyms

Useful language from Module 11

Wordlist

accounts	facial bruising	listen for	spill
amusement park	fall off	locker room	splint
assembly point	fall over	lose one's balance	stool
baby grand piano	fire alarm	lump	theme park
bandage	fire drill	minor injuries	throughout
be hospitalised	fire exit	movable barrier	thumb
bend one's knees	fire extinguisher	nationwide	toothache
big toe	first aid	obstacle	trip over a wire
bruise (n + v)	get the sack	on offer	twist one's ankle
by mistake	go on rides	plaster	university campus
canteen	hallways	pool table	warehouse
cement factory	hard hat	procedure	waste material
choke	hazard	protective mask	water consumption
clock in	health and safety	recreational	wear protective
clot	heat exhaustion	amenities	clothing
crutches	high voltage	reduce the risk	weights machine
dehydration	high-heel shoes	rowing machine	wrist
do some exercise	injury	safety inspection	
drop sth	invoice	safety officer	
DVT (deep vein	laboratory	sign in / out	
thrombosis)	lava	solid waste	

Expressions

be over a certain height
dried fruits and nuts
ensure the safety of sb
for safety reasons
get an electric shock
in case of fire
the knife slipped
wear a white coat in the lab

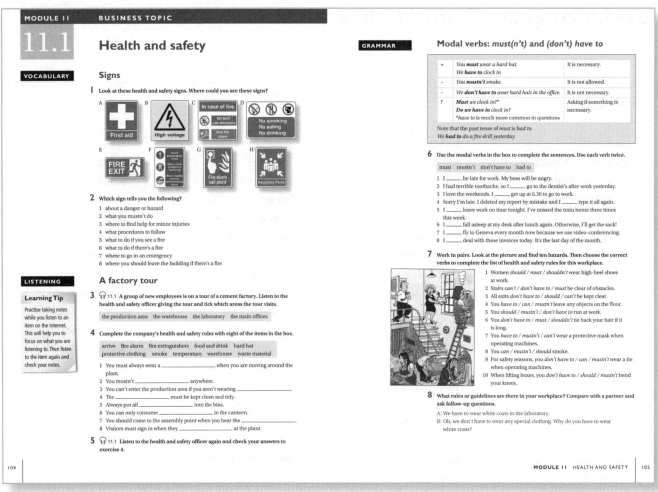

Signs

VOCABULARY

1 Ask students to look at the health and safety signs. Ask them if they are familiar with any of these. Also ask them if any of these signs are present either in the building where they are now or in their workplace. Discuss where you might see them.

2 Students work in pairs and do exercise 2.

Answers
1 B   2 D   3 A   4 F   5 G   6 C   7 H   8 E

Draw students' attention to the Learning Tip. You may want to add that downloading podcasts from the Internet is easy and a lot of programmes are free. Students can create a listening bank by saving the files and listening to them whenever they want so that they can practise note taking.

A factory tour

LISTENING

3 🎧 11.1 Ask students to look at the title. Elicit the names of the different areas or departments that you can find in factories, eg: *loading bay, warehouse, production floor, reception, administration, offices, canteen, showroom,* etc. Write any new words on the board and check that students know what *cement* is.

Play the recording. Students tick the words in the box as they listen.

11.1 Listening script

Good morning, everyone. I'm Alistair Patterson, and I'm responsible for health and safety here at the plant. Before we start the tour of the plant, please put on your jackets and the hard hats. Remember that you must always wear a hard hat when you are moving around the plant. OK, good. Is everyone ready? I'll take you around the main production lines first. Then we'll visit the warehouse, and we'll finish the tour back here in the main office building …

Now, obviously, you mustn't smoke in the production area – in fact, there is no smoking allowed anywhere. Until last year, we had a special smoking area outside the office building, but now the whole plant is a no-smoking zone. As you can see, the main hazard here is the machinery. That's why you should always wear protective clothing. In fact, you can't enter this area if you aren't wearing jackets and hard hats ...

Well, here we are in the warehouse. There are a lot of fire hazards in the warehouse, and so this area must be kept clean and tidy at all times. If you're working here, always put all waste material into the bins. There are fire extinguishers on the walls, and the fire exit is on the left. Can you see it? It's quite clearly marked. Please remember, we don't allow any food or drink in the warehouse area. You can only eat or drink in the canteen ...

Now just before we go back into the main office building, can you see the sign on the wall here? This is the main assembly point, where you should come if there is an emergency – a fire, for example. We do regular fire drills, and you should come here to this assembly point when you hear the fire alarm. This is the way we check that all employees and visitors are safe. That's why visitors must always sign in when they arrive at the plant, and sign out when they leave. We have to know who is on site at all times. Now, are there any questions ...

Answers
the production area
the warehouse
the main offices

4 Students work alone to do this task. Don't check answers at this stage as this will be done in exercise 5.

5 🎧 11.1 Students listen and check their answers in exercise 4.

Answers
1 hard hat
2 smoke
3 protective clothing
4 warehouse
5 waste material
6 food and drink
7 fire alarm
8 arrive

Extension
Ask students which of the ten options in the box they left out (*fire extinguishers, temperature*).

Modal verbs: *must(n't)* and *(don't) have to*

GRAMMAR

6 Go through the information about *must(n't)* and *(don't) have to*. Point out the meanings of *must* and *have to* in the phrases in the right-hand column.

Students work alone to do the exercise and then check their answers with a partner.

Answers
1 mustn't
2 had to
3 don't have to
4 had to
5 must
6 mustn't
7 don't have to
8 must

7 Ask students to describe the cartoon. Elicit actions that must(n't) / (don't) have to be done in this workplace, and also elicit the names of the objects. Then students work in pairs and do exercise 7.

Answers
 1 shouldn't
 2 must
 3 should
 4 mustn't
 5 mustn't
 6 must
 7 have to
 8 mustn't
 9 mustn't
10 should

Extension
Tell students to read the sentences again and decide whether the rules are part of health and safety or are common sense. Have a class discussion. In some cases, the sentences are both:
Health and safety rules: 1, 2, 3, 4, 6, 7, 8, 9
Common sense: 1, 5, 10

8 Ask two students to read the dialogue. Elicit suggestions about why someone might have to wear a white coat. Ask students what rules or guidelines there are in their workplaces or educational establishments. Tell them to discuss and compare the rules with a partner.

Photocopiable activity
See page 180.

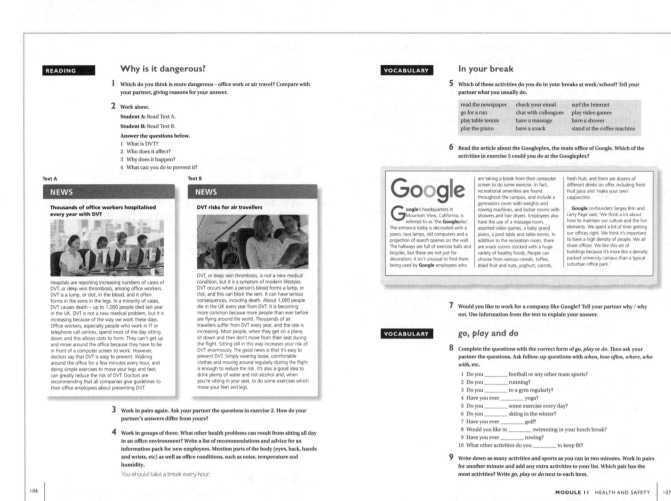

Why is it dangerous?

READING

1 Write on the board *office work* and *air travel* and ask students which they think is more dangerous and why. Elicit students' ideas. Write relevant key words under each heading.

2 Put students into pairs. Tell them to read their texts and find the answers to the questions.

3 In their pairs, students ask each other the questions and listen to their partner's answers. Then discuss the answers with the whole class.

Answers

1 DVT stands for deep vein thrombosis. It's a clot or a lump that can form in the veins in the legs when you sit in one place for a long time.
2 It affects office workers, people who work in IT, in telephone call centres and air travellers.
3 It happens when you sit in one place for a long time.
4 To prevent DVT, you can walk around the office or the aeroplane for a few minutes every hour, do simple exercises to move your legs and feet while you are sitting in your seat, and wear loose, comfortable clothes. Drinking plenty of water and no alcohol is also very important.

4 Brainstorm with students what other health problems can result from sitting all day in an office environment, eg: *bad blood circulation, headaches, stiff neck, aching wrists, backache, stress, sore throat, eye ache,* etc.

Then students work in small groups and write a list of recommendations.

Possible answers

Drink plenty of water.

If you spend hours in front of the computer, look away from time to time and focus on something in the distance.

Take a break every hour and do some relaxation exercises.

Extension

Ask students to carry out some research on health and safety rules in the office.

In your break

VOCABULARY

5 Students work in pairs and do exercise 5. Ask students to list any other activities they do in their breaks at work, or when they study at home.

6 Ask students to read the article and underline all the activities that Google™ employees can do during their breaks. Then they can tick the activities listed in exercise 5.

Answer
You could do all of the activities listed in exercise 5, except reading the newspaper, checking your emails and surfing the Internet. Remember you're having a real break!

7 Students work in pairs or in small groups and discuss the question in exercise 7. Ask the students if they know of another company that has the same philosophy as Google.

go, play and do

VOCABULARY

8 Ask students to think of some collocations for *go, play* and *do*. Elicit students' answers orally.

Then students work alone to do exercise 8.

After checking answers, tell students to interview each other.

Answers
1 play
2 go
3 go
4 done
5 do
6 go
7 played
8 go
9 been
10 do

9 Tell students to take a sheet of paper and divide it into three columns. Each column has one heading: *GO, PLAY, DO*. Ask students to write as many expressions as they can in two minutes. One rule is that they can't use the expressions already used in exercise 8. When they've finished, ask students to work in pairs for another minute and add any other expressions they hadn't written before.

Possible answers

GO	PLAY	DO
cycling	basketball	aerobics
dancing	cards	karate
fishing	chess	meditation
horse-riding	cricket	sport
sailing	tennis	the gardening
canoeing	volleyball	judo

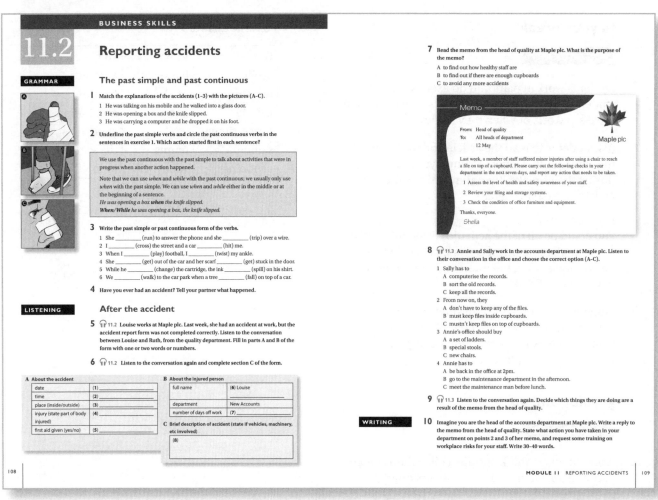

Student's Book pages 108 and 109

The past simple and past continuous

GRAMMAR

1 Ask students to look at the three pictures and to match them with the three sentences.

Answers
1 C   2 A   3 B

2 Students do the activity and answer the question.

Answers
1 He (was talking) on his mobile and he <u>walked</u> into a glass door.
2 He (was opening) a box and the knife <u>slipped</u>.
3 He (was carrying) a computer and he <u>dropped</u> it on his foot.

The action in the past continuous started first.

Extension
Ask students to read the information about the past continuous and past simple. Then ask students to rephrase sentences 1 and 3 in exercise 1. Point out the use of the comma in sentences starting with *While / When*.

1 When / While he was talking on his mobile, he walked into a glass door.

3 When / While he was carrying a computer, he dropped it on his foot.

3 Students work alone to do the exercise.

Answers
1 was running, tripped
2 was crossing, hit
3 was playing, twisted
4 was getting, got
5 was changing, spilled / spilt
6 were walking, fell

4 Students work in pairs and tell their partner about any accident they have had.

Photocopiable activity
See page 181.

After the accident

LISTENING

5 🎧 **11.2** Read through the instructions with students. As you play the recording for the first time, students fill in parts A and B.

11.2 Listening script

R = Ruth L = Louise

R Hi, Louise. Have you got a few minutes? It's about the accident you had the other day.

L Yes, I'm not too busy at the moment. What do you need to know?

R You said that there were some mistakes in the copy of the accident report that you got. Can I check it with you?

L OK, fine. It was only a couple of things.

R Yes, but I think we should just check everything. It was on Tuesday, wasn't it? That was May the 5th.

L Yes, that's right, Tuesday the 5th.

R And it says here that it happened at 3 o'clock. Is that right?

L No, it isn't. It was just before lunch, so it was about 1 o'clock.

R OK, let's change that from 3 o'clock to 1 o'clock. And you fell over here in the office?

L I was right here at my desk. I was standing on that chair to get a file from on top of the cupboard.

R Really? And what happened? Did you lose your balance?

L Yes, I was trying to reach the file, and I lost my balance and fell off the chair. And the file fell off the cupboard and hit me on the head!

R Did you hurt yourself badly?

L No, I was really lucky – it was just a small cut on my head, nothing serious.

R And Jane gave you first aid?

L Yes, Jane gave me first aid, and then I went home. I took the afternoon off.

R OK. Now, is this the correct spelling of your surname, R–A–L–P–H?

L No, it's R–E–L–P–H.

R OK, let me change that as well. R–E–L–P–H. And you're the accounts assistant, aren't you?

L Yes, but it's new accounts, actually. We're a separate section.

R Oh yes, that's right. So, you were off work for the afternoon and ...?

L Yes, just the afternoon. I came back the next day. That was yesterday morning. I'm fine.

R Aha ... Now, last section ... description of the accident. It says here 'the employee was standing on a chair to reach files which are kept on top of a cupboard. She was hit by a file which fell off the cupboard.' That's all correct, isn't it?

L Yes.

R Did you hurt yourself anywhere else, apart from your head?

L No.

R OK. Thanks for your time, Louise. Can you sign there to show that ...

6 🎧 11.2 Students listen again and fill in part C.

Answers

1 Tuesday 5 May
2 1pm
3 inside / office
4 head
5 yes
6 Relph
7 half
8 The employee was standing on a chair to reach files which are kept on top of a cupboard. She was hit by a file which fell off the cupboard.

7 Ask one student to read the memo out loud.

Answer
C

8 🎧 11.3 Play the recording once for students to choose the correct option.

11.3 Listening script

A = Annie S = Sally

A Sally, are you coming for lunch?

S Hi, Annie. Yes, but I just have to put these files away first.

A What are you doing?

S I have to sort all these old records and files, and decide which ones we should keep and which ones we can throw away.

A Wow, that's going to take you ages!

S I know. Plus, I've only done a few and I'm bored already.

A But why are you doing it? Whose idea was that?

S Oh, Mike says there isn't enough space to keep everything. He got a memo from the quality department. From now on, we mustn't keep files up on the top of cupboards like this.

A Oh, that's because Louise fell off a chair last week, isn't it? The man from maintenance came to check our office yesterday. He said we should buy those special stools to stand on when we can't reach things that are too high.

S Oh, yes, I know the stools you mean. We've got one somewhere, I think. Oh, I think I'll leave this for after lunch. Let's go.

A Come on then, I haven't got much time. I have to be back at two to meet the maintenance man again. He's going to fix some broken lights, or something ...

Answers
1 B   2 C   3 B   4 A

9 🎧 11.3 Play the recording again.

Possible answers

They are reviewing the filing and storage systems.

They are checking the conditions of office furniture and equipment.

They mustn't keep files on the top of cupboards.

10 Students write a reply to the memo in exercise 7. This can be set for homework.

Sample answer

> Dear Sheila
>
> This week, we started to review our filing system and we checked all office equipment. There are a few problems that maintenance can solve easily.
>
> However, I think my department needs some training on health and safety.
>
> Mike

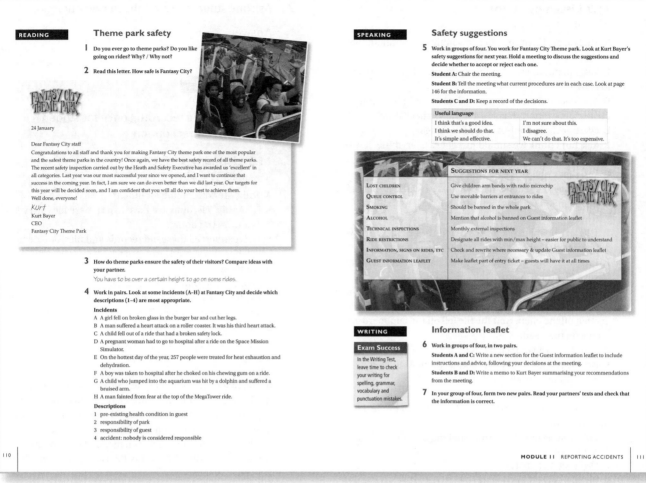

Theme park safety

READING

1 Ask students to think about theme parks. Ask them to name some famous ones, known internationally (eg: Disneyland™, Disneyworld™, Universal Studios™, Legoland™), or well known in the students' countries. Then ask the questions in exercise 1.

2 Ask one student to read the letter out loud to the class. Elicit students' answers on how safe Fantasy City is.

Answer
Fantasy City is the safest theme park in the country. It has been awarded excellent marks in all categories.

3 Students brainstorm ideas for exercise 3. For more ideas visit: www.saferparks.org

Possible answers
You have to dress sensibly.

You have to be over a certain age to go on some rides.

You have to read the safety signs.

You have to identify the ride operators in case of an emergency.

You have to double check that safety belts and safety equipment are safely adjusted.

Don't go on rides you are afraid of.

If you have any health problems, such as asthma or epilepsy, always go on gentler rides and always stay with a person you know and trust.

4 Students work in pairs and do exercise 4. Allow students plenty of time to discuss which descriptions are most appropriate.

Possible answers
A 2
B 1
C 2
D 3
E 4
F 3
G 3
H 4

Safety suggestions

SPEAKING

5 Students work in groups of four. They read the situation and instructions and hold a meeting to discuss the suggestions. This discussion activity is similar to Speaking Test Part Three, where students have to discuss a situation, using a prompt sheet, and reach a decision.

Point out the Useful language for students to use in their discussion. These are general phrases for agreeing and disagreeing, and students should practise using these in preparation for Speaking Test Part Three.

Information leaflet

WRITING

6 Students remain in their groups from exercise 5, and produce a piece of written work based on their discussion and the decisions they agreed at the meeting.

Students A and C write instructions and advice to be included in the *Guest information leaflet*. They can refer to the information on page 146 of the Student's Book.

Students B and D write a memo summarising the recommendations from the meeting.

7 Students swap partners, still in their groups of four, and check the information produced by the other pair.

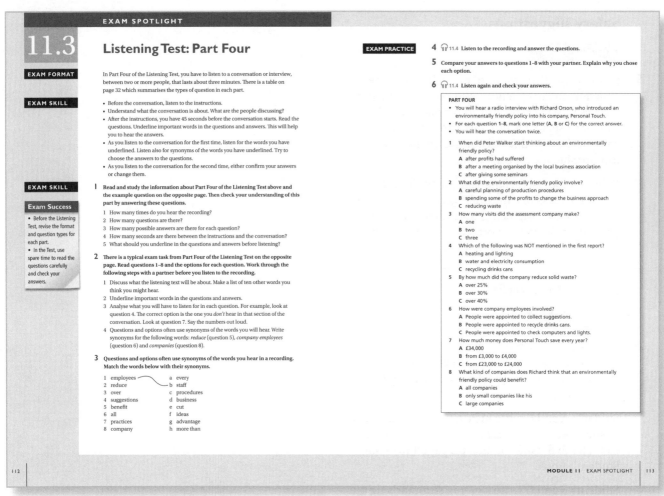

Student's Book pages 112 and 113

Listening Test: Part Four

EXAM FORMAT

Read the opening description of this part of the exam with the students.

Extension
Ask them to circle relevant key words as you read through, eg: *two or more people, three minutes, 45 seconds before conversation starts, synonyms.*

EXAM SKILL

1   Ask students to read the information about Part Four of the Listening Test. There is a sample question on the opposite page that students should refer to. Ask students to check details of the Part Four Listening Test against the sample question. After that, ask for volunteers to answer the questions.

Answers
1 Twice
2 Eight
3 One
4 45 seconds
5 Important words

2   Ask students to form pairs. Ask them to read the introduction to the Listening Test before creating a list of ten words that they expect to hear.

Then ask them to underline any words in the questions and answers that they should listen out for. Ask them to discuss what they think each question requires them to do.

Pairs should then work together to think of words or phrases that could mean *reduce, company employees* and *companies.* Go through the answers as a class. Some possible answers are written below.

reduce: *become smaller, shrink, lessen*

company employees: *staff, workers*

companies: *businesses, corporations, organisations*

3   Students should work individually to search for synonyms for each word.

Answers
2 e   3 h   4 f   5 g   6 a   7 c   8 d

4   🎧 11.4 Play the recording for the exam task twice, as in the exam. Students answer the eight questions in the task on page 113. Don't check answers at this stage as this will be done in exercise 5.

11.4 Listening script

I = Interviewer   R = Richard

I I'm talking today to Richard Orson, who introduced an environmentally friendly policy into his company, Personal Touch, which makes objects for the home. Welcome, Richard.

R Hello.

I Tell me, have you always promoted environmentally friendly business practices?

R No, quite the opposite. I used to be convinced that it was bad for business. I thought that you couldn't be environmentally friendly and maintain profits at the same time.

I So what changed your mind?

R Who, actually. It was my production manager, Peter Walker. He went to a meeting organised by our local business association. At the meeting, Peter heard about how cutting waste would benefit the environment, and it would also reduce costs. Well, afterwards, Peter started thinking more about the environment. And he attended some free seminars, where he learnt how to prepare an environmentally friendly policy.

I What did you think about this?

R I didn't know very much about it. It was only when he had produced his policy that he showed it to me. But his arguments were convincing, and I had to listen to what he was saying.

I And what was he saying?

R That we could save money by cutting the amount of waste we produced.

I Well, it sounds easy in theory, but how did you decide where to cut waste?

R We brought in a company to assess our work procedures. That was in 2015. Then we asked them back in 2016 and again in 2017. The first report the company produced explained how we could reduce water consumption, use paper more carefully and cut photocopying, electricity and heating costs. We followed their suggestions, and in the first year, we were able to cut our energy bills by 17 per cent.

I That is a lot.

R Yes, but the biggest difference was in the amount of solid waste. We used to produce over 40 tonnes a year, and this has fallen to less than 30 tonnes.

I So you've made a cut of more than 25 per cent.

R That's right. Of course, the only way to achieve these reductions was to get the whole staff involved. We had some meetings early on with everyone to tell them what we intended to do. We appointed people, one person for each office, to check that the lights and PCs were switched off at the end of the day. We started a scheme to encourage staff to suggest new ways of reducing waste. And we provided bins for drinks cans to be recycled. This doesn't save us any money, but it does make staff more aware of environmental issues. Twice a year, we email all staff an update on what we have achieved, and we remind them of our targets for cutting waste. And finally, each department is monitored to see where cost savings can be made.

I And how much do you think you save in money terms?

R We save between three and four thousand pounds a year.

I That's not bad for a small company like yours.

R Exactly. And you know what? Every company could do what we've done, and make similar, or even greater savings. It just makes good business sense.

I Yes, I can see that. Well, thank you, Richard.

5 Students work in pairs and compare answers. They have to explain why they chose each option.

Answers
1 B   2 C   3 C   4 C   5 A   6 C   7 B   8 A

6 Play the recording again for the students to listen and check their answers.

Extension

After checking the answers, play the recording again and ask students to write the exact words that were used in the recording next to each correct answer. Alternatively, they can find the exact words used by reading the script on page 161 of the Student's Book.

Overview

12.1   Business topic: The job market

LISTENING   **Job satisfaction**

GRAMMAR   **The second conditional**

SPEAKING   **Working abroad**

READING   **Relocation**

VOCABULARY   **Getting a job**

SPEAKING   **Problems at work**

12.2   Business skills: Job applications

READING   **An advertisement**

WRITING   **A covering letter**

LISTENING   **A job interview**

WRITING   **Interview follow-up**

12.3   Exam spotlight: Reading Test Parts Six and Seven

Cloze practice

Predicting words

Extracting information from written tests

Useful language from Module 12

Wordlist

accompany	department	job-related skills	recruitment
accounts clerk	desirable	knowledgeable	register
adapt	destination	language	represent
advertisement	determined	legible	restrictions
application form	editor	lottery	rumours
approval	enclosure	maintain	salary
aspect	excellent	media	satisfaction
attachment	expand	medical	self-motivated
attentive	expensive	merge	skilled
attitude	exploitation	migrant	somewhere
beach	export contract	multiple-choice	sponsor
benefit	exposure	newspaper	survey
contraction	financial services	noisy	tourism
co-ordinator	flexitime	parent company	traffic
covering letter	generous	post (job / position)	uniqueness
cruise ship	global marketplace	PR co-ordinator	unlikely
current	graduate	predict	vacancy
CV (curriculum vitae)	health care	product launch	visa
degree (qualification)	identity	prospects	weak
	imaginary	public relations	well-organised
	integrate	qualifications	well-qualified
dental	interpreter	qualities	

Expressions

attention to detail
do the lottery
fulfil a contract
holiday packages and services
How does your experience match this position?
medical and dental care
on a good salary
pay and conditions
Please do not hesitate to ...
relocate a department to (place)
salary and benefits package
She's on a good salary.
This is an equal opportunity advertisement.
working under pressure

12.1 The job market

LISTENING

Job satisfaction

1 Work in pairs. Tell your partner what you like about your current job/position. Is there anything you don't like about it? What would you like to change?

2 🎧 12.1 Listen to an interviewer asking five people about job satisfaction. What do the people talk about? Write the interview number next to the topic.

salary	work colleagues	working from home
holidays	flexible hours	overtime
promotion	unemployment	responsibility at work

3 🎧 12.1 Listen to interviews 1–4 again. For each person, complete the notes using one or two words.

Reason for the change
Person 1   to save _____ and _____
Person 2   to have more time with _____
Person 3   to _____ for her hotel room
Person 4   to use his _____

4 Work in pairs. What other benefits are there from the changes the people would like to make? Think of two benefits for each person. Then compare your ideas with a new partner.

GRAMMAR

The second conditional

5 Read the sentences and underline the *if*-clauses. Then answer the questions below.

1 I would keep in touch by email if I didn't go to the office every day.
2 If I worked flexitime, I would come to work earlier.
3 If I could go on holiday in June, the beaches wouldn't be so full of noisy children.

A Which form of the verb is used in the *if*-clause?
B Do the sentences refer to events in the past or to imaginary/unlikely situations?
C Does a second conditional sentence always begin with *if*?
D Which sentences have a comma?

6 Match the beginnings of the sentences (1–6) with the endings (A–F) to make complete sentences.

1 If I took my holidays in September,   A if I worked at home.
2 If I worked flexitime,   B the beaches would be empty.
3 I would save money on petrol   C I would avoid the traffic.
4 If I earned more money,   D I wouldn't do the lottery every week.
5 I would make big changes   E I would be very unhappy.
6 If my work colleagues left the   F if my boss gave me more responsibility.
  department,

7 Complete these sentences using the correct form of the verb.

1 I'd really like that job. If I _____ (have) more experience, I _____ (apply) for it.
2 I've never been to China. If I _____ (can) speak Chinese, I _____ (look) for a job there.
3 He _____ (stay) until the end of the meeting if he _____ (not / have) a flight at 6pm this evening.
4 It's going to be difficult to get a visa. It _____ (be) easier if you _____ (have) a sponsor.
5 She's on a good salary here. She _____ (change) jobs if she _____ (want) more money.
6 An interpreter will be very expensive. If they _____ (speak) Russian, they _____ (not / need) one.

8 Put the verbs in the correct form and answer the questions for yourself. Then ask your partner.

1 What you / change about your current job? _____
2 If you / not work in this company, where you / work? _____
_____
3 If you / can, / you / work from home? _____
4 What / be the advantages of working from home? _____
_____
5 If you / can have any job, what it / be? _____
6 If you / lose your job, what you / do? _____

9 If you were the managing director of the company where you work, what would you do? Compare your ideas with two other students.

Student's Book pages 114 and 115

Job satisfaction

LISTENING

1 Draw students' attention to the photo. Ask them what they think is happening (people are being interviewed in the street). Students work in pairs to discuss what types of interviews are carried out in the streets (market research, news interviews).

Tell students that the interview in the photo is about job satisfaction. Ask students, in their pairs, to write down some questions that the interviewer might ask, eg: *What do you do? How long have you been a …? Do you work part-time / full-time? Do you like your job?* Students then interview each other using the questions in exercise 1 and the additional questions they have written down.

2 🎧 12.1 Ask students to look at the items in the box. Then play the recording once, without stopping. Students note what the people talk about. Then ask them to identify the phrases that helped them with the answer.

12.1 Listening script
I = Interviewer   M = Male   F = Female

1
I Excuse me. I'm asking people about their jobs. Would you change anything if you could?
F Oh yes, I'd like to work from home. I could quite easily do my job from home, without going to the office. I would save time and money if I didn't go to the office every day. And I could keep in touch with the office by email or by phone. Of course, I'd have to go to the office occasionally, maybe once a week, or once a fortnight, but that wouldn't be so bad.

2
I Hello, I'm interviewing people about job satisfaction. Are you happy in your job?
M Yes, I am, most of the time.
I If you could change one aspect of your job, what would it be?
M I suppose I'd like to change the hours that I work. I'd prefer to work flexitime. The office hours are from 9am to 5pm, but at these times, the traffic is terrible. It takes me over an hour to get to work in the morning. If I could, I'd come to work earlier, around 7.30, and leave earlier, around 3.30, maybe. I would have more time with my children if I left work earlier.

3
I Hello. I'm interviewing people about job satisfaction. If you could change one thing in your job, what would it be?

F Only one thing? Well, I'm quite happy with everything ... except for the holidays. In my company, everyone has to take their holidays in July or August. But this is when the schools close for the summer holidays, so all the families go away in these months, and everything is more expensive. If I could go on holiday in June, or September, I would pay less for my hotel room. That would be great. And, of course, the beaches wouldn't be so full of noisy children.

4

I Hello. I'm asking people about their jobs. Would you change anything in your job?

M I suppose there are some things I would change, if I could. For example, I'd like to have more responsibility, you know, and work more independently. At the moment, my boss doesn't let me do anything without his approval. I basically follow his orders, all the time. But I'd like to have the opportunity to use my experience and to show him what I can do.

I Thank you.

5

I Excuse me. I'm asking people about their jobs. Are you happy with your job?

M I haven't got a job. I'm unemployed.

Answers
1 working from home (*I'd like to work from home*; *I could easily do my job from home.*)
2 flexible hours (*flexitime*; *I'd come to work earlier ... and leave earlier.*)
3 holidays (*everyone has to take their holidays in July or August*; *If I could go on holiday in June ...*)
4 responsibility at work (*I'd like to have more responsibility*; *to show him what I can do.*)
5 unemployment (*I haven't got a job*; *I'm unemployed.*)

3 🎧 **12.1** Ask students to read the instructions and the notes. Play the recording again for students to complete the notes.

Answers
Person 1: time, money
Person 2: his children
Person 3: pay less
Person 4: experience

4 Ask students to work with a new partner. For each person in exercise 3, students should suggest two more benefits resulting from the changes the people would like to make.

Ask students to change partners again and compare their ideas. Collect feedback from the class.

The second conditional

GRAMMAR

5 Students do this exercise alone. Then they can compare their answers with a partner.

Answers
1 ... if I didn't go to the office every day.
2 If I worked flexitime ...
3 If I could go on holiday in June ...

A The past simple.
B Imaginary/unlikely situations.
C No.
D The sentences that begin with the *if*-clause – Sentences 2 and 3.

6 Students work in pairs. Student A covers phrases (A–F) with a sheet of paper, and Student B covers phrases (1–6). They then take turns to read one of their sentences, and their partner completes the sentence.

Answers
1 B   2 C   3 A   4 D   5 F   6 E

7 Students work in pairs. Ask them to do the exercise orally first, and then to write the correct forms of the verbs in the spaces.

Answers
1 had, would apply
2 could, would look
3 would stay, didn't have
4 would be, had
5 would change, wanted
6 spoke, wouldn't need

8 Students work alone. Ask them to write the questions out in full on a piece of paper. Tell them to answer the questions for themselves first, and then to work in pairs. They interview their partner and write down their answers to the questions.

Answers
1 What would you change about your current job?
2 If you didn't work in this company, where would you work?
3 If you could, would you work from home?
4 What would be the advantages of working from home?
5 If you could have any job, what would it be?
6 If you lost your job, what would you do?

9 Students work in groups of three and discuss the question. When they've finished, ask the groups to describe their ideas to the class.

Alternative
If you have pre-work students, ask: *What would you do if you were the managing director of ...* (name a famous company that students would know about). Ask students to walk around the class, exchanging their ideas with the other students.

Photocopiable activity
See page 182.

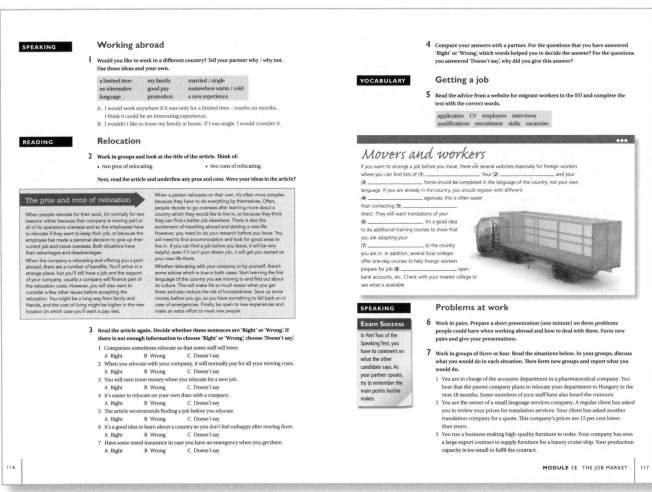

The pages shown are:

Working abroad

SPEAKING

1   Ask students to read the phrases in the box and the sentences below. In pairs, students talk about working abroad.

Then ask a few students to explain what their partners told them, eg:
Federica said she wouldn't work in a different country, because she would miss her friends.

Relocation

READING

2   Ask students to look at the article's title. Clarify the meaning of 'relocation'. Then ask students to think of advantages and disadvantages of relocating. Write the answers on the board for all to see. Then ask students to see if they can find their answers in the text.

In the article:

Pros of relocating: a job and the support of the company, exciting, learn about a new country, starting a new life, new experiences.

Cons of relocating: a long way from family and friends, new cost of living, homesickness.

3   Ask students to read the questions. If they think they know the answers, they can put a mark beside the correct ones. Then ask students to read the text more carefully, and to underline the information in the text that answers the questions. Don't correct answers at this stage, as this will be done in exercise 4.

4   Students discuss their answers to exercise 3 with a partner. Then check answers with the class.

Answers
1 C
2 B (*... usually a company will finance part of the relocation costs.*)
3 C
4 B (*When a person relocates on their own, it's often more complex ...*)
5 A (*If you can find a job before you leave, it will be very helpful ...*)
6 A (*... find out about its culture. This will make life so much easier ... reduce the risk of homesickness.*)
7 C

Getting a job

VOCABULARY

5 Ask students to read the words in the box, and then to do the exercise alone. They should then check their answers with a partner.

Answers
1 vacancies
2 CV
3 application
4 recruitment
5 employers
6 qualifications
7 skills
8 interviews

Problems at work

SPEAKING

6 Read the instructions together with students. Allow a few minutes for students to prepare their presentations in pairs. Then read the Exam Success tip with students.

Students change partners and give their presentations to each other. The student who's listening should comment after their partner has given their presentation.

7 Students work in groups of three, or four. They discuss the three situations and decide what they would do.

Students then form new groups of three or four. The groups discuss the various solutions to each situation.

Alternative
If the class is large, choose students to present their group's solutions to the class.

BUSINESS SKILLS

12.2 Job applications

READING

An advertisement

1 Tell your partner about your first job. Explain what it was, how much you earned and how you got the job.

2 Read the job advertisement for a position in public relations and say which paragraphs give information about these areas.

A the company _____
B contact details _____
C the salary _____
D the position _____
E the candidate _____

Ref. 786459
Date posted: 25 April
Closing date: 19 May
PUBLIC RELATIONS CO-ORDINATOR

1 We are a leader in professional and consumer hair care products and are looking for a creative and dynamic public relations co-ordinator.

2 The ideal candidate will have a degree, plus at least two years of working in public relations. You will also have excellent IT and communication skills, and be self-motivated and well-organised. You should be fluent in French and English.

3 The responsibilities will include: co-ordinating product launches, maintaining contacts with editors, writing articles for the media and planning PR strategies for maximum media exposure. You will also be responsible for the development of a new company website.

4 We offer a competitive salary and excellent benefits, including medical and dental health care, and the opportunity to work for a rapidly expanding company.

5 Qualified candidates should send a covering letter and CV to Carolina Arnaud, HR manager: c.arnaud@système.fr

This is an equal opportunity advertisement.

Learning Tip

Read a wide variety of text types, including advertisements, lists, timetables, catalogues, etc. Try to identify the important information in each one.

3 Read the advertisement again and complete the notes.

Company name _____
Job title _____
Qualifications required _____
Experience required _____
Skills required:
• job-related skills _____
• languages _____
• personal qualities _____
How to apply _____

4 🎧 12.2 Listen to the conversation between Jenny and Maria, two PR assistants in a cosmetics company. Has Jenny got the qualifications, experience and skills required?

5 Do you think Jenny is a suitable candidate for the position? Why? / Why not?

WRITING

A covering letter

6 Read these guidelines for writing a covering letter. Is anything missing?

A covering letter should
• give your contact details
• give the name and address of the person you are writing to
• state the reason for writing
• give brief details of qualifications and skills
• explain why you are the right person for the job
• explain why you want the job
• refer to attachments or enclosures, such as your CV
• use a formal style

7 Read the covering letter that Jenny sends to Système. Does it follow the guidelines in exercise 6?

Dear Ms Arnaud

I am writing to apply for the post of public relations co-ordinator currently advertised on The Independent website (Ref. 786459).

I have worked in public relations for four years, since I completed my degree in French and German. Currently, I am a PR assistant with Gloss Cosmetics, where I am responsible for organising our participation in trade shows, as well as assisting in product launches.

I am creative and self-motivated, and I enjoy working with people. I am looking for a position with more responsibility, where I can use my language skills.

I attach my CV. If you require any additional information, please do not hesitate to contact me.

I look forward to hearing from you.

Yours sincerely
Jenny Hamilton
jhamilton@gloss.co.uk
(44) 610 739 433

---

8 What differences are there between a covering letter sent through the post and an emailed letter?

9 Choose one of the job advertisements on page 147, or find one online or in a newspaper. Write a covering letter to accompany your application form or CV. Use the sections in *italics* in the letter in exercise 7 as a guide.

10 Work in pairs and exchange your letters. Has your partner followed all the points in the guidelines in exercise 6?

An advertisement

READING

1 Students work in pairs to talk about their first jobs. Then ask a few students to tell the class about the jobs they discussed.

Alternative
With pre-work students, ask them to talk about what type of job they hope to find, how they might find this job, and the minimum salary below which they wouldn't accept a job, giving reasons.

2 Tell students to close their books. Ask them what they understand by the phrase *public relations* and ask them if they think that public relations is important, and why.

Write these five topic areas in a vertical list on the board:
– the company
– contact details
– salary
– the position
– the candidate

Choose five students to read the five paragraphs. The rest of the class must listen and identify the topic of each paragraph.

Then ask students to open their books, and to look at the advertisement. Ask them when the advertisement appeared (25 April), and when the applicants must send their CV (by 19 May).

Answers
A 1   B 5   C 4   D 3   E 2

3 Refer students to the Learning Tip. Then ask students to read the advertisement carefully, and to complete the notes.

Answers
Company name: Système (See domain name in contact email address.)
Job title: public relations co-ordinator
Qualifications required: university degree
Experience required: two years of working in public relations
Skills required:
• job-related skills – excellent IT and communication skills
• languages – fluent French and English
• personal qualities – self-motivated and well-organised
How to apply: send covering letter and CV to HR manager, Carolina Arnaud

154

4 🎧 12.2 Read the instructions together with students. Then play the recording for students to answer the questions.

12.2 Listening script

M = Maria   J = Jenny

M Hey, Jenny. Have you seen *The Independent*'s job pages today? There's an advert for a PR co-ordinator at Système.

J Système? Wasn't that the company on the stand next to us at last month's Fashion Fair?

M Yes, that's the one. They're looking for a PR co-ordinator. It sounds pretty good. You should apply!

J What are they asking for?

M A degree and two years' experience in PR. So that's OK. You're a graduate, and you've been working here more than two years, haven't you?

J Yes, and I worked at L'Oréal before I came here.

M So your French is excellent, of course!

J Well, of course! What does the advert say about the actual job?

M Let's see … co-ordinating product launches … contacts with editors … writing articles for the media and planning PR strategies. Oh, and developing a website. What do you think? You could do all that!

J Well, I don't know a thing about websites! But the rest sounds really interesting, doesn't it?

M I'm sure you won't need any technical knowledge for the website – it would be more about the ideas for the site.

J Yes, you're probably right. What else do they want?

M You should be 'self-motivated and well-organised'. Well, I think you're both of those things. And it also says 'excellent IT and communication skills'.

J IT skills? Oh, I'm not sure about this.

M I'll tell you what – I'll email the page to you and you can read it yourself. I would apply if I were you – you're always saying how bored you are here!

J OK, then. Thanks, Maria. I'll have a look at it and we can talk about it at lunchtime.

Answers

Jenny has got the qualifications and experience. The only thing she lacks is the IT skills.

5 Students discuss the question.

Possible answer

Jenny has everything except the IT skills. Although the advertisement specifies 'excellent IT skills', these may be more desirable than necessary, and she could learn these on the job. Therefore, she may be a suitable candidate. However, if the IT skills are necessary, it is unlikely she will be offered the job.

A covering letter

WRITING

6 Ask students what a covering letter is. (A letter sent together with a CV to explain what is being sent.) Then ask students to read the guidelines and answer the question.

Answer

The guidelines are complete, but students may suggest more specific details.

7 Ask students to read the covering letter alone, and then to compare their ideas with a partner.

Answer

The covering letter does follow the guidelines. However, it could perhaps explain in more detail why Jenny is the right person for the job, and address the points mentioned in the advert (*communication skills, well-organised, fluent in French and English*).

8 Students discuss the question.

Answer

The differences concern the use of the postal addresses of the person to whom the letter is sent and the writer of the letter.

9 Read the instructions with the class. Students should write a covering letter structured like the one in exercise 7.

This activity can be given as homework.

10 When students have finished writing, they should exchange their letter with a partner, and assess it according to the guidelines. Students can make suggestions for improving their partner's letter.

Choose a few students to read out their covering letters. If they've found a job advertisement online or in a newspaper, ask them to read the advertisement out. Also ask them why they chose that particular advertisement.

LISTENING

A job interview

1 Work in pairs. Read these questions from an interview for the post of marketing assistant. Decide if the interviewer (I) or the candidate (C) would ask each question.

1 What do you enjoy most about your current job?
2 How do you deal with difficult situations in your current job?
3 Where would I be based?
4 Why would you like to work here?
5 What responsibilities would I have?
6 What would you like to be doing in a few years' time?
7 How does your experience match this position?
8 Would I be able to use my language skills?
9 What qualities do you bring to this position?
10 What would you say were your weak points?
11 What kind of training would be available?
12 Could you tell me something about the pay and conditions?

2 Add two more questions to the list in exercise 1.

3 🎧 12.3 Listen to an interview and tick the questions you hear in the list above.

4 🎧 12.3 Listen to the interview again and choose the correct option (A–C).

1 What does Philip say about his current job?
  A He likes the variety.
  B He enjoys meeting lots of people.
  C He enjoys the routine.
2 What does he say about routine administrative tasks?
  A He doesn't do that kind of work.
  B He wouldn't like to do an administrative job.
  C He thinks they are important.
3 Why would he like to work for the company?
  A He wants to earn more money.
  B He wants more responsibility.
  C He doesn't want to work for a big company.
4 What would he like to do in the future?
  A He'd like to manage his own team.
  B He'd like to run his own business.
  C He'd like to stay with the company.
5 What qualities does he offer?
  A He is creative and competitive.
  B He is well-qualified and knowledgeable.
  C He is determined and motivated.
6 What are his weak points?
  A He doesn't have any.
  B He isn't always patient.
  C He doesn't like impatient people.

5 Would you give Philip the job of marketing assistant? Why? / Why not?

6 Work in groups of four, in two pairs. Choose a job that one of you does, or a job that you would like to do.
  Pair A: Work together to prepare interview questions. Use ideas from exercise 1.
  Pair B: Prepare for the interview using ideas from exercise 4 to help you.

7 In your group of four, form two new pairs. Carry out the interviews. Is the candidate successful?

WRITING

Interview follow-up

8 Look at the Useful language box. Read the beginnings of sentences from a letter following a job interview. Which ones could be used in a letter offering someone a job? Which could be used in a letter turning down a candidate?

> **Useful language**
> I am writing …
> I am pleased to inform you that …
> I regret to tell you that …
> We would like you to …
> Please confirm …
> We will keep your details …
> We look forward to …
> We wish you luck in your ….

9 In pairs, write suitable endings for the sentences in the Useful language box.

10 Do you think Philip got the job? If you think he did, write an email to Philip telling him:
  • that his application was successful
  • the date the company would like him to start work
  • that he should reply by email to confirm his acceptance of the position offered
  If you think Philip didn't get the job, write him an email:
  • thanking him for attending the interview
  • telling him that his application was not successful
  • informing him that you'll keep his CV in your files

120 / MODULE 12 JOB APPLICATIONS 121

Student's Book pages 120 and 121

A job interview

LISTENING

1 Students work in pairs to do the exercise.

Answers
1 I 2 I 3 C 4 I 5 C 6 I
7 I 8 C 9 I 10 I 11 C 12 C

2 Students work in pairs to add two more questions to the list in exercise 1. Then ask students for their ideas. You could write any interesting or unusual questions on the board.

Possible questions
How long have you worked in you current job?

What would you hope to achieve in your first three months?

Who would I be responsible to?

Who would be assessing my performance?

3 🎧 12.3 Play the recording for students to tick the questions they hear that are listed in exercise 1.

12.3 Listening script
I = Interviewer   **P** = Philip

I Good morning. Philip Barras, isn't it? Please take a seat.
P Yes, that's right. Good morning.

I Well, Philip, I see from your CV that you have some experience working in marketing.
P Yes, I have. I've worked in the marketing department of a large sportswear company for the last year.
I Can you tell me what you enjoy most about your current job?
P Yes, well … I've learnt a lot working with the sales and marketing team. I like the variety – you know, it's not always the same routine. And the people on the team are great – everyone works together and helps each other. I enjoy the satisfaction – when we meet our targets, I mean … it's very satisfying.
I And what about the routine tasks, the administration and so on?
P Yes, I have to do that do, but it's not a problem. I think every job has … well, a boring part. I'm quite well-organised, and actually I think it's important to do the routine things well, too.
I I see. Now, why would you like to work here?
P Well, I think there are two reasons, mainly. The job looks very interesting – some of the areas are similar to what I do now, but with more responsibility. So I think it will be a challenge, but it will be exciting. And then … in a big company like this, I think I'll have more opportunities to learn new things.
I So, looking to the future, what would you like to be doing in a few years' time?
P I'd like to be in charge of my own account, and I'd like to manage my own team.

I OK, good. So what qualities do you bring to this particular position?

P Well, as you can see, I'm quite ambitious! I'm creative and enthusiastic – obviously I don't know everything about your products, but I do have a few ideas already about the marketing possibilities. I'm quite competitive – I like to meet targets and goals, as I said earlier.

I And what would you say were your weak points?

P Ah, that's a difficult question to answer. I suppose I can be impatient, sometimes.

I Hmm … Let's talk in a bit more detail about what this position involves …

Answers
Questions 1, 4, 6, 9, 10

4 🎧 12.3 Ask students to read the questions first. If they can answer a question, they should mark the answer they think is correct. Then play the recording for students to check their answers.

Check their answers. If students haven't answered correctly, play the recording again, stopping at the points where the answers come up.

Answers
1 A   2 C   3 B   4 A   5 A   6 B

5 Students discuss the question. Collect ideas about whether Philip is right for the job.

Answer
So far, Philip appears to be a suitable candidate.

6 Put students into groups of four, and then divide the groups into two pairs. Each group decides on a job. Pair A prepares interview questions, using the ideas from exercise 1, and Pair B prepares for the interview, creating a profile for the candidate and using the ideas from exercise 4.

7 In their groups, students work with a different partner from the one they worked with in exercise 6. One pair are the interviewers, the other pair are the candidates. They carry out the interview using the questions and the profile they created in exercise 6.

Ask the interviewers if they think their candidate was successful, and to explain why or why not.

Interview follow-up

WRITING

8 Students work in pairs. Ask them to look at the Useful language phrases, and decide if the sentence beginnings are for a letter offering a job, or for a letter turning down the candidate.

Answers
Offering: *I am pleased to inform you that …, We would like you to …, Please confirm …, We look forward to …*

Turning down: *I regret to tell you that …, We will keep your details …, We wish you luck in your …*

Offering and turning down: *I am writing …*

9 Students work in pairs to complete the sentences in the Useful language box in exercise 8 with a suitable ending. Collect students' ideas.

Possible answers
I am writing to thank you for attending the interview on 3 June.

I am pleased to inform you that we would like to offer you the post of head of marketing.

I regret to tell you that your application was unsuccessful.

We would like you to start working on 14 March.

Please confirm that you wish to take up this offer.

We will keep your details on our files.

We look forward to having you on our team.

We wish you luck in your search for employment.

10 Although students can work in pairs to write this email, both students should write so that they both keep a copy.

Sample answers

> Dear Mr Barras
>
> I am pleased to inform you that your interview for the post of marketing assistant was successful.
>
> We would like you to start working here on Monday 13 October.
>
> Please send an email to confirm that you accept the post offered.
>
> Yours sincerely
> Sandra Richards

> Dear Mr Barras
>
> I am writing to thank you for attending the interview on 5 September.
>
> I regret to tell you that your application was unsuccessful. However, we will keep your CV on our files, in case a suitable post becomes vacant.
>
> Yours sincerely
> Sandra Richards

Photocopiable activity
See page 183.

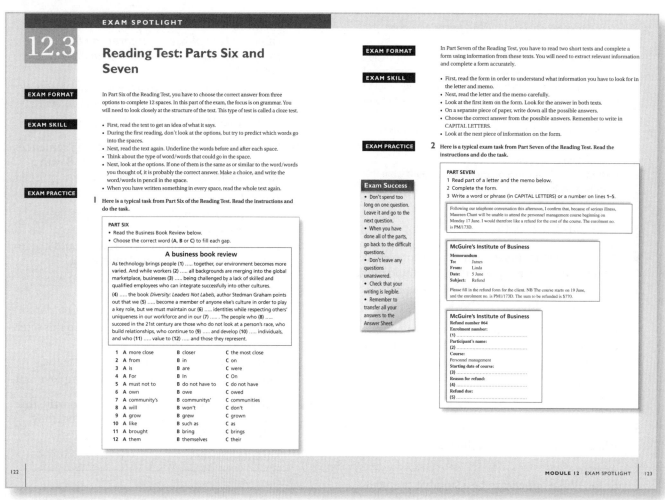

Student's Book pages 122 and 123

Reading Test: Part Six

EXAM FORMAT

Read the opening description of this part of the exam with the students.

EXAM SKILL

Ask students to read the information. They then describe to a partner how to approach this part of the test. If they need to, they can refer back to the information in their books.

EXAM PRACTICE

1 Students do this task individually, as if they were taking the exam. Ask them to time themselves, ie, the time they take to read the text and answer the questions. Tell students to write the starting and finishing time at the top of the page and keep a record of how long they take to do each exercise. By the end of the book, they'll have an idea of how to manage their time when they do the Reading and Writing parts. When they've finished, they can check their answers with a partner.

Answers
1 B 2 A 3 B 4 B 5 B 6 A
7 C 8 A 9 A 10 C 11 B 12 B

Reading Test: Part Seven

EXAM FORMAT

Read the opening description of this part of the exam with the students.

EXAM SKILL

Ask students to read the information. They then describe how to approach this part of the test to a partner. If they need to, they can refer back to the information in their books.

EXAM PRACTICE

2 Read the Exam Success tip together with the students. Students do this task individually, as if they were taking the exam. Ask them to time themselves, as with the Reading Test Part Six.

When they've finished, they can check their answers with a partner.

Answers
Enrolment number: (1) PM1/173D
Participant's name: (2) MAUREEN CHANT
Starting date of course: (3) 19 JUNE
Reason for refund: (4) SERIOUS ILLNESS
Refund due: (5) $770

Photocopiable activities and Workbook answer key

1.1   World of work

Play this game in groups of four to six. Shuffle the cards and deal them out. The first player puts down a card to begin a sentence. The next player must put down a card which can follow grammatically, or miss a turn. Continue in this way to make grammatically correct sentences. The winner is the first person to get rid of their cards.

Our company	always	organises
great parties	three or four times	a year
My boss	doesn't	often
say hello	in	the morning
I	often	check
my email	every	ten minutes
In our department, we	never	have
meetings	in	the afternoons
I	rarely	meet
my work colleagues	at	weekends
My colleagues	sometimes	do
work at home	several nights	a week
My office	usually	closes
for the holidays	every	August

1.2   Personal and professional details

Read your role card and complete the last section. Do not show other people your card.

You work for Bixco, a multinational company that makes snacks and soft drinks. You are attending the welcome dinner of your company conference. Talk to as many people as you can and find someone who does a similar job to you. Which office do they work in?

Student A

You work in Stockholm. You're a sales representative. You visit clients (shops and supermarkets) every month and you promote new products to clients. Outside of work, you enjoy playing chess and _____.

Student B

You work in Vancouver. You're an IT support assistant. In your job you deal with employees' IT problems by telephone. You also write instructions for in-company software applications. Outside of work, you like opera and _____.

Student C

You work in Dublin. You work in the sales and marketing department, you're the department secretary. Part of your job is to deal with correspondence and make travel arrangements for the sales team. Outside of work, you do martial arts and _____.

Student D

You work in Stockholm. You are the financial controller of the company's Northern and Eastern Europe division. You're responsible for the division's accounts. You give authorisation for payments and other movements of money. Outside of work, you go skiing regularly and _____.

Student E

You work in Dublin. You're the quality assurance manager for the Western Europe division. You co-ordinate all the activities to ensure that the quality system works. Outside of work, you enjoy painting and _____.

Student F

You work in Dublin. You work in the sales department. You show product samples to company customers (supermarkets and petrol stations) and you meet customers regularly. Outside of work, you like playing volleyball and _____.

Student G

You work in Stockholm. You work in the communications and information technology department. You design software for use in the company, and you analyse the C&IT needs of company departments. Outside of work, you enjoy learning languages and _____.

Student H

You work in Vancouver. You are the office administrator for the IT department. You're responsible for the general administration of the department. You spend a lot of time organising meetings for the IT team. Outside of work, you play chess and _____.

Student I

You work in Dublin. You work in the accounts department. You're the deputy manager. Part of your job is to control payments to suppliers. You also manage all the incoming finances from customers. Outside of work, you enjoy playing chess and _____.

Student J

You work in Vancouver. You're an assistant in the quality department. You monitor the quality of raw ingredients and the finished products. Outside of work, you like mountain climbing and _____.

2.1   Work in progress

1   Work with a partner. Look at the picture and spot ten odd things. Write ten sentences about the things.

2   Work with another pair. Tell each other about the odd things in the picture. Don't show your picture until you have finished. How many things are different?

1   Work with a partner. Look at the picture and spot ten odd things. Write ten sentences about the things.

2   Work with another pair. Tell each other about the odd things in the picture. Don't show your picture until you have finished. How many things are different?

2.2   Making arrangements

1   Play this game in groups of three. Shuffle the Arrangements cards and deal them out. Place the Excuses cards face down in front of you.

2   Student A, choose one of your Arrangements cards. Student B, take an Excuses card from the pile. Student A must try to make an arrangement with Student B using the prompt on the Arrangements card. Student B makes an excuse or agrees, according to the prompt on the card. If they make an arrangement, Student A gives Student B the card. If they don't make an arrangement, Student C takes a card from the Excuses pile and Student A tries to make the same arrangement with him/her. Place the used Excuses cards at the bottom of the pile.

3   Take turns at trying to make an arrangement with the other members of the group until all the cards are used. The winner is the player who gives away most Arrangements cards.

Arrangements

Monday am meet new head of department	**Monday pm** go to staff training	**Tuesday am** visit new clients
Tuesday pm do stock-taking	**Wednesday am** attend new product launch	**Wednesday pm** discuss sales targets with team
Thursday am interview candidates for PA job	**Thursday pm** chair design meeting	**Friday am** go to planning meeting
Friday pm set up MD's leaving party	**Saturday am** back up computer files	**Saturday pm** attend MD's leaving party

Excuses

take the day off	have an operation
visit head office	watch football final on TV
get married	pick up new car
inspect new branch premises	Confirm arrangement. Ask for details.
meet mother for coffee	Confirm arrangement. Ask for details.
present new season's products to sales team	Confirm arrangement. Ask for details.
wash hair	Confirm arrangement. Ask for details.
hand in resignation	Confirm arrangement. Ask for details.
exhibit paintings in local gallery	Make an excuse.

3.1   Company biography

1   Work in a group of four, in two pairs. Pair A, read the information sheet for Papaya and change the verbs to the past simple tense. Pair B, read the information sheet for Fresco and change the verbs to the past simple tense.

2   Each student from pair A then works with a student from pair B. The A students have two minutes to tell the B students as much as they can about Papaya, while each B student completes a Papaya worksheet. Then each B student tells their A student partner about Fresco, while the A students complete the Fresco worksheets.

3   In your group of four, compare your notes and decide who communicated the most information.

Company name	Papaya
Founded by	Joseph Pickering
Type of company	Public limited company
Products/services	Travel: Papaya Airlines, Papaya Trains and Papaya Coaches (long distance bus routes) Communications: local radio stations, mobile phone and Internet provider
First business activity	begins selling second-hand vinyl records when still at school
Expanded	starts own record label in 1996
Notable successes	sells record label for £2.58m in 2002

Key dates/achievements
2004 sets up Papaya Coaches (low cost travel to European capitals)
2008 company value is £11m, rises to £278m after one year as public company
2012 Papaya Airlines launches £200 London–New York airfare
2016 Papaya Mobile UK market share reaches 67%
Number of employees 13,500 worldwide

Company name	Fresco
Founded by	Roland and Bertrand Siddell (brothers)
Type of company	Limited company
Products/services	Supermarket chain. **Financial services:** insurance, credit card, personal banking
First business activity	sell fruit and vegetables at a market stall in 1948
Expanded	buy two vehicles to travel to more customers in 1952
Notable successes	take over 23 food and non-food retailers from 1960–1970

Key dates/achievements
1972 Fresco introduces the first self-service store in the UK
1975 annual sales reach £1m
1980 builds the first hypermarket in the UK
2002 annual sales rise to £1bn
2014 launches 'carbon footprint' policy to reduce Fresco pollution
Number of employees 8,000

Company name	Papaya
Founded by	....
Type of company	....
Products/services	Travel: ....
	Communications: ....
First business activity	....
Expanded	 1996
Notable successes	 2002

Key dates/achievements
2004 ....
2008 company value ....
.... London–New York airfare
2016 .... 67%
Number of employees 13,500 worldwide

Company name	Fresco
Founded by	....
Type of company	....
Products/services	....
First business activity	....
Expanded	....
Notable successes	 1960–1970

Key dates/achievements
1972 ....
1975 .... £1m
1980 .... hypermarket ....
.... annual sales ....
.... 'carbon footprint' policy
Number of employees ....

3.2   Company performance

1   Work in groups of three. Shuffle the cards and put them face down in front of the group. Student A, turn over two cards. If the cards are synonyms, make a sentence using one of the words. If students B and C accept your sentence as correct, you can keep the pair of cards and go again. If the cards do not match, or the other students don't accept your sentence, replace the cards in the same positions.

2   Each student takes turns until all the cards are matched. The student with the most cards wins.

fall	decrease	rise	increase
drop	go down	employees	staff
manufacture	produce	supply	distribute
run	manage	sell	market
customers	clients	grow	expand
found	set up	turnover	revenue
provide	give	partner	associate
founder	creator	products	goods

4.1   International business

1   Work in groups of three. Shuffle the cards and put them face down in front of the group. Student A, take a card and read it out; then follow the instructions on the card. Student B or C, take the other role. If the result of the conversation is positive, Student A keeps the card. If not, place the card at the bottom of the pile.

2   Take turns and continue until there are no cards left. The player with the most cards wins.

You need to leave at lunchtime today, to go to a meeting at your child's school. Ask your supervisor for permission.	You work in a shop and see a customer with a broken leg having problems on the stairs. Offer to help.
Your driving test is next Friday and you have a lesson every morning from 9am–10am. Ask your boss for permission to arrive late.	You're in the company canteen and you see the head of your department. Offer to buy him/her something to eat or drink.
The football team you support arrives at the airport this afternoon after winning the European Championship; you want to be there. Ask your supervisor for time off.	You see a new member of staff standing at the printer, tearing up pieces of paper. Offer some help.
Your kitten is ill and needs medication every four hours. Ask your boss for permission to bring him to the office this week.	You are interviewing someone in the street for a market research survey. Request his/her full name, address and date of birth.
It's your brother's birthday. He lives in Japan. Your phone is out of order. Ask your boss for permission to phone him from work.	Your colleagues stand just outside the office door to smoke. Your desk is next to the door. Make a request.
Your colleague has to make 100 phone calls this week. Offer to help.	You are behind with your work, but you've got a meeting scheduled with a very boring client. Ask a colleague for help.
Your colleague is feeling ill. Offer to take him/her to hospital.	Your car is in the garage, so you need a lift to work for a week. Ask a colleague for help.

4.2   Business communications

Work in a group of four. Take a card each.

1   Read the message on your card; then make phone calls according to the instructions. Student A, phone Student C. Student B, phone Student D. Students C and D, take the message and note down the information.

2   Now swap pairs. Student C, phone Student B. Student D, phone Student A. Students A and B, take the message and note down the information.

3   Work in pairs, AB and CD.

Students A and B, you both work for Sound Electronics. Compare all the information you have and discuss the service you have had from PNI Wholesale. Decide what is the best action for your business to take.

Students C and D, you both work for PNI Wholesale. Compare all the information you have and discuss the quality of your service to Sound Electronics. Decide what is the best action for your business to take.

Student A: Sam, Sound Electronics

Sam

A delivery of DVD players came yesterday, but three boxes of model 96D are missing. They are on the delivery note (EG704/80). Can you phone Bill at PNI Wholesale and find out what the problem is? Tell him we need the DVDs before 15 Feb.

Thanks

Carol

Student B: Jackie, Sound Electronics

Jackie

PNI Wholesale sent us three invoices in December for the same goods. The invoices are 238/07 for €1,398, 240/07 for €1,003 and 243/07 for €2,300. Can you phone PNI Wholesale and speak to Bill, and find out which one is correct?

Thanks

Carol

Student C: Fran, PNI Wholesale

Fran

Can you do me a favour and phone Carol, at Sound Electronics? They still owe us €2,300 from December. The invoice number is 243/07. Find out if there's a problem and remind her that our new bank account number is 2100 19 9887 287464.

Thanks

Bill

Student D: Jo, PNI Wholesale

Jo

The new delivery driver has mixed up some deliveries. Can you phone Carol, at Sound Electronics, and ask her to fax a copy of delivery note EG704/80 to us at 0116 938 887? Tell her we hope to get everything sorted out by Friday (the 16th).

Thanks

Bill

5.1   Career choices

Take a bingo card each. Listen to the sentences and look on your card for the infinitive of the past participle in each one. If you have a match, cross out the verb. When you have crossed out all the verbs on your card, shout 'Bingo!'.

be

build

cut

deal

grow

keep

lose

take

write

---

build

speak

give

go

lead

lose

make

sell

win

---

be

speak

cut

feel

grow

hide

keep

rise   write

---

deal

hide

go

rise

say

spend

take

think

win

5.2   Achievements and plans

Student A: The entrepreneur

You are a successful entrepreneur and a TV company is going to make a documentary about your life and work. Read and complete the information about yourself below with your own ideas. Then answer the journalist's questions.

> You began work at the age of _____. Your first company was
> _____. Your first success was _____. Over
> the years, you have made $_____ and your company has taken
> over _____ companies. You've set up businesses in
> _____ countries and given jobs to _____.
> On a personal level, you've met _____ and you've
> _____. You have some regrets, in both your business life and your
> personal life, for example _____. On the other hand, you've had
> some unique experiences, such as _____.
> At this stage, you have lots of plans. You're going to _____ this year
> and in the next five years you're going to _____. One thing you
> definitely aren't going to do is _____.

Now write two more sentences about your achievements and / or plans for the future.

- -

Student B: The journalist

You are a journalist for a TV company. You're going to interview an entrepreneur for a documentary on his/her life and work. Prepare questions using these prompts. Then do the interview.

> What / first job?
> What / first company?
> What / first big success?
> How much money / make?
> How many companies / take over?
> How many countries / operate in?
> How many people / employ?
>
> Ever / meet / famous people?
> Any interesting personal experiences?
> Any regrets?
> What plans / have / immediate future?
> What / do / in the long term?
> Any comments?

Now add two more questions to ask about the entrepreneur's achievements and / or plans for the future.

6.1   Business travel

Work in a group of four.

1   Read the lines of text from two different newspaper reports, one on business travel and one on family travel. Put the lines of text into the two groups.
2   Sequence the lines in each report to give complete texts.
3   Pair A, take the business travel report. Pair B, take the family travel report. In each case, read the report again and write six questions that the original survey asked.
4   Work with someone from the opposite pair. Interview each other using your questions.
5   Re-form your pairs A and B, and report the answers to the questions.

A leading travel group reported today that despite new technology such as video-

conferencing, business travel is continuing to rise. 60% of the business people questioned

said that they had travelled for business in the last month, and of these, 75% said that they

usually travelled by plane. About 40% reported that they used low-cost airlines,

but only 10% said they could remember the name of the last company they flew with. However,

nearly 80% said that they were happy with the quality of service they received and that

in their companies, business travel would increase, not decrease, in the next ten years.

One of the big budget airlines has reported this week on a survey into family travel

trends. Of those who replied to the survey, 85% said that their families enjoyed

travelling, and a similar number said that they usually took an annual holiday. Over 60%

of the families said that they were going on a trip abroad this year, but only 20% said that

they could speak another language. Asked if the availability of budget air fares would

affect their holiday destinations, 45% said that it would. Finally, about 15% said that

they would go on several short breaks instead of one long summer holiday.

6.2   Travel arrangements

1   You are part of a team that organised a celebrity awards ceremony last week. Some things did not go well. Read the email that your colleague sent you before the ceremony, and the notes you made on each item after the ceremony.

2   Hold a meeting with your two colleagues to find out why things went wrong and what you could change for the next ceremony. Be prepared to explain any problems they say you were responsible for.

Kris Campbell

From: Jay
To: Kris
Date: 11 March
Subject: Update on arrangements for awards ceremony, 14th March:

The police are arranging an escort for the limousines.   *OK!*
There are security cameras in the street and in the hotel.   *None in the hotel!*
The security firm is checking the building on the afternoon of the 13th.   *Too early, needs to be same day.*
No public guests will be in the hotel.   *OK!*
The weather report says it will be fine all day on the 14th.   *It rained all day!*

Jay Brown

From: Alix
To: Jay
Date: 12 March
Subject: Update on arrangements for awards ceremony, 14th March:

The invitations were hand-delivered to all the guests last week. *Two winners did not get their invitations until 13th March!*
The press passes will be ready on the morning of the 14th.   *OK!*
The awards are locked up in the hotel safe.   *The safe wasn't locked.*
The clips of the nominated films are ready.   *OK!*
We can give the winners' envelopes to the presenters before the ceremony. *Chaos! Too much was going on.*

Alix Waters

From: Kris
To: Alix
Date: 13 March
Subject: Update on arrangements for awards ceremony, 14th March:

Everything is on schedule at the hotel.   *OK!*
The seating arrangements were organised yesterday.   *Chaos! Nobody knew where to sit.*
The presenters will arrive at 8pm on the 14th.   *Too late. The ceremony started before they had all arrived.*
The final rehearsal is from 6pm to 7pm today.   *OK!*
The red carpet can't be put down until the afternoon of the 14th.   *Too many crowds outside by that time.*

7.1 Products and services

Work in a group of four. You work for a large insurance company. You are going to choose a bonus gift for branch managers (and their partners) who reached their sales targets last year.

1 Decide what is important and appropriate when choosing this type of bonus.

2 Form two pairs in your group. With your partner, discuss the packages sent by the travel agency and choose one of them, making a note of your reasons.

3 In turn, each pair present the package they have chosen to the other pair, giving the reasons. If you choose different packages, continue the discussion and agree on one only. If both pairs choose the same package, present your decision to another pair in the class.

Package 1

St Petersburg, Russia
Accommodation: two nights in 4-star hotel.
Sightseeing: UNESCO World Heritage city including Winter Palace, scene of 1917 revolution, Peterhof, summer residence of Tsars. Visit to the Hermitage, one of world's largest collections of European Art.
Evening: folk music and dance

Package 2

Chamonix, France
Accommodation: two nights in top-class chalet.
Activities: skiing (all levels) and winter sports at site of first winter Olympic games. Paragliding in spectacular setting of Western Europe's highest mountain, Mont Blanc.

Package 3

Porto, Portugal
Accommodation: two nights in 3-star hotel in UNESCO World Heritage area of old town.
Sightseeing: bridges across the River Douro (designed by Eiffel); river trip up Douro to typical restaurant for supper. Visits to the port wine lodges and wine-tasting at wine museum.
Shopping: traditional Portuguese crafts

7.2   Orders and contracts

Work in groups of three.

1   Shuffle the cards and place them face down in a pile. Student A, take a card and read it out to the other students. Toss a coin to see how long you must talk about the subjects on the card: heads means 30 seconds, tails means one minute. Student B, keep time. Student C, think of one question to ask Student A at the end of the time.

2   You get three points if you are still speaking at the end of the time, but if you hesitate a lot or repeat things, you get two points. If you stop speaking before the end of the time, you get one point.

3   Take turns and continue until one player gets ten points and is the winner.

sports cars motorbikes quad bikes	Monopoly dominoes chess	microwaves dishwashers freezers
hotel bed & breakfast self-catering	digital cameras video cameras mobile phone cameras	pizzas burgers sandwiches
safaris cruises caravanning	mobile phone smart TV radio	credit cards debit cards cash
perfumes alcohol tobacco	laptops desk tops tablets	books newspapers magazines
mobile phones email web cameras	a diary USB stick fitness tracker	suitcases backpacks handbags

8.1   Manufacturing processes

1   Work with a partner. Take a card and brainstorm everything you know about the process
    on the card.
2   Use the prompts on the card and prepare a two-minute presentation on your process.
3   Give your presentation to another pair.
4   Listen to another presentation and ask two questions at the end.

Estate agent: selling a house

advert / write   contract / sign

viewings / arrange   house / advertise

photographs / take   house / value

offer / make   offer / accept

Car dealer: buying a new car

financial arrangement / explain

car / deliver   cheque / clear

new car / test drive   contract / sign

old car / inspect   old car / value

registration papers / organise

Bank manager: opening an account

account number / assign   card / issue

sample signature / take   application / make

PIN number / give   forms / fill in

money / deposit   identity / check

HR manager: hiring new staff

candidates / select   contract / sign

applications / receive   interviews / hold

job / accept   offer / make

job / advertise   start date / agree

8.2   Problems and solutions

Work in a group of three. Share the dominoes equally. Do not let the other student see your dominoes. Student A, put down any domino. Student B, add one correct domino to either side of A's domino to complete the sentence. If you can't go, Student C continues. The first player to use all their dominoes wins.

are dealt with immediately.	The toys are being made		under licence	Production is increased		when demand goes up.	We try to solve
problems at once.	**All our shoes**		**are handmade.**	**The goods have been sent**		**by road.**	**When ice heats up,**
it melts.	**The paint is going to be produced**		**on an automated line.**	**The problem**		**was detected last night.**	**The raw materials will be kept**
in the warehouse.	**Quality was monitored**		**at every stage.**	**The manager should be told**		**as soon as possible.**	**The extra demand**
can't be met in time.	**Materials are delivered**		**to the loading bay.**	**The assembly line**		**can be run 24 hours a day.**	**When water is heated to 100°C,**
it boils.	**We didn't find anything**		**wrong with the machine.**	**Orders have been received**		**from several new customers.**	**The disaster was avoided**
by prompt action.	**Improvements can be seen**		**immediately.**	**If we get extra orders,**		**we increase our output.**	**System problems**

9.1   The future

1   Complete the sentence *If* … at the top of the sheet with a prediction. Pass the sheet to your left.
2   Read the sentence and then complete the next sentence *And if* … with a possible consequence. Fold the paper down along fold 1. Pass the sheet to your left.
3   Read the sentence beginning *And if* … and then complete the next sentence *But if* … with your prediction. Fold the paper down along fold 2, so that only the sentence beginning *But if* … is visible. Pass the sheet to your left.
4   Continue in this way until the sheet is finished.
5   Unfold the sheets and read out the chain of predictions to your group. Choose the most interesting one.

If …

··· fold 1 ···

And if …

··· fold 2 ···

But if …

··· fold 3 ···

On the other hand, if …

··· fold 4 ···

and then if …

··· fold 5 ···

However, if …

··· fold 6 ···

So to sum up, if …

9.2   Meetings

1   Work in groups of three. Look at the case study together. Then take a role card each.
    Read your role cards and hold the meeting.
2   Write a bullet-point action plan.
3   Present your action plan to another group.

Case study: Funplay Toys Inc.

Your company, Funplay Toys Inc, is a manufacturer and distributor of children's toys. It is an established company, making some of the best-selling and classic children's toys on the market in your country. Some of your toy characters have TV spin-offs and one, 'Fun Bear', is also licensed to a food manufacturer to promote breakfast cereals.

In recent years, to keep costs down, you have moved toy production to China, where 80% of the world's toys are made. The quality of the goods has been consistently excellent, and you have maintained your strong market share. Now a consumer group has shown that the paint used in the imported toys is above the safety limits for toxicity. You are not the only toy company affected by this crisis.

Hold a meeting to:
- discuss what you should do in this situation
- discuss the advantages and disadvantages of each person's ideas
- write an action plan

Chief executive

Here are some ideas you have considered before the meeting. Add one more idea of your own.

- Recall all the affected toys.
- Visit the factories in China.
- Make a public statement.
- Run our own tests on the toys.
- Make a list of which products are affected.
- ■

Quality manager

Here are some ideas you have considered before the meeting. Add one more idea of your own.

- Ask Chinese supplier for information.
- Review quality assurance procedures.
- Call a press conference.
- Change production to a different contractor.
- Recall all the affected toys.
- ■

Communications director

Here are some ideas you have considered before the meeting. Add one more idea of your own.

- Recall all the affected toys.
- Write an open letter to customers, full page in main national newspapers.
- Give instructions to retailers.
- Brief sales staff on the situation.
- Change production to a different contractor.
- ■

10.1 Career development

Student A

1 Work with a partner (another Student A). Write the correct relative pronoun in each sentence below.
2 Work with Student B. Read out each complete sentence. Student B has to choose the correct option a, b or c in each case. (The correct answers are in **bold**.)
3 Now answer Student B's questions. The winner is the person who gets most answers right.

1 A place _____ goods are mass-produced is **a) an assembly line**, b) a workshop or c) a trading estate.

2 A course _____ you do at university over three or more years is a) a career, b) a diploma or **c) a degree**.

3 A leader _____ is fascinating and appealing can be described as a) self-confident, **b) charismatic** or c) authoritative.

4 A person _____ bank account is in 'negative numbers' is a) in the black, b) in the green or **c) in the red**.

5 A person _____ you employ to do a specific, short-term job is a) a supplier, b) a dealer or **c) a sub-contractor**.

6 The money _____ a public company pays to shareholders is called a) a bonus, **b) a dividend** or c) a share.

7 A place _____ raw materials are kept is called a) a loading bay, b) a storeroom or **c) a warehouse**.

8 The person _____ runs a meeting is a) the speaker, b) the leader or **c) the chair**.

Student B

1 Work with a partner (another Student B). Write the correct relative pronoun in each sentence below.
2 Work with Student A. Answer Student A's questions.
3 Now read out each of your complete sentences to Student A, who will choose the correct option a, b or c in each case. (The correct answers are in **bold**.) The winner is the person who gets most answers right.

1 A person _____ does work for a series of different companies is called **a) a freelancer**, b) a sole trader or c) a partner.

2 The money _____ a company makes after costs is a) turnover, **b) profit** or c) benefits.

3 A person _____ job involves building relations with the media is a) a PA, **b) in PR** or c) in HR.

4 A leader _____ has lots of energy and ideas can be described as **a) dynamic**, b) communicative or c) ambitious.

5 The term _____ is used when two companies join together to form a new company is a) a joint venture, b) a takeover or **c) a merger**.

6 A place _____ a customer can buy in bulk is a) a retailer, **b) a wholesaler** or c) an outlet.

7 A number of people _____ work together on a project can be called **a) a team**, b) a group or c) a band.

8 The department of a company _____ a brand image is created is a) Sales, **b) Marketing** or c) Advertising.

10.2 Organising a conference

1 Work alone. Read each box in the grid and prepare the questions you'll need to ask to find out the information.
2 Walk around the classroom and chat to your classmates. You aren't allowed to start your conversation with your questions: first you should introduce yourself and make small talk. Your aim is to get three names in a row, either horizontal, vertical or diagonal. Write the names in the spaces. You can only ask each person one question, then move to another person.
3 When you have three names in a row, sit down.

Grid A   Find someone who ...

accepts your invitation to go out for a meal	has been to a place where it rarely rains	can recommend some interesting local dishes
has a similar family background to you	would like to travel more, and find out why	knows someone who you work or study with (not in this class)
is free this weekend	has read a book which you enjoyed	accepts your offer of a guided tour of the local area

Grid B   Find someone who ...

accepts your invitation to the cinema	has been to a place where it rains a lot	can recommend some interesting local sights
owns something that you would like to own	travels a lot, and find out why	knows someone who you work or study with (not in this class)
is free after class today	likes a film which you didn't enjoy	accepts your offer of a game of golf

11.1   Health and safety

1   Work with a partner. Decide if the modal verbs in sentences 1–12 are grammatically or logically correct or incorrect. For the incorrect sentences, write the correct modal verb(s).

2   Work with the rest of the class. In your pairs, you have €500 to invest. You can invest all or part of this money by saying if the sentences are correct or incorrect. You can invest in multiples of €50. If you make a good investment (ie your answer is correct), you double your money. If you are wrong about the sentence, you lose the amount you invested.

3   For each incorrect sentence, you can make an additional investment, based on what you think is the correct modal verb. The pair that has the most euros at the end wins.

1   Everyone knows you should use the lift in a fire.

2   If you finish the job early, you don't have to stay until 6pm, just go.

3   An EU report recommends that the working week can be reduced.

4   According to the law, lorry drivers have to rest every four hours.

5   She must give up her desk job after she developed repetitive strain injury in her wrist.

6   Do you have to have an eye test every year in your job?

7   When people can smoke at work, everybody benefits.

8   How much paternity leave should new fathers be entitled to?

9   From 1 July, all public transport operatives will must submit to regular drug testing.

10   A: In my opinion, you must be forced to retire from your job because of your age.
B: I agree. It should be your choice what you do.

11   Since the new management arrived, we must work flexitime if we want.

12   What training did you have to do to become an air traffic controller?

11.2 Reporting accidents

1   You are in the Accident and Emergency department of your local hospital. Take a role card and write your own name on the card. Read about your accident and think of two more details about what happened.
2   Talk to all of the other patients while you're waiting to be seen. Tell them why you are there and listen to their stories. Try to memorise everything you hear.

Name: _____	Name: _____	Name: _____	Name: _____
You're a flight attendant. While you were closing the overhead lockers after the passengers got off, the plane suddenly moved sideways and the first aid box fell on your head.	You're a film reviewer for a local newspaper. You were laughing so much at a re-issued Marx Brothers' film that you broke a rib.	You were going into the office kitchen to have your afternoon coffee when you slipped on the wet floor, fell onto the open dishwasher and cut your arm on a knife.	You were arguing with colleagues about the strength of men and women. You were trying to tear up the telephone book to prove your point, when you dislocated your shoulder.
Name: _____	Name: _____	Name: _____	Name: _____
You're a sports equipment retailer. While you were demonstrating how to use a climbing safety harness, you broke your finger on the fastener.	You own a flower shop. You were spraying your stock of houseplants with insecticide when you developed an allergic reaction to the product.	You're an accountant. When you were hurrying to finish this month's accounts, you stapled some invoices to your hand.	Your workplace was on the TV news. You were running into your office to see yourself on screen, when you tripped and broke your toe.

3   Work with a partner. You're the last people waiting at A&E. The hospital receptionist has accidentally deleted the records from today's A&E patients. Offer to help by filling in the missing details on the A&E record sheet before the next shift starts.

NAME	INJURY	HOW IT HAPPENED

12.1   The job market

Play this game in a group of six. Number yourselves 1–6. Shuffle the cards and place them face down in the middle.

1   One player takes a card and rolls the dice. Read the card out to the group, inserting the name of the person who corresponds to the number on the dice. (If you roll your own number, roll again.) Give the answer you think that person would give, giving your reasons.

2   The other players can agree or disagree with the first player, giving their own opinions. The person whose number was rolled should say nothing.

3   Now the person whose number was rolled can give their own answer to the question on the card. If the player who turned over the card was right, they get two points. Any other players who got the answer right get one point.

4   In turn, take a card and throw the dice until you have used all the cards or time is called. The winner is the player with the highest score.

If _____ could change one thing about his/her job or studies, what would it be?	If _____ could work abroad, would he/she prefer the Far East or North America?
If _____ was looking for a new job, would he/she be attracted more by a high salary or interesting work?	If _____ had to go on a business trip to Japan, would he/she learn some Japanese, use an online translation site or rely on his/her English?
If the Cambridge Business English exam was tomorrow, what would _____ do tonight?	If the next English class was cancelled, what would _____ do?
What company car would _____ drive, a sports car or an eco car?	What would _____ do if he/she had a year's paid holiday?
What would _____ do if he/she was late for an important interview or meeting?	What would _____ spend a €2,000 bonus on?
What would be the best gift for _____, a cookery book, a bicycle or a GPS?	Where would _____ live, if he/she could go anywhere?
Where would _____ suggest for an evening out with colleagues?	Would _____ enjoy running his/her own business?

12.2 Job applications

Work in groups. Listen to the questions. If your group knows the answer, make your group's 'noise'. If you answer correctly, you get two points. If another group goes first and answers wrongly, you can answer correctly for one point. For each point, colour in one coin. The first group to complete the euro symbol wins the game.

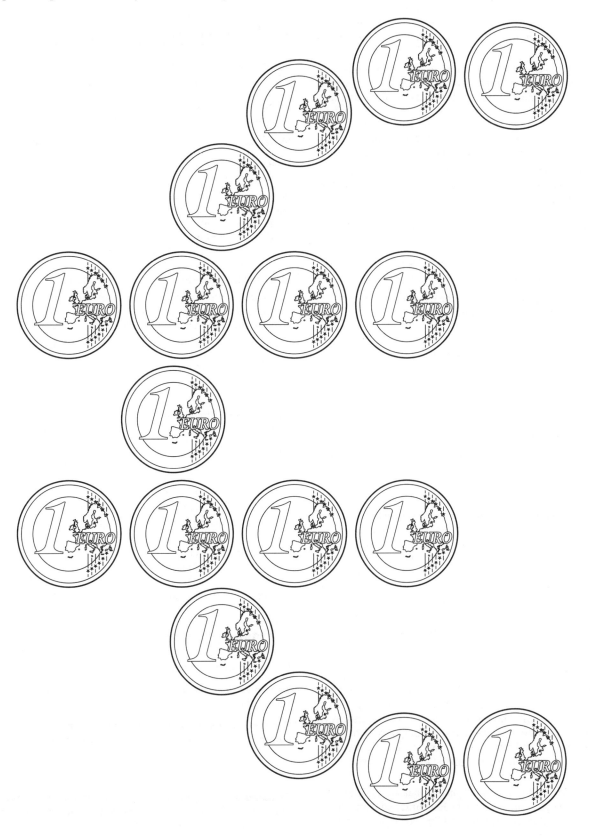

1.1 World of work

Summary of activity: Card game

Language practice: Present simple, adverbs of frequency, other expressions of frequency

Preparation for Speaking Test: Grammatical accuracy and business vocabulary

When to use: Any time after 1.1

Procedure: Photocopy and cut up one worksheet (instructions and cards) for each group of four to six students. Shuffle the sets of cards.

Put students into groups of four, five or six. Give each group a set of instructions and shuffled cards. With the whole class, read through the instructions and check that these are understood. Tell students to place each completed sentence down so that you can check as you circulate. Remind students that the objective is to use all the cards first, and that the sentences must be grammatically coherent but they can be illogical.

For groups that finish quickly, ask students to tell each other one true thing (to do with their work, study or personal life) for each of the frequency adverbs in turn. Alternatively, if groups have only made a few sentences, ask them to construct the original sentences. (The worksheet is laid out in order so can be used as a key.)

Feedback: Ask students for any interesting sentences, then ask if they can work out what the original sentences were.

Teacher role: Circulate and check the completed sentences, noting any problems for the feedback stage.

1.2 Personal and professional details

Summary of activity: Mingle activity; exchanging personal & professional information

Language practice: Personal information, language for job titles and responsibilities, and company departments

Preparation for Speaking Test: Part One: Giving personal information

When to use: Any time after 1.2

Procedure: Photocopy and cut up one worksheet (instructions and role cards) for each group of students. The groups should be as large as possible, with an even number of students up to a maximum of ten in each group. For example, if you have 16 students, have two groups of eight, rather than one of ten and one of six. (You can discard the bottom rows of cards: note that the cards match up in pairs on each row.)

With the whole class, review ways of greeting and responding to people (see page 8 of the Student's Book). You may wish to write some of these on the board for students to refer to during the activity.

Organise the class according to the sets of cards you have made. Give out one set of material to each group and tell one student in each group to read out the instructions to their group. Then check the instructions with the whole class. Give students a couple of minutes to prepare their roles and to check any necessary vocabulary with you before starting the activity. Remind students that the objective is to talk to as many people as they can to find their counterpart.

If possible, divide the classroom space so that the groups will not get mixed up during the activity. Encourage students to move around within their groups and find out about as many people as possible.

When students find their counterpart, they should stay together and introduce each other to other people, and try to find people with similar interests outside of work.

Feedback: Ask some of the students to introduce themselves and their counterpart to the class.

Teacher role: Monitor and give help during the preparation stage, tell students about their next 'task' when they've found their counterpart.

2.1 Work in progress

Summary of activity: Picture game

Language practice: Present continuous

Preparation for Speaking Test: Interactive communication, grammatical accuracy

When to use: Any time after the grammar section in 2.1

Procedure: Photocopy and cut up one worksheet (instructions and pictures) for each pair of students.

Put the students into pairs. Before giving out the pictures, ask students to imagine what their office colleagues (for in-work students), or another group of students (for pre-work students), are doing right now. Tell the pairs they have two minutes to write down as many ideas as they can think of, using the present continuous tense. After two minutes, elicit one or two ideas and find out which pair has the most ideas.

Give each pair the instructions and a picture. Tell students to look at the picture to see if any of their ideas match the activities there, and then follow the instructions.

For step 2, make sure that the two pairs have different pictures.

Feedback: Ask students to tell you the differences between the pictures, encouraging them to use the present continuous to do this.

Teacher role: Circulate and give any help as needed, monitoring students' use of the present continuous.

Answers:
top picture: cat asleep in in-tray, telephone upside down, man wearing pyjamas, man asleep on desk, person asleep on filing cabinets, woman doing yoga, couple spreading picnic blanket, couple cuddling, man reading car magazine, man playing computer game, man making sandwich

bottom picture: man eating hot meal on desk, man drinking from upside down cup, couple spreading picnic blanket, couple cuddling, man reading car magazine, woman on very high swivel chair, man asleep on desk, person asleep on filing cabinets, man making sandwich, woman doing yoga

2.2 Making arrangements

Summary of activity: Card game

Language practice: Present continuous with future time expressions

Preparation for Speaking Test: Part Three: Interactive communication, discourse management, grammatical accuracy

When to use: Any time after 2.2

Procedure: Photocopy and cut up one worksheet (instructions and cards) for each group of three students. Keep each set of cards (Arrangements and Excuses) separate.

Put the students into groups of three. If you have extra students, this activity will work better with pairs, rather than groups of four, in which case students simply alternate the roles.

Give each group a set of instructions and cards. Tell students to read the instructions and check that these are understood. Demonstrate the activity with a confident student to establish that students can use the present continuous from the prompts on the cards, eg, *Are you free to meet the new head of department on Monday morning? No, I'm taking the day off.*

Tell students that they should add as much detail as they can to the prompts on the cards: times, locations, etc. Remind students that the object of the game is to give the Arrangements cards away by getting one of the other players to agree, so they should try to persuade them. The other player should try to justify their excuse even if it's unbelievable.

Stop the game after 15 minutes or when most of the groups have used all their cards. Students who finish quickly can write a follow-up confirmation email to one of their group, for one arrangement (as in exercise 4, page 20 of the Student's Book).

Feedback: Find out which players won and which, if any, excuses were not successful. Share any useful expressions you heard in use.

Teacher role: Circulate and give any help as needed, monitoring the students' use of the present continuous. Note any useful expressions that students use, to share with the class at the feedback stage.

3.1 Company biography

Summary of activity: Timed information gap presentation

Language practice: Past simple, dates and numbers, company activity vocabulary

Preparation for Speaking Test: Part Two: Mini-presentation, giving information and expressing opinions

When to use: Use any time after 3.1

Procedure: Photocopy and cut up two worksheets for every four students. If you have extra students, you will need extra gapped fact sheets. You will also need a timer (eg a watch or a mobile phone).

Put students into groups of four, and divide them into A and B pairs. The A pair have an information sheet each for Papaya and a worksheet each for Fresco. The B pair have a Fresco information sheet each and a Papaya worksheet each. Each pair also has one set of instructions. Tell students to read the instructions together and check that these are understood.

Give students enough time to complete the first stage (instruction 1), changing the present simple verbs into past simple ones.

Then explain that the partners compete to present the most information in two minutes to the other members of their group.

You can organise this so that all pairs work simultaneously and you keep time, or the pairs can time themselves.

Tell the students to check the information they've written against the original fact sheet. The groups can then discuss which company they'd prefer to work for.

Feedback: Find out about areas of difficulty, such as numbers, dates or vocabulary.

Follow-up: Students can write up their notes into a short text if written consolidation is needed.

Teacher role: Act as timekeeper. Monitor for any remedial work.

3.2 Company performance

Summary of activity: Pelmanism game

Language practice: Business vocabulary – verb and noun synonyms

Preparation for Speaking Test: Part Two: Speaking from written prompts, business vocabulary

When to use: Any time after 3.2

Procedure: Photocopy and cut up one worksheet for each group of three students. (The activity will work equally with pairs, if you prefer.) Shuffle the cards.

Give one set of material (instructions and 32 cards) to each group. Tell students to read the instructions and check that these are understood. You may wish to demonstrate with a good student if students are not familiar with the game.

The items are arranged on the worksheet in order of suggested matches; this can be used as a key. However, there is some overlap which will not affect the outcome if all the matches are made correctly.

Groups that finish quickly can look at the cards again and decide which are verbs, which are nouns, and which can be both.

Feedback: Find out any disputed matches and discuss with the whole class. Check the classification into verbs, nouns and 'both'. Go over any problem areas you noted as you monitored the activity.

Teacher role: Circulate and solve any disputes over the sentences that students produce.

4.1 International business

Summary of activity: Card game: mini role plays

Language practice: Modal verbs and other expressions for permission, offers and requests

Preparation for Speaking Test: Part Three: A conversation between candidates, functional language and strategies, interactive communication, discourse management

When to use: Any time after 4.1

Procedure: Photocopy and cut up one worksheet for each group of three students.

Put the students into groups of three. If you have extra students, have groups of four rather than pairs.

Review the use of modal verbs for permission, offers and requests (page 36 in the Student's Book) and elicit further expressions that can be used for these functions. Write these on the board so that students can refer to them during the activity.

Give each group a set of instructions and cards. Tell students to read the instructions and check that these are understood. For each card, the student can choose one of the other two students in the group to role-play the situation with. Remind students that the aim is to collect the cards by getting a positive result, ie getting someone to agree to their request, give them permission or accept their offer.

You can ask students who finish quickly to think of their own real situations (at work or as students) and make two of their own requests or offers to their classmates.

Feedback: Find out which were the most difficult tasks, and who was the most persuasive person in each group.

Teacher role: Circulate and give any help with language as needed.

4.2 Business communications

Summary of activity: Phone call role play followed by discussion

Language practice: Expressions for phone calls and messages, giving and understanding specific information, expressions for checking information

Preparation for Speaking Test: Part Three: Interactive communication, pronunciation – word stress and individual sounds

When to use: Any time after 4.2

Procedure: Photocopy and cut up one worksheet for each group of four students.

Put the students into groups of four. If you have an odd number of students, double up on one of the role cards. Both students can note down the information when they receive a phone call, but only one will be able to make the call.

With the whole class, review the expressions for telephoning in exercise 1, page 38 and for telephone messages in exercise 6, page 41 of the Student's Book.

Give the instructions and four role cards to each group. Tell students to read and do each instruction in turn. They do not have to read all of the instructions at once. The two phone calls in each of steps 1 and 2 can be carried out simultaneously.

When all four phone calls have been made and the messages taken, tell students to read instruction 3 and work with their partner to compare the information and decide what action to take. Give students a maximum of five minutes for this.

Feedback: Ask some pairs to tell the class what they decided and why. Find out how many students made mistakes in writing down the numbers.

Teacher role: Monitor and help with ideas as necessary in step 3.

5.1 Career choices

Summary of activity: Bingo game

Language practice: Past participles of irregular verbs

Preparation for Speaking Test: Grammatical accuracy, business vocabulary

When to use: Any time after the grammar section in 5.1

Procedure: Photocopy and cut up one worksheet (bingo cards + instructions) for each group of four students.

Give out one set of material to each group and tell one student in each group to read out the instructions to their group. You may wish to check the instructions with the whole class.

Read out the sentences in the Teacher's role section, or if you prefer, simply read out the words in bold. Students listen for the verb in the present perfect and cross out the matching infinitive on their cards. Check the matches of the winning student by asking them to say both the infinitive and the participle of the verbs they have crossed out.

To play the game again, give out new cards and read the words or sentences in a different order.

Follow-up: Students can use the verbs on their cards to test each other on the past participles – the quickest one to answer gets a point, until all the verbs are read out.

Teacher role: Act as 'caller' reading out sentences and checking answers.

*Have you **been** to the new office yet?*

*The head of department has **gone** to see the supplier.*

*They've **kept** records since 1923.*

*We've **made** record profits this year.*

*Our company has **led** research in this field for decades.*

*Has the team **thought** of a solution to the problem yet?*

*They've **lost** money again this quarter.*

*We've completely **sold** out of that model, I'm afraid.*

*We've **dealt** with many problems like this before.*

*They've **won** a major contract to supply a large supermarket chain.*

*They've **built** a new factory to replace the one that burned down in the fire.*

*Costs have **risen** but our prices have stayed the same.*

*The company has **written** to everyone explaining the new policy.*

*He hasn't **said** anything about the changes yet.*

*The company has **hidden** the extent of its losses from the shareholders.*

*Have we **spent** all of the marketing budget?*

*I've **felt** strange all morning, since I ate that sandwich.*

*Management has **given** everyone an excellent bonus.*

*Sales have **grown** by over 100% in the last year.*

*The board has **taken** a difficult decision.*

*They've **cut** prices by 10% in the summer sale.*

*We've **spoken** to the customer about the delay.*

5.2 Achievements and plans

Summary of activity: Pairwork: role play information gap

Language practice: Present perfect simple, *going to* for plans

Preparation for Speaking Test: Part Three: Conversation between candidates, interactive communication and grammatical accuracy

When to use: Any time after the grammar section in 5.2

Procedure: Photocopy enough worksheets for one role card per student.

Put the students in pairs and give two copies of the same role card to each pair, making sure you have matching numbers of A and B roles. If you have an extra student, have three Student Bs. You may wish to match weak students with stronger students for this preparation stage. Equally, you can give the entrepreneur role card to the more imaginative students in the class. The students work together to prepare their roles as entrepreneurs and journalists. The entrepreneurs can choose to base themselves on real life entrepreneurs (Bill Gates, etc.) or invent their own characters.

Tell the students to form new pairs so that each entrepreneur (Student A) is working with a journalist (Student B). Again, you may wish to designate the pairs according to your students' abilities. If you have an extra student, there will be one group with two journalists.

The journalists should take notes of the answers given during the interview.

Students who finish quickly can draw up a list of up to ten questions they would like to ask an 'achiever' in the public eye, choosing someone from the field of business, government, sport, etc. As other students finish, they can compare lists.

Feedback: Ask some of the journalists to tell the class one or two things about the people they interviewed. Ask quick finishers about their follow-up questions and have the others speculate on the answers if appropriate.

Follow-up: Student B's notes can be used to write up a short description (or blurb) for the documentary. Student A can rewrite their own information in the 3rd person, or can use the notes from a different pair of students.

Teacher role: Monitor and give help with ideas (Students A) and accuracy (Students B) during the preparation stage.

6.1 Business travel

Summary of activity: Pairwork reading and information gap

Language practice: Reported speech and direct speech

Preparation for Speaking Test: Part Three: Conversation between candidates, grammatical accuracy

When to use: Any time after the grammar section in 6.1

Procedure: Photocopy and cut up one worksheet (instructions and 14 lines of text) for every four students. You can make an additional copy (not cut up) to be used as a quick reference to check the sequenced texts.

Put students into groups of four and give a set of material to each pair. (If you have extra students, the activity will also work with groups of three instead of pairs in steps 3–5.)

Tell students to read the instructions and check that these are understood. Tell students that they will work as a group for steps 1 and 2, and in pairs after that. In step 3, if your class is likely to have difficulty writing direct questions give them the questions from the answer key to use in their study. In step 4, pre-work students will need to invent a business persona if they are in pair B, answering the business travel questions.

Feedback: You can collate the original 12 survey questions on the board, for discussion or a written follow-up.

Follow-up: Ask students to write a short paragraph reporting the class replies to one of the surveys.

Teacher role: Circulate and help as necessary, try to keep the pairs working at the same pace in steps 3–5.

Possible answers:

Business travel survey:
1 Have you travelled for business in the last month?
2 How do you usually travel? / What form of transport do you usually use?
3 Do you use low-cost airlines?
4 Who / Which company did you last fly with?
5 Are you happy with the quality of service you receive?
6 Do you think business travel in your company will increase or decrease over the next ten years?

Family travel survey:
1 Does your family enjoy travelling?
2 Do you usually take an annual holiday?
3 Are you going on a trip abroad this year?
4 Can you speak any foreign languages?
5 Will the availability of budget air fares affect your holiday destination?
6 Will you go on several short breaks or one long summer holiday?

6.2 Travel arrangements

Summary of activity: Case study discussion

Language practice: Reported speech

Preparation for Speaking Test: Interactive communication, grammatical accuracy

When to use: Any time during or after 6.2

Procedure: Photocopy and cut up one worksheet for every three students.

Give the instructions and three role cards to each group. Tell students to read the instructions together. Tell them to take a role card each and spend three minutes preparing for the meeting. They should use reported speech to introduce the information on their cards. For example: *Jay, you said there were security cameras in the hotel, but there were none!* Each person must improvise a reason for the problems.

Tell groups they have ten minutes to list what went wrong and why.

Groups that finish quickly can work out what they are going to do next year to avoid the problems.

Stop the meetings when the time is up or when most groups have covered all the points.

Feedback: Ask some students to report the best excuses for the problems.

Teacher role: Monitor and give help with vocabulary as necessary during the activity.

7.1 Products and services

Summary of activity: Business scenario, group discussion and presentation

Language practice: Comparatives and superlatives, agreeing / disagreeing / stating opinions

Preparation for Speaking Test: Part Two: Giving presentations, *What is important when …*; **Part Three:** Discussing a scenario, interactive communication between candidates

When to use: Any time after 7.1

Procedure: Photocopy and cut up one worksheet for every two students.

Divide the class into groups of four. (You can also organise the activity as pairwork, where each member of a pair presents the decision to a new partner in step 3.) Give two sets of instructions to each group. Ask students to read the instructions and step 1, and tell them that they have up to five minutes for their discussion.

As the groups finish the first task, give a set of package cards to each pair and tell them to continue with step 2. After five minutes, give the pairs two minutes to finalise their discussions before going on to step 3.

Feedback: Ask some of the students which package they chose and why.

Follow-up: For a written follow-up, students can write an email to the branch managers congratulating them and telling them about the bonus package.

Teacher role: Monitor and give help and ideas as necessary during the activity.

7.2 Orders and contracts

Summary of activity: Speaking game

Language practice: Comparative and superlative forms

Preparation for Speaking Test: Part Two: Mini-presentations from prompts, discourse management

When to use: Any time after 7.2

Procedure: Photocopy one worksheet for each group of three students. Cut the cards up and shuffle them. Each group will also need a coin and a timer (eg a watch or a mobile phone). Put the students in groups of three and give a set of material (instructions and cards) to each group.

Tell students to read the instructions and check that these are understood. Tell them that they can compare the items on the cards or simply talk about them. If a student doesn't like the topics on the card, they can put it back in the pile and take the next one. They can only do this once. At the end of the time, Student C should ask his/her question, and Students B and C decide if Student A should get one, two or three points.

Groups that finish quickly can take any unused card and individually prepare the topics for one minute, then speak for one minute in turn. This is similar to Part Two of the Speaking Test.

Feedback: Find out what students found most difficult about the speaking activity and discuss how to deal with this. Ask students to compare speaking with or without preparation.

Follow-up: If you wish to do a written follow-up, students can choose one of the cards and write a paragraph comparing the three items.

Teacher role: Circulate and note any areas that individual students need to work on, such as linkers, vocabulary, fillers, grammatical accuracy.

8.1 Manufacturing processes

Summary of activity: Mini-presentations in pairs

Language practice: The passive

Preparation for Speaking Test: Part Two: Mini-presentations, long turns, listening and commenting on presentations

When to use: Any time after the grammar section in 8.1

Procedure: Photocopy and cut up one worksheet for every two students.

Put students into pairs and give the instructions and role cards to each pair. If you have an extra student, either have a group of three or have a strong student work alone.

Tell students to read the instructions and check that these are understood. Give the pairs a few minutes for the brainstorming in step 1 and five minutes to prepare their presentations.

For the presentations, you can put students into new pairs to give the presentation individually, or they can do a presentation as a pair to another pair. Put students into pairs with students who have chosen a different process.

After they have done the presentation once, they should repeat step 3 with a new pair.

Feedback: Discuss any areas students feel that they need to improve on.

Follow-up: If you wish for a written follow-up, students can write a paragraph about the process they presented or one they heard about.

Teacher role: Monitor and help with vocabulary and the passive construction. Try to keep the pairs working at the same pace. Note any useful expressions either to share with the class at the feedback stage, or that students need in order to make their presentations more fluent.

8.2 Problems and solutions

Summary of activity: Dominoes game

Language practice: Collocations with the passive, *when* and *if*, supply and demand, production philosophies, problems and solutions

Preparation for Speaking Test: Business vocabulary, grammatical accuracy

When to use: After 8.2

Procedure: Photocopy and cut up one worksheet for every three students.

Put students into groups of three and give one set of dominoes and instructions to each group. If you have an extra student, have two pairs rather than a group of four.

Tell students to read the instructions and check that these are understood.

Students who finish quickly can ask you to check their domino chain.

Teacher role: Monitor and check that students are putting the correct dominoes down, and help with any problems.

9.1 The future

Summary of activity: Chain writing game

Language practice: First conditional

Preparation for Speaking Test: Grammatical accuracy, interactive communication

When to use: Any time after 9.1

Procedure: Photocopy and cut up one worksheet for each student.

If you have a large class, put students into two groups. Arrange the seating in a circle or similar, so it will be clear which way the sheets get passed at each stage of the writing activity.

Before giving out the instructions and sheet, ask students to suggest topics that are in the news, or that have current relevance for them at work (for in-work students), or in their studies (for pre-work students). Write these topics on the board, asking students to give some background details for each suggestion. Then demonstrate the activity: choose one topic and write *If …* on the board, to elicit a prediction, eg *If the opposition wins the election, taxes will go up.* Then write *And if …* and elicit a prediction that follows the first, eg, *And if taxes go up, I won't be able to buy a new car.* Show students how to fold the paper and explain that they must be able to see the previous sentence only.

Give each student a set of instructions and a sheet. Tell students to choose a topic from the board and complete the first sentence on that topic. Each sentence should follow on from the sentence before.

For stage 5, students should work in groups of four or five to read out the chains and choose the most interesting / bizarre / optimistic / pessimistic one.

Feedback: Ask one or two students to read out the chains they chose as most interesting. Correct persistent errors, if there are any, in the grammar.

Follow-up: Depending on the topics, make a note to check some of the predictions at a future date.

Teacher role: Monitor, especially in the first two steps, to make sure the students fold the sheet correctly.

9.2 Meetings

Summary of activity: Case study discussion

Language practice: Functional language for meetings, agreeing and disagreeing

Preparation for Speaking Test: Part Three: Interactive communication, prioritising from a list of prompts

When to use: This activity can be used for pre-work students instead of exercise 8 on page 89 of the Student's Book. For in-work students, it can be used any time after 9.2.

Procedure: Photocopy and cut up one worksheet for each group of three students.

Put students into groups of three. If you have extra students, have groups of four rather than a pair, and give out two Communications director role cards. Give the instructions, case study notes and three role cards to each group. Tell students to read the instructions and the case study notes together. Tell them to take a role card each and spend five minutes preparing for the meeting.

Tell the groups they have ten minutes to discuss their ideas and write their action plans. Stop the meetings when the time is up or when most groups have their action plan ready.

Ask one member from each group to present their action plan to another group.

Feedback: Have a short discussion on the similarity or differences between the action plans.

Follow-up: For a written follow-up, students can write a press release or other written communication according to their action plans.

Teacher role: Monitor and help with vocabulary or ideas as necessary.

10.1 Career development

Summary of activity: Grammar worksheet followed by multiple-choice questions in pairs

Language practice: Relative pronouns: *who, which, where, whose, that*

Preparation for Speaking Test: Grammatical accuracy, business vocabulary including commonly confused words

When to use: Any time after 10.1

Procedure: Photocopy and cut up one worksheet for each pair of students.

Put students into pairs and give each pair two copies of the same worksheet. Tell students there are two stages to the activity. In stage one, they should read and do instruction

1 with their partner. You may wish to check answers to this section as a whole class before students move on to stage two (see answers below).

For stage two, tell students to read instructions 2 and 3, and make sure they form new pairs so that students are in A/B pairs.

As pairs finish, they can review any items that they got wrong. The original pairs can reform to compare their scores.

Feedback: Check the correct relative pronouns were used.

Teacher role: Circulate and give help as needed.

Answers:

Student A:

1 where	2 that / which
3 who / (that)	4 whose
5 who / (that)	6 that / which
7 where	8 who / (that)

Student B:

1 who / (that)	2 that / which
3 whose	4 who / (that)
5 that / which	6 where
7 who / (that)	8 where

10.2 Organising a conference

Summary of activity: *Find someone who ...* mingle activity

Language practice: Relative pronouns, offers and invitations, small talk

Preparation for Speaking Test: Part One: Giving personal information and expressing personal opinions; **Part Three:** Interactive communication, discourse management

When to use: Any time after 10.2

Procedure: Photocopy and cut up one worksheet for every two students.

Tell students that they are at a conference and give them a couple of minutes to invent a name and an identity. Alternatively, they can be themselves.

Give each pair of students a set of instructions and one grid each. There are two versions of the grid so that sometimes the students will have to answer an expected question. If you prefer students to prepare their questions in pairs they should work with another student who has the same grid.

Tell students to read the instructions and check that these are understood. Give students a time limit of a few minutes to work alone and prepare their questions for the 'mingle' activity. Tell students that they should only answer direct questions; if someone simply reads out the text on the grid they should not answer. Also, they should not answer more than one 'grid' question at a time.

Students who finish quickly should sit down and write a note to one of the people they spoke to, inviting them to meet again.

Feedback: Ask some of the students to tell the class one or two things about the people they spoke to. Find out if there were any questions that had no 'results'.

Follow-up: All students can write a note, as for the quick finishers, and then exchange the notes.

Teacher role: Circulate and take note of any remedial work that needs to be done on speaking in general.

11.1 Health and safety

Summary of activity: Grammar worksheet followed by class game

Language practice: Modal verbs: *must, (don't) have to, can, should*

Preparation for Speaking Test: Grammatical accuracy, business vocabulary

When to use: Any time after the grammar section in 11.1

Procedure: Photocopy one worksheet for each pair of students.

You may wish to revise modal verbs with the whole class before the activity if several lessons have elapsed since doing the grammar section of Unit 11.

Put students into pairs and give a worksheet to each pair. Tell students to read instructions in step 1 and tell them they have five minutes to complete the worksheet.

Tell students to read instructions for steps 2 and 3, and demonstrate the activity by writing the sentence below on the board. Ask students, in their pairs, to decide if the sentence is correct or not.

You have to take the first aid course; it's voluntary.

Tell each pair to write down how much money they want to invest, and then ask each pair to tell the rest of the class the amount of their investment and if they think the sentence is correct or incorrect. The pairs who said *incorrect* win double the amount they invested. The pairs who said *correct* lose the amount they invested. Then ask for investments on the correct version (answer: *don't have to*) in the same way.

Repeat with sentences 1–12. With small classes, you can keep a record of investments on the board, otherwise each pair should keep a record of their investments.

Answers:

1 mustn't, shouldn't	7 can't, mustn't
2 ✓	8 ✓
3 should	9 will have to
4 ✓	10 A: shouldn't
5 had to	11 can
6 ✓	12 ✓

Teacher role: Make a note of the sentences that cause most difficulty for any remedial work.

11.2 Reporting accidents

Summary of activity: Role play 'mingle' followed by pairwork

Language practice: Past simple and past continuous

Preparation for Speaking Test: Part Two: Speaking from written prompts, interactive communication, discourse management

When to use: Any time after section 11.2

Procedure: Cut worksheets into two halves: instructions 1 and 2 plus role cards; instruction 3 plus the A&E record sheet. Photocopy enough copies of the top half for every eight students, and enough copies of the bottom half for every two students. Cut up the individual role cards.

Put students into groups of eight. If you have one or two extra students, repeat some of the role cards. Alternatively, have groups of seven or six and discard one or two of the cards.

Give each group instructions 1 and 2, and a set of role cards, face down. Ask one student to read the instructions 1 and 2 to the group, and check that these are understood. Tell students they have 15 minutes to talk to all the other patients.

After 15 minutes, or when students have exchanged information, tell students to find a partner. Give each pair a sheet with instruction 3 and the A&E record sheet. Tell students that it's now a race to fill in the sheet. When the first pair finishes, everyone should stop. Then check the information and give one point for each correct fact, up to a maximum of 24 points. The pair with the most points wins.

Follow-up: Ask students to relate any anecdotes about incidents or accidents they know.

Teacher role: Check any vocabulary problems in the preparation stage. Monitor students and note any general remedial work on speaking that needs to be addressed before the Speaking Test.

12.1 The job market

Summary of activity: Card game

Language practice: The second conditional

Preparation for Speaking Test: Part Three: Conversation between candidates, interactive communication, discourse management, grammatical accuracy

When to use: Any time after the grammar section in 12.1

Procedure: Photocopy and cut up one worksheet (instructions and cards) for each group of six students. You'll also need a dice for each group, or students can use small pieces of paper numbered 1–6.

Put students into groups of six. The activity will also work with smaller groups, in which case the players should number themselves accordingly and roll the dice again if they roll numbers that are not in their group.

Give each group a set of instructions and cards. You can introduce the game by asking students how well they think they know each other now that the course is almost over. This game will reveal all! Tell students to read the instructions and check that these are understood.

Stop the game after 15 minutes or earlier if the groups are recycling the cards.

Feedback: Find out which students appear to know their colleagues best, which were the most difficult questions to answer, etc.

Teacher role: Circulate and give any help as needed, noting how well students use the conditional form in their answers.

12.2 Job applications

Summary of activity: Group game to revise language, and knowledge of the Cambridge Business English exam

When to use: After 12.2

Procedure: Photocopy one sheet for each group. Groups can be between two to four students. Each group will need its own whistle, bell, cup of coins or similar to make a noise.

Each group competes against the others to answer the questions asked by the teacher. There are 12 language questions and 16 questions about the exam, which you can read out in any order. Tick each one as you use it.

Read out a question and let each group confer. When they have the answer, they should use their bell, whistle, etc. They should not call out the answer until you ask them. Award two points for a correct answer. If the first group gets the answer wrong, ask the other groups for their answer. Give one point for each correct answer. Alternatively, allow the first group to answer, but don't comment on their answer; then ask the other groups to give their answers, and give points to all the correct answers with an extra point for the first group.

For each point, the groups 'colour in' a coin to complete the euro symbol. The first group to complete the euro symbol wins the game.

Language questions:
1 Change this sentence into reported speech beginning *He*: *I would like to change my flight.*
2 Change this sentence so that it is true: *Trains are as fast as planes.*
3 Complete this sentence in a logical way: *If I didn't speak English, …*
4 Complete this sentence with an appropriate modal verb: *You ____ use the lift in a fire.*
5 Is this sentence grammatically correct? (For an extra point, correct it.) *If the bad weather will continue, we won't sell many bikinis.*
6 Is this sentence grammatically correct? (For an extra point, correct it.) *I had a teacher what was very motivating.*
7 Put the adverb *usually* in the correct place: *I am at my desk at 8am.*
8 Put this sentence into the past simple tense: *Our profits grow every year.*
9 Say four verbs that collocate with money.
10 What's the missing preposition? *We have a sales meeting ____ the end of the month.*
11 Which noun collocates with these verbs: *cause, solve, deal with, avoid, detect*?
12 You are with people you don't know well. Ask to borrow a pen.

Questions about the exam:
1 Can you talk about your home in Part One of the Speaking Test?
2 Correct this statement: *Part Two of the Listening Test has multiple choice answers.*
3 How long do you get to transfer your answers to the Answer sheet in the Listening Test?
4 How many parts are there to the Speaking Test?
5 How many tests does the exam have? Name them.
6 How many words should you write in Part One of the Writing Test?
7 In the Speaking Test, what should you do if you don't understand the examiner?
8 In which part of the exam do you have to produce a piece of internal communication?
9 True or False? Part Five of the Reading Test is multiple choice.
10 True or False? The examiner doesn't join in Part Three in the Speaking Test.
11 True or False? The Listening Test lasts 40 minutes.
12 True or False? The Speaking Test lasts five minutes.
13 True or False? There are six parts in the Reading Test.
14 True or False? You can write your answers in pencil.
15 What kind of task do you do in Part Seven of the Reading Test?
16 What's the format of Part Two of the Speaking Test?

Answers to language questions:
1 He said he would like to change his flight.
2 Trains aren't as fast as planes. Planes are faster than trains. Trains are slower than planes.
3 If I didn't speak English, I wouldn't be here, I would start to learn, I wouldn't be doing this job, etc.
4 mustn't, shouldn't, can't
5 No. 'If the bad weather continues, we won't sell many bikinis.'
6 No. 'I had a teacher who was very motivating.'
7 I am usually at my desk at 8am.
8 Our profits grew every year.
9 spend, lose, save, make, earn, win, etc.
10 at
11 problem
12 'Could I borrow a pen, please? / Could you lend me a pen, please?'

Answers to questions about the exam:
1 Yes
2 Part One and Part Four of the Listening Test have multiple choice answers.
3 Ten minutes
4 Three
5 4: reading, writing, listening, speaking
6 30–40
7 Ask them to repeat or ask a question to check your understanding.
8 Writing Part One
9 True
10 False. He/She can join in, and asks questions at the end.
11 True
12 False – about 12 minutes
13 False – there are seven
14 True
15 Transferring information to complete a form or notes
16 A mini-presentation

Workbook answer key

MODULE 1

1.1
World of work

1
A retail manager
B office manager
C tourism officer

2
0 A (*I'm responsible for the success of the shop – meeting our sales targets, basically*)
1 B (*I work a typical working week, Monday to Friday*)
2 C (*I talk to people of different nationalities every day*)
3 C (*I answer people's queries*)
4 B (*I'm usually at my computer most of the day*)
5 A (*I work long days ... On a typical day, I get here early in the morning*)

3 **Text A**
0 organise special promotions
1 check deliveries
2 help staff
3 manage staff
4 process salaries
5 supervise day-to-day work

Text B
6 check accounts
7 process accounts
8 supervise staff
9 deal with payments
10 reduce office costs

Text C
11 answer queries
12 give information
13 set up exhibitions
14 lead tours
15 represent the town / country

4
0 work
1 has
2 is
3 deal with
4 is
5 counts
6 don't like
7 don't often have
8 knows
9 are
10 try

5
0 Do you *usually* drive to work?
1 He doesn't *usually* work late.
2 I *never* work at weekends.
3 He visits clients *twice a month*.
4 I am *normally* at my desk by 8am.
5 Do they give press conferences *every week*?
6 She isn't *often* behind schedule.
7 We *often* finish work early *on Fridays*.
8 Our department *sometimes* organises training sessions *at weekends*.
9 He is *occasionally* late for work *on Mondays*.

6
1 check personal emails at work
2 X and Y
3 take too long for lunch
4 X
5 Y

7
In Company X, employees rarely take a day off when they are not sick.
In Company X, staff often use the office stationery for their personal use.
In Company X, people sometimes copy the office software for their personal use.
In Company Y, employees often take a day off when they are not sick.
In Company Y, staff sometimes use the office stationery for their personal use.
In Company Y, people never copy the office software for their personal use.

1.2
Personal and professional details

1

day	see	pen	eye	go	you	car
A	B	F	I	O	Q	R
H	C	L	Y		U	
J	D	M			W	
K	E	N				
	G	S				
	P	X				
	T	Z				
	V					

3

/z/ as in *goes*	/s/ as in *works*	/ɪz/ as in *finishes*
tries	gets	organises
opens	checks	manages
enjoys	helps	processes
gives	visits	arranges

4 1 Hi, Anya. Nice to see you again.

2 Hello, I'm Ross McGovern.

3 Excuse me, are you Bart Roland?

4 Hello, Ms Wiseman. How are you?

5 Excuse me, is your name Delemus?

6 Good morning, my name's Maya Lund.

5 1 F 2 C 3 A 4 B 5 E 6 D

6 0 What time do you start work?

1 What do you do?

2 Who do you work for?

3 Do you like your job?

4 Where is your studio?

5 Why is it in Paris?

6 How often do you show your collection?

7 Are you ambitious?

8 Where are you from?

9 Who buys your designs?

7 **Sample answer:**

Raffi is from Birmingham. He's a fashion designer and he works for YSL™ in Paris. His studio is in Paris, because Paris is the fashion centre of the world. He loves his job and he's very ambitious: he wants to have his own fashion label. He shows his collection twice a year, in spring and in autumn, and lots of celebrities and film stars buy his designs.

8 Hi everyone

I'm Katherine, but my **friends** call me Kate. My name is **English**, but I'm from Lisbon. I'm **a** lawyer and I work in the head **office** of the Legal Department at PLA. I specialise in insurance contracts. In my spare time, I like marathon **running** and **photography**. You can see my pictures if you click <u>here</u>. I hope you like them!

1.3
Reading Test: Part One

1 1 B

2 Option A says 'mornings only' but the text doesn't specify mornings.

Option C says 'delivers' but the shop accepts deliveries.

3 **Text 2**

1 C

2 Option A says 'present' identity documents, whereas the text says 'have your photo taken for your conference ID badge'.

Option B says 'leave' but the text gives instructions for arriving because it says 'sign in' and 'welcome pack'.

Text 3

1 A

2 Option B says 'mornings' but the text says '16.30–17.30', which is the afternoon.

Option C says 'at half past six', which is 18.30.

Text 4

1 C

2 Option A says 'open throughout February' but the text says 'closed'.

Option B says 'closed on the first of February' but the text says 'closed for holidays from 2/2'.

MODULE 2

2.1
Work in progress

1 0 is delivering

1 are extending

2 are looking

3 are improving

4 is holding

5 are using

6 isn't working

7 is visiting

8 is co-ordinating

9 am giving

10 are doing

2 **Possible answers:**

0 On Day 1, he's having a breakfast meeting with the IT manager, Australia.

1 In the morning, he's meeting the department heads until lunchtime.

2 In the afternoon, he's giving a presentation of the project to local staff.

3 On Day 2, he's with the IT manager in the morning and they are visiting the Sydney offices and factories.

4 After that, he's interviewing local staff.

5 On Day 2 in the afternoon, he's discussing the project schedules with the IT manager. / They are discussing the project schedules.

6 On Day 4, he's leaving for Bangkok in the evening.

3 1 D2 2 A1 3 F2 4 E1 5 C3 6 B3

4 **Project manager**

0 employ project staff

1 set targets for each phase of the project

2 hold meetings with management

3 complete project on schedule

Team leader

4 supervise the work of the team

5 give weekly updates to project manager

6 meet deadlines agreed with project manager

7 hire temporary staff if necessary

5 1 B Wrong (*I'm having a great time here at Mulligan!*)

2 B Wrong (*Next week I'm spending* three days *with the traders in the front office*)

3 C Doesn't say (*Are you* thinking about *applying for a permanent job …?*)

4 C Doesn't say

5 A Right (*first, I have to finish my degree!*)

6 1 option

2 clients

3 great

4 traders

5 short-term

6 degree

2.2
Making arrangements

1 1 E 2 D 3 A 4 C 5 B

2

09.15	nine fif<u>teen</u>
12.30	twelve <u>thir</u>ty
2.20	two <u>twen</u>ty
6.19	six nine<u>teen</u>
13	thir<u>teen</u>
90	<u>nine</u>ty
18	eigh<u>teen</u>
80	<u>eigh</u>ty

1 **first** syllable: <u>*twenty*</u>, <u>*thirty*</u> etc

2 **second** syllable: *thir<u>teen</u>, four<u>teen</u>* etc

4

19th Jan	the nine<u>teenth</u> of <u>J</u>anuary
30th Sept	the <u>thir</u>tieth of Sep<u>tem</u>ber
13th Jul	the thir<u>teenth</u> of July
17th Feb	the seven<u>teenth</u> of <u>Feb</u>ruary
18th Dec	the eigh<u>teenth</u> of De<u>cem</u>ber
15th Oct	the fif<u>teenth</u> of Oc<u>to</u>ber
30th Nov	the <u>thir</u>tieth of No<u>vem</u>ber
20th Aug	the <u>twen</u>tieth of <u>Au</u>gust

5 1 at

2 on

3 in

4 in

5 at

6 at

7 in

8 on

9 on

10 in

6 and **7**

A

From: Managing Director

To: all_staff@mail

Subject: Phyllis Adcock

As you may know, Phyllis Adcock is leaving the company at the end of the week. I invite you all to join Phyllis, myself and the rest of the management team <u>on Friday lunchtime</u>, for <u>an informal leaving party</u>. Drinks and snacks will be served <u>in the board room</u> <u>from 1pm</u>. Please be prompt.

B

From: Tessa Faulks

To: bwoodcock@woodcock.org

Subject: Presentation

Many thanks for the invitation to your presentation on Tuesday 12th. I'm afraid I'm visiting our Italian subsidiary next week, so I won't be able to attend.

Good luck with the presentation.

8 **Sample answer:**

Dear Tessa

I'm giving a presentation on 'New Markets' next week and I would like to invite you to attend. It's on Tuesday 12th, in the main meeting room at Head Office.

I hope you can come.

Brenda Woodcock

9 **Sample answer:**

Dear Phyllis

I have received an invitation from the MD to your leaving party. I'm afraid I'm visiting the American operation next week, so I won't be able to attend. I'm sorry to miss your party. I wish you all the best for the future.

Regards

Anna

10 I am writing to invite you to our annual seminar on Future Trends in IT. This year the seminar is taking place at the Science Museum, **on 17th July**. **It starts at 10am**. It is open to all IT professionals, and it is of particular interest to IT systems managers. Please confirm your attendance. Registration closes **on 10th July**.

2.3
Writing Test: Introduction

1 A Part One (*the text is shorter – 30–40 words, and more informal. It is clearly to someone in the same company*)

B Part Two (*this text is longer – 60–80 words, and more formal*)

2 3 (*1 does not match because the note does not say where the meeting is, or ask the colleague to call for more information. 2 does not match because the memo is written to Fiona, not to the department. It does not mention punctuality.*)

3 Sample answers:

1 Hi Bill

I have a marketing meeting this afternoon, but I'm leaving early to catch the flight to London. Can you take my place at the meeting? It's in room 2.2 at 3pm. Give me a call if you need any information.

Thanks

David

2 Hello everyone

I've arranged a meeting with the IT manager to discuss our ideas for improvements to the internal email system. She will be here on Thursday morning at 09.30. Please don't be late.

Regards

Sue

MODULE 3

3.1
Company biography

1
- 0 developed
- 1 crashed
- 2 invented
- 3 formed
- 4 signed
- 5 began
- 6 forced
- 7 launched
- 8 ended
- 9 merged
- 10 bought

2
1 What did Henry Ford produce?
2 When was the Wall Street Crash?
3 What was the aim of the EEC?
4 Where did colour TV broadcasts begin?
5 Was 'New Coke™' a success?
6 How long did the dot-com boom last?

3
1 He / Henry Ford produced cars.
2 It / The Wall Street Crash was in 1929.
3 The aim of the EEC was to promote free trade in Europe.
4 They / Colour TV broadcasts began in Europe.
5 No, it wasn't. / 'New Coke' wasn't a success.
6 It / The dot-com boom lasted five years.

6 1 B 2 A 3 C 4 B 5 C

7 **Paragraph 1**
ended
made
marketed

Paragraph 2
expanded
acquired
launched

Paragraph 3
persuaded
developed

3.2
Company performance

1
1 sold
2 produced
3 designed
4 imported
5 marketed
6 published

2

/d/ **as in** *planned*	/t/ **as in** *produced*	/ɪd/ **as in** *started*
designed	crashed	distributed
manufactured	developed	expanded
merged	forced	imported
organised	launched	marketed
supplied	published	provided

3 Sample answer:

ExxonMobil™ is a public company. It began operations in 1999 after Exxon and Mobil merged. Its original name was Standard Oil. Its headquarters are in Texas, in the United States. The CEO is Darren Woods. The company produces fuels, lubricants and petrochemicals and it had a revenue of $237.1 billion USD in 2017. It has around 70,000 employees.

4 Business is **beginning** to recover from the stock market mini-crash last **Wednesday**. The index **rose** by three points yesterday, and there was an increase in activity in all sectors. Experts **say** that the fall in share prices last week was not a real crash, but part of a normal **cycle** and not unusual in **October**.

5

			L				
	R	O	S	E			
			V				
		S	T	E	A	D	Y
		T	L				
		E					
		A			I		
		D	O	W	N		
		I			C		
		L			R		
		Y		F	E	L	L
					A		
					S		
					E		

6

Graph 2 (Text A)

Graph 5 (Text B)

Graph 1 (Text C)

Graph 4 (Text D)

Graph 3 (Text E)

Graph 6 (Text F)

3.3

Listening Test: Part One

2 A 3

B 1

C 2

D 4

Possible answers:

Words <u>not</u> connected to topics:

A invent, office, safe

B application, fly, time

C computer, paper, share

D material, memo, system

MODULE 4

4.1

International business

1 1 B

2 F

3 C

4 E

5 D

6 A

2 manufacturer → freight forwarder → carrier → wholesaler → retailer → consumer

3 A (A Scandinavian success story)

4 1 people

2 Exports

3 goods

4 companies / firms / brands

5 successful

5

verb	noun – thing	noun – person
compete	competition	competitor
consume	consumption	consumer
export	export(s)	exporter
import	import(s)	importer
produce	product	producer
retail	retail	retailer
sell	sales	seller
ship	shipment	shipper
supply	supplies	supplier
transport	transport	transporter

6 1 Can

2 couldn't

3 can

4 couldn't

5 can, can't

6 could

7 can't

8 could

7 1 should

2 can't

3 Should

4 can

5 Couldn't

6 couldn't

7 Should

8 should

8 2, 3, 5

4.2

Business communications

1 1 C

2 D (*introduces the reason for writing*)

3 F (*gives further details*)

4 E (*introduces second point*)

5 B (*suggests possible action*)

6 G

7 A

2 1 J Hallcro

2 invoice 982/08

3 four PC monitors

4 claims procedure

3   **Sample answer:**

Dear Sir or Madam

I am writing about your invoice 982/09 for the transport of our office furniture to new premises on 4th and 5th March. The original quotation for this work was €2,750. However, the invoice you sent us is for €1,500. I think this is a mistake. In addition, the move took two days, not one. Could you please check your records and send me the correct invoice?

Yours sincerely

5   **Possible answers:**

0 Don't worry, I'll take it.

1 I'll photocopy it now.

2 I'll finish early tomorrow.

3 I'll tell the manager.

4 I'll be ready in time.

6   0 in<u>crea</u>se

1 <u>ex</u>ports

2 im<u>port</u>

3 <u>tra</u>nsport

4 <u>pre</u>sent

5 <u>de</u>crease

6 <u>re</u>cord

7 per<u>mit</u>

7   **Correct order:**

B Good morning, Westco Transport.

D I'm afraid she's not in her office at the moment.

F Would you like to leave a message?

E Who's calling, please?

A Does she have your number?

C I'll ask her to call you when she gets back.

8   **Westco Transport**

Telephone Message

Message for: Simone

Name of caller: Mark Bashir

Company: Hi-Flyers

Tel./Email: –

Message: Please call him back

4.3
Speaking Test: Part One

2   1 I **am** from Bilbao. / I**'m** from Bilbao.

2 I'm **a** marketing assistant.

3 I'm doing a **degree** in economics.

4 I **work** for a small family business.

5 My company's name **is** Gratton.

6 **I** agree with you, a small town is better.

7 I **don't** like working in a large company.

8 I like working there **very much.**

3   1 C   2 C   3 B   4 A   5 B

6 B   7 C   8 A   9 A

MODULE 5

5.1
Career choices

1   1 C Doesn't say

2 A Right (*And contrary to what some people might say, a gap year doesn't have to be a wasted year.*)

3 C Doesn't say

4 B Wrong (*… your CV will look better if you gained some work experience … The combination of such work experience and the fact that you've lived abroad could make your CV stand out.*)

5 C Doesn't say

2   1 stand out

2 career path

3 internships

4 in high demand

5 skill

6 turn

7 contrary

8 earns a living

3   grow

4   1 earn   2 lost   3 spent

4 save   5 lent   6 win

5   0 She has phoned the suppliers.

1 She hasn't sent them the new contract.

2 She has booked a flight to Glasgow.

3 She has written up the minutes from yesterday's meeting.

4 She hasn't spoken to the office manager about the security door.

5 She hasn't given the IT manual back to Sara.

6 She hasn't bought a birthday card for the MD.

6   1 C Have you been to Venice?

2 F Has Alistair gone to Venice?

3 A Have we used this supplier before?

4 B Has the new boss been to the office today?

5 E Haven't you finished the accounts yet?

6 D Have you been here for a long time?

7   1 yet (*used with negatives or questions*)

2 yesterday (*finished times, not used with present perfect*)

3 already (*used with positive sentences*)

4 last week (*finished times, not used with present perfect*)

5 ever (*wrong position in sentence*)

6 ever (*used with questions or negatives*)

8 1 took over   2 has fired   3 has closed
    4 has cut   5 have never seen   6 said
    7 have had   8 rose

5.2
Achievements and plans

1 He's going to give away all of his money.

2 1 A, B, E, F
    2 C, D, G, J
    3 H
    4 I

3 He founded 11 companies.
    He has been on the list of the UK's ten richest people for
    18 years.
    He has sold all the shares in his companies now.
    His companies expanded into 25 countries.
    They employed more than 50,000 people.
    They have never made a loss.
    They increased their turnover by 700%.
    The share price has risen steadily since 1987.
    Investors have made a lot of money.

4 In Sir Cameron's 40-year career, he invented 46 successful
    products and he founded 11 companies. His companies
    expanded into 25 countries and they employed more than
    50,000 people. They have never made a loss. His companies
    increased their turnover by 700% and the share price has
    risen steadily since 1987. Investors have made lots of
    money. Sir Cameron has been on the list of the UK's ten
    richest people for 18 years, but he has sold all his shares in
    his companies now.

5 Sir **Cameron's** other achievements include a knighthood
    from Queen Elizabeth II and the **French** Légion d'honneur.
    He has also sailed around the world **three** times, and in
    1988, he **climbed** Mount Everest. He has **set** up a number
    of foundations to help children in need, and now he **plans**
    to give most of his fortune to these organisations.

6 1 are going to do
    2 are going to add
    3 is going to mean
    4 isn't going to be
    5 are going to introduce
    6 are we going to start
    7 are going to modify
    8 are we going to get

8 <u>twenty</u>-<u>seven</u> per <u>cent</u> 27%
    three <u>quarters</u> ¾
    <u>nine</u> hundred and <u>fifty</u>-<u>five</u> 955

<u>fif</u>teen thousand, <u>three</u> hundred and <u>nine</u>ty 15,390
<u>eight</u> hundred <u>thousand</u> 800,000
<u>thir</u>ty-<u>eight</u> <u>mill</u>ion 38,000,000
<u>six</u> and a <u>half</u> 6½
<u>nine</u>ty-<u>nine</u> per <u>cent</u> 99%
<u>eight</u> hundred and <u>thir</u>ty 830
<u>twelve</u> thousand, <u>three</u> hundred and <u>seven</u>ty-<u>seven</u> 12,377

5.3
Reading Test: Part Four

2 3, 5, 7

3 2, 4

4 1, 6

5 1 Right
    2 Wrong
    3 Doesn't say
    4 Wrong
    5 Doesn't say
    6 Right
    7 Doesn't say

7 1 C   2 F   3 A   4 G   5 E   6 D   7 B

MODULE 6

6.1
Business travel

1 1 C   2 F   3 D   4 B   5 E   6 A

2 1 C   2 A   3 E   4 D   5 B   6 F
    1 The taxi driver said it was €25 and there was a €10
       supplement for the suitcases.
    2 The travel agent said I could pick up my tickets at the
       airport.
    3 The security officer told me to remove my jacket before I
       came through the security gate.
    4 The check-in clerk said I was too late to check in. The
       flight was already boarding.
    5 The conference organiser told me to wait for the
       conference representative at the meeting point.
    6 The airline representative told me there was a technical
       problem with the plane and they were working on it (at
       that moment).

3 **Sample answer:**
    Ms Vine, this is Tom. I spoke to the travel agent about trains
    to Valencia and he said the service was excellent. He said
    they had just started a new service. He said there were
    frequent trains and they were really comfortable. He also
    said it took about three hours from Barcelona and no trains

had arrived late since the new service began. He said you could book in advance or you could buy a ticket on the day and it was very popular with business travellers. Do you want me to cancel your air ticket and book you on the train?

4 1 take off
    2 business
    3 boarding pass
    4 flight attendant
    5 check in
    6 luggage

5 1 C
    2 A
    3 L
    4 H
    5 I

6 0 Mr Nielsen is the **passenger**.
    1 Mr Nielsen's flight with Justgo Airlines was **cancelled**.
    2 Mr Nielsen **wrote** to complain to the airline.
    3 Justgo went bankrupt **before** Mr Nielsen made his complaint.
    4 Justgo **didn't make** alternative travel arrangements for Mr Nielsen.
    5 True

6.2
Travel arrangements

1 0 We have booked
    1 We now need
    2 and one more
    3 Could you confirm
    4 Payment details are
    5 I write to confirm
    6 Please quote this number
    7 If you are going to
    8 I can also confirm that the

2 Dear Ms Marino
I write to confirm the additions to your booking, reference 983UT. I have reserved two single rooms for 10th–12th May and one double room for 12th May. The additional cost is €390 in total. Please note that you must present the same credit card on arrival at the hotel.
We look forward to seeing you on 10th May.
Best regards
Florence Bruce

3

			¹C	O	N	F	E	R	E	N	C	E	R	O	O	M		
			L															
			E															
		²L	A	U	N	D	³R	Y										
			N					O										
			E		⁴P	O	O	L										
			R				M											
							S											
							E											
					⁵P	O	R	T	E	R								
							V											
					⁶M	I	N	I	B	A	R							
							C											
⁷I	N	T	E	R	N	E	T	C	O	N	N	E	C	T	I	O	N	

4 1 I'd like to book a seat
    2 would you like to fly?
    3 There's / There is
    4 It leaves at 20.05.
    5 I'll check (the) availability.
    6 Could you make me a reservation
    7 What's the passenger's name
    8 Would you like me to spell
    9 Do you have an account
    10 Would you like me to send you

5 **Sample answer:**
Dear Guy
Just to let you know that I'm arriving in Geneva on 12th November, at 11pm local time. Could you meet me at the airport?
Looking forward to seeing you.
Many thanks
James

6

●●○	○●○
passenger	arrival
company	connection
conference	departure
customer	equipment
excellent	
Internet	
manager	
newspaper	
technical	
telephone	

6.3
Writing Test: Part One

1 B (*A is too informal; C is too formal for a memo to another member of staff; B is neutral.*)

2 Sample answers:

1 Dear all

This year's annual party is on 29 December at the Grand Hotel. All staff and their partners are invited.

Remember to confirm your attendance to me by email before 10 December, please.

Thanks

Sandra

2 To: all staff

From: Hotel Manager

I have received a letter from the Franklin Trust thanking us for the excellent service and facilities we provided for the conference last week. Well done, everyone. You did a very professional job.

Thanks again, everyone, for your hard work.

Angela

MODULE 7

7.1
Products and services

1 1 C 2 D 3 C 4 C 5 B 6 C 7 D 8 D

2 0 System A is the smallest.

1 System A is the noisiest.

2 System C is the quietest.

3 System A is the easiest to install.

4 System C is more expensive than System B.

5 System C is easier to maintain than System B.

3 1 less expensive

2 quicker

3 more comfortable

4 more interesting

5 better

6 more convenient

4 0 smaller

1 better than

2 as popular as

3 more convenient than

4 easier

5 more appropriate than

6 more entertaining than

7 wider

8 more expensive than

5 1 €1,000 per year

2 ten

3 problems with parking and driving fines

4 €100

6 1 A and   2 B can   3 A The   4 A as
5 C their   6 C quickest   7 A does   8 B more

7 **Client consultation record**

Name of client:	Simon Westgate
Date of enquiry:	11/02/19
Annual contract number:	9934/HT
Nature of enquiry:	driving fine / traffic fine
Previous consultations this year:	no

7.2
Orders and contracts

1 A table (4), chairs (3)

B chairs (3)

C fridge (5), cool box (2)

D fridge (5)

E microwave oven (1)

2 1 big   2 round   3 many   4 small
5 bigger   6 wide / deep 7 deep / wide
8 wider   9 best   10 much

3

adjective	noun
long	length
wide	width
deep	depth
high	height
heavy	weight
old	age

4 different (*the vowel sound in 'height' is* /aɪ/, *as in 'high'. The vowel sound in 'weight' is* /eɪ/, *as in 'wait'.*)

5 1 S (/aɪ/)   2 D (/eɪ/ and /eə/)   3 S (/eɪ/)   4 S (/aɪ/)
5 D (/əʊ/ and /aʊ/)   6 S (/ɜː/)   7 S (/iː/)   8 S (/ɜː/)

6 **Possible answers:**

1 The cheapest system is Supahome.

2 It takes between a morning and two days to install the systems.

3 SureSafe gives the most protection.

4 Supahome and Protektor use a PIN code control system. SureSafe has a PIN code and a remote control.

5 The best level of guarantee and after-sales service is with SureSafe.

6 SureSafe is the best value for money.

7 **Sample answer:**

We looked at three different home security systems, Supahome, Protektor and SureSafe. The cheapest system is Supahome, at €400. SureSafe costs €475 and the most expensive system is Protektor, at €500. It takes between a morning and two days to install the systems.

SureSafe gives the most protection; it covers all zones. Protektor covers the doors and windows, but Supahome only covers the front door. Supahome and Protektor use a PIN code control system. SureSafe has a PIN code and a remote control. The best level of guarantee and after-sales service is with SureSafe. The guarantee is for ten years, and there is a free callout service for two years. On the other hand, Supahome and Protektor give a guarantee for five years, and only give six months and one year free callout. In conclusion, SureSafe is the best value for money.

8 We have received your call about a fault on **your** system. Our **technician** will visit as soon as **possible**. Please call 079 878 464 to **arrange** a time.

7.3
Listening Test: Part Two and Part Three

2 1 A H
2 C F
3 E I
4 D G
5 B J

MODULE 8

8.1
Manufacturing processes

1 1 are made
2 were designed
3 has been delayed
4 will be supplied
5 was sent
6 can't be increased

2 1 The film is being produced by an independent studio.
2 The special effects were designed by a studio in Belgium.
3 The animation sequences are filmed in the UK.
4 The actors' voices can be recorded in any location.
5 The soundtrack will be added at the end of filming.
6 About 90% of the film has been completed now.
7 The copies will be produced in Spain.
8 The film is going to be released on Christmas Eve.

3 1 make
2 can be taken
3 is informed
4 can't be provided
5 is received
6 hasn't been filled in
7 can be delayed
8 is sent
9 decide
10 takes

11 is accepted
12 is usually paid

4 C to give information

5 1 C (*The milk was sold to a large commercial dairy.*)
2 A (*it was our responsibility to make sure there were no problems with the milk quality.*)
3 B (*The whole place was automated. …. Nothing was wasted at all.*)
4 A (*organic dairy farming producing high quality, specialist cheeses.*)
5 C (*the Internet means they can reach a much wider market …*)

6 1 handmade   2 order
3 demand   4 supply
5 automated   6 output
7 warehouse   8 delivery

8.2
Problems and solutions

1 1 problem
2 opportunities
3 succeed
4 way

2 1 stop / prevent
2 so that
3 to
4 to
5 stops / prevents
6 so that
7 stops / prevents
8 so that
9 stop / prevent
10 to

3 1 G 2 D 3 C 4 H 5 E 6 B 7 F 8 A

4 1 <u>air</u> conditioning
2 <u>conference</u> phone
3 <u>smoke</u> detector
4 <u>maintenance</u> manager
5 <u>barcode</u> scanner
6 <u>quality</u> control
7 <u>optical</u> cell
8 <u>business</u> school

5 1 D 2 E 3 F 4 B 5 A 6 C

6 1 There is no E98 flavouring.
2 a mistake with the orders
3 contact the purchasing department

7 Sample answer:

The production manager has informed me that there was no delivery of E98 flavouring last week, and there is no stock. Could you check on this order and all other flavourings orders, please? If there is no E98 on order, please order some urgently.

Could you also inform me of the expected delivery dates for the flavourings?

Many thanks

Tina

8 The new product brochure **was** discussed at yesterday's meeting with the owners and **the** following suggestions were made:
- reduce the size of the catalogue **by / to** ten pages
- use full colour
- put the catalogue **on** the website

Could you discuss the first two points **with** our usual printer and look into what's involved with the third? Get quotations and let me know something by the end of the week **if** possible.

Sam

8.3
Speaking Test: Part Two and Part Three

2 A 1, 7, 9
B 3, 6, 10, 12, 13
C 4, 8, 15, 16
D 2, 5, 11, 14

MODULE 9

9.1
The future

1 1 will
2 will
3 won't
4 will
5 will
6 won't
7 will
8 will

2 1 When will it be in the shops?
2 Why won't it be available before Christmas?
3 How much will it cost?
4 Where will it be on sale?
5 How will it work?
6 Who will it appeal to?

3 1 We'll sell more in Asia and Africa if it's solar-powered.
2 If we don't use aluminium, it will be much cheaper to make.

3 If we use recycled plastic, we'll reduce our CO_2 emissions.
4 The costs will be lower if we don't use so much packaging.
5 We'll have a bigger impact if we advertise on the Internet.
6 It won't be in the shops for Christmas if we don't increase production.

4 1 C use / will get
2 A continues / will pollute
3 D rise / will be
4 B will set / do not increase

5 emissions = gases released when something is burned
fuels = materials which provide energy when they are burned
carbon-based fuels = oil, coal and gas
biofuels = fuels made from renewable resources
crops = plants which are grown on a large scale, usually for food
solvents = chemical compounds used to dissolve oil and other substances

6 1 A to
2 B for
3 B are
4 C of
5 A are
6 C other
7 C cheaper
8 A in

7 1 C 2 D 3 F 4 A 5 B 6 E

8 1 rate
2 venture
3 future
4 technology
5 factor
6 cost

9.2
Meetings

1 1 If
2 before
3 If
4 if
5 until
6 As soon as

2 1 **Block** the main entrance.
2 Lift the machinery **before** the water gets in.
3 Switch off the electricity **if** the water starts to come in.
4 **Move** equipment into the loading area.
5 **Decide** when to make an announcement to the staff.

3
  1 agenda
  2 arrange
  3 departmental
  4 minutes
  5 attend
  6 hold

4 and **5**

Dear Ms Wilkes

Please accept my **apologies** for the problems you have had with your new QX motorbike. <u>I know that your bike was ordered on 2nd March and delivery was expected the last week in March, and it's the end of April now</u>. Unfortunately, the delivery of your bike has **been** delayed.

<u>The problem isn't really our fault</u>. The delay is due to production problems at the factory. <u>I sent a couple of emails last week to try to find out what the situation is</u>. We have been told that these problems have now been solved and that normal production **will** start again next week.

<u>Well, I hope so, don't you</u>? We will contact you as soon as we **have** a definite delivery date for your bike.

In addition, QX would like to offer you a 10% discount on our range of motorbike **accessories**. <u>I'm really sorry about everything</u>.

Yours sincerely
E. Bridge
Motorbike Central

6 **Short vowels:**
  1 list
  2 will
  3 hit
  4 mat
  5 cat
  6 this
  7 chip
  8 Tim
  9 hop
  10 bin

7
sh<u>i</u>pment	S
gr<u>ee</u>n	L
n<u>ee</u>d	L
k<u>ey</u>	L
pred<u>i</u>ct	S
c<u>o</u>st	S
c<u>au</u>sed	L
l<u>a</u>ws	L
l<u>o</u>ss	S
comp<u>e</u>te	L
str<u>o</u>ng	S
st<u>o</u>rm	L
f<u>a</u>ll	L
pr<u>o</u>blem	S
f<u>o</u>rty	L

9.3
Reading Test: Part Five and Part Six

1 C is correct. Statements B and C are both true according to what the text suggests, but they are not reasons why 'nobody wants to be a farmer'.

2 2 A (*They take out loans from the banks … their income is not guaranteed.*)   3 B (*crops depend on the weather.*)

3
  4 B with
  5 B lower
  6 C will happen

MODULE 10

10.1
Career development

1 **teachers**
  lecturers
  speakers
  trainers
  tutors

  classes
  courses
  lectures
  seminars
  sessions
  workshops

  education
  professional development
  training

2
  1 which
  2 who
  3 who
  4 where
  5 which
  6 which
  7 which
  8 which

3
  0 I work for a man who values education.
  1 I studied at a business school **which** has an international reputation.
  2 I work with a colleague **who** studied at the same school.
  3 I did a degree **which** helped me in my profession.
  4 I had a tutor **whose** lectures were inspirational.
  5 I work for a company **which** has offices all over the world.

6 My office is in a business park **where** there are lots of facilities.

7 I met a client **whose** company is very successful.

8 I work in a building **where** smoking is not allowed.

4 Sentences 1, 2, 3 and 5. (*You are less likely to use 'that' in sentence 2, as 'colleague' refers to a person, so 'who' sounds more natural.*)

5 1 *Don't Just Manage, Lead!* is a course (which) many managers find useful.

2 Francis Baker is a creative director who has worked for leading advertising agencies.

3 The course (which) I took last year was called *Effective Communicating*.

4 Professional development is something (that) companies often neglect.

5 I'm going back to the college where I did my first degree.

6 The woman (who) I spoke to about the course was very helpful.

7 The tutor who interviewed me was quite friendly.

8 The amount of work (that) you have to do is reasonable.

6 A An online course

B An activity weekend

C A development day

7 1 B (*I was in a group with people who are quite dynamic and confident at work …*)

2 A (*I can … see how things work in practice in my job.*)

3 C (*It was all very mysterious …*)

4 A (*I can study the theory … We do a lot of case studies …*)

5 C (*You discovered that … others are great at listening …*)

6 B (*I went on a team-building weekend … we made a great team …*)

8 **Text A**

great

patient

good at motivating (us)

good at organising (time)

understanding

Text B

competitive

dynamic

confident

Text C

good at communicating

great at listening and explaining

10.2
Organising a conference

1 1 When we decide the dates, I'll **book a room / book rooms** at the hotel.

2 It's organised by a local **development agency** which has experience in the area.

3 I've **confirmed the dates** of the conference for late May.

4 Until we **finalise the budget**, we won't know how much we can spend on catering.

5 We've received completed **registration forms** from all the participants now.

6 How much have we budgeted for the **speaker's fee**? John Cruz looks great, but expensive.

2 and **3**

1 E   4 A   2 D   5 B   3 C

4 **Sample answer:**

Dear Mr Ellacott

I attended your talk on Internet advertising at the Northern Chamber of Commerce and I thought it was very relevant and interesting.

I am currently organising a development day on the topic of 'Marketing and the Internet' for a group of about 40 staff. I would be delighted if you could deliver your talk as part of the event. I enclose details of the event and of our company.

Please confirm your availability and your fee.

Yours sincerely

6 1 C H   2 A H   3 D V   4 E H   5 B V

7 1

A *We're thinking of* going out for dinner tonight. Are you free?

B *Good idea.* Which restaurant did you have in mind?

2

A *Would you like to* try this dish?

B *It looks* very nice. What is it made of?

3

A *Can I offer you* some more wine?

B *Thanks, but* I think I'll just have water now.

4

A *Have you been* to any of the typical tourist sites here? What do you recommend?

B *I'm afraid* I haven't. I haven't had very much free time.

5

A *Would you like to* join us for a drink?

B *It's very kind of you to* ask, but I think I'll go back to the hotel now.

8

/z/ as in *speakers*	/s/ as in *workshops*	/ɪz/ as in *classes*
clothes	budgets	businesses
cultures	dates	conferences
fees	hosts	courses
sessions	networks	offices

10.3
Writing Test: Part Two

1 The answer received a low mark because it copied too much from the instructions. You should try to express the same ideas in your own words.

2 Ask what kind of courses they offer: 6, 8, 10
Ask for a quotation for a group of 25: 1, 4, 5
Find out if there are any restrictions on participants: 2, 3, 9
Find out about available dates: 7, 11, 12

3 **Sample answer:**
Dear Mr Yardley
I am organising some training for administrative staff and I see from your website that you run residential weekend courses.
I would like to know if you have courses suitable for a group of young administration workers, on team-building skills. Could you let me know prices for groups of up to 25 people and also if the activity courses are suitable for people with disabilities?
Please send me a list of the dates that you have courses available.
Thank you in advance.
R Brooke

4 **Sample answer:**
Dear Ms Brooke
Thank you for your enquiry about our courses. We offer a team-building activity weekend which is suitable for people working in most areas of business. Please see the enclosed leaflet which gives full details, and the restrictions on participants. The price will be €2,500–€3,000, with a 10% deposit to be paid at the time of booking. There is a 5% discount on bookings made over two months in advance. Please also see our website OutdoorBusiness.co.uk.
Best regards
Tom Yardley

MODULE 11

11.1
Health and safety

1 1 B 2 A 3 B

2 1 mustn't
2 had to
3 have to
4 must
5 mustn't
6 don't have to

3 1 mustn't
2 don't have to
3 should
4 don't have to
5 don't have to
6 can't

4 1 had to
2 don't have to
3 can't
4 should
5 have to
6 mustn't

5 1 B Wrong (*The traditional image of the gym has changed completely.*)
2 A Right (*open all day, every day from 06.30 …*)
3 C Doesn't say
4 C Doesn't say
5 A Right (*our shop can provide you with quality sports clothes and equipment.*)

6

go	play	do
swimming	football	yoga
rowing	golf	aerobics
climbing	baseball	exercises
cycling	hockey	karate
jogging	tennis	Pilates
running	volleyball	t'ai chi
skiing		
surfing		

7 1 **play** is used before games with rules.
2 **go** is used before activities ending in *-ing*.
3 **do** is used before activities with names that are nouns.

11.2
Reporting accidents

1 1 B 2 D 3 F 4 A 5 C 6 E

2 1 was carrying / dropped
2 was walking / fell
3 was using / broke off / cut
4 splashed / was trying
5 knocked over / was driving / fell
6 was washing / slipped / hurt

4 **Possible answers:**

1 'You have to / should / must wear appropriate clothing.'
2 Parking permits must be displayed.
3 Children should not / must not be left alone.
4 'We can't give refunds if you don't have the receipt.'
5 Membership fees must be paid on time.
6 Armbands must be worn by all children under 12.

5 **Sample answers:**

1 We provide lockers for all clients.
2 Please place all your personal possessions in the lockers and remember to lock them.
3 Outdoor footwear should not be used in the green zone.
4 All pool users should shower before entering the pool area.
5 In the gym, some equipment must be booked in advance.
6 Ask at reception.
7 Children are welcome at certain times.
8 They must be accompanied in all zones.

6 **Caesar** Sportswear has acquired the sports chain GetFit, after the announcement that GetFit was **facing** bankruptcy. GetFit has 89 retail outlets across the country, and currently it is not **known** if Caesar Sportswear intends to **close** these branches or rebrand them as Caesar stores. A spokeswoman for Caesar Sportswear said, **'**We **must look** at the situation in more detail before we can take any decisions.**'**

11.3
Listening Test: Part Four

1 1 C 2 B 3 A

Question 1:

A: It's now official that the company is going to be split into two separate divisions.

Question 2:

A: Well, obviously there's going to be a reduction in the number of employees, both here in Europe and in North America.

Question 3:

B: I suppose so – but we've just invested a lot of money in retraining staff in Europe, with the intention of expanding the Internet side of the business …

2 In 1, option A is incorrect because neither *take over* nor *competitor* are mentioned in the text. Option B is incorrect because *merge* is not mentioned. In addition, options A and B both refer to other companies, but no other companies are mentioned in the text.

In 2, option A is incorrect because *reduction* means the opposite of *employ more*. Option C is incorrect because the text says the company will reduce the number of employees in North America, not send people there.

In 3, option B is incorrect because they don't have to train staff; they *have just trained* staff. Option C is incorrect because the text says they have invested in training but doesn't mention money specifically.

MODULE 12

12.1
The job market

1 1 E 2 F 3 B 4 C 5 A 6 D

2
1 was not / wasn't
2 would work / 'd work
3 would enjoy / 'd enjoy
4 would be
5 would give
6 did not work / didn't work
7 would be / 'd be
8 could / would be able to
9 would enjoy / 'd enjoy
10 was not / wasn't / weren't
11 would do / 'd do
12 would not like / wouldn't like
13 did not have / didn't have
14 would do / 'd do
15 would not like / wouldn't like / don't like

3
0 0 If I knew someone there, it would be easier.
1 C If she wasn't happy here, she would look for another job.
2 F If he worked harder, he would get better results.
3 E If he spoke Russian, he would apply for a job as a tour guide.
4 A If it had a branch in Germany, I would apply for a transfer.
5 B If his boss left, he would leave too.
6 D If the salary was better, I wouldn't consider leaving.

4
1 qualifications
2 employers
3 vacancies
4 interview
5 application
6 recruitment

5
1 A would be
2 B who
3 C had to
4 B to
5 C decided
6 C until
7 A lots
8 C any

12.2
Job applications

1

[1]S	E	L	F	[2]C	O	N	F	[3]I	D	E	N	T	
				R				N					
				E				D					[4]R
				A		[5]F	L	E	X	I	B	L	E
		[6]P		T				P					L
	[7]M	O	T	I	V	[8]A	T	E	D				I
		S		V		M		N					A
		I		E		B		D					B
		T				I		E					L
		I				T		N					E
		V				I		T					
		E				O							
					[9]P	U	N	C	T	U	A	L	
						S							

2 1 A 2 F 3 G 4 D 5 E 6 C 7 B 8 H

3 **Sample answer:**

Dear Mr Brown

Thank you for your application for the post of credit card assistant controller at Winthrop Bank.

I would like to invite you to attend an interview for this position. The interview will take place at Winthrop Bank's head office at Winthrop House in York, at 09.45 on 2nd September. Please confirm your attendance by telephoning Susan on extension 1356 on the number at the head of this letter.

I look forward to meeting you.

Yours sincerely

F. Brierley

4 **Possible answers:**

0 Where did you see the job advertised?

1 Do you have any experience in tourism?

2 What were your responsibilities?

3 What qualities do you need in this job?

4 Why would you like to work for this company?

5 What would you say your weak points were?

6 What kind of training would I get?

7 Where would I be based?

8 Can I ask you about salary and conditions?

5 1 I'd <u>like</u> to apply for this job.

2 She <u>would</u>n't <u>like</u> to work there.

3 We'd pre<u>fer</u> to finish early.

4 I <u>would</u>n't con<u>sid</u>er working from home.

5 They <u>would</u>n't inc<u>rease</u> his salary.

6 He'd <u>look</u> for another job.

12.3
Reading Test: Part Seven

3 1 564430009

2 DAVID DUNLOP

3 078 287 6478

4 DUNLOP ASSOCIATES ARCHITECTURE AND DESIGN

5 MORDEN PLACE, GLASGOW